# THE MORALITY
# OF PUNISHMENT

PATTERSON SMITH REPRINT SERIES IN
CRIMINOLOGY, LAW ENFORCEMENT, AND SOCIAL PROBLEMS

*A listing of publications in the* SERIES *will be found at rear of volume*

PUBLICATION NO. 116: PATTERSON SMITH REPRINT SERIES IN
CRIMINOLOGY, LAW ENFORCEMENT, AND SOCIAL PROBLEMS

# THE MORALITY OF PUNISHMENT

## WITH SOME SUGGESTIONS FOR A GENERAL THEORY OF ETHICS

BY

## A. C. EWING

Litt.D. (Cambridge); Fellow of British Academy;
Honorary Fellow of Jesus College, Cambridge

WITH A FOREWORD BY
DR. W. D. ROSS

REPRINTED WITH A NEW PREFACE BY THE AUTHOR

MONTCLAIR, N. J.
PATTERSON SMITH
1970

*Originally published 1929 by*
*Kegan Paul, Trench, Trubner & Co., Ltd.*

*Reprinted 1970, with permission of*
*Routledge and Kegan Paul, Ltd.*

*Patterson Smith Publishing Corporation*
*Montclair, New Jersey 07042*

*New material copyright © 1970 by*
*Patterson Smith Publishing Corporation*

SBN 87585–116–9

Library of Congress Catalog Card Number: 70–108233

This book is printed on three-hundred-year acid-free paper.

TO MY FATHER

## PREFACE TO THE REPRINT EDITION

ALTHOUGH this book was first published forty years ago, when I read it through again on the occasion of the publication of this new edition, I discovered to my amazement that I was still in complete agreement with the views on punishment I expressed there (except perhaps for certain slight differences as to degree of emphasis). I do not say this by way of a boast; I am not at all certain that it is to my credit as a philosopher, and I fear most of the present generation at least would definitely think not; but I state it simply as a fact, whatever inference the reader may be inclined to draw from it. At any rate it seems to show that at the time I wrote the book my thought on the subject of punishment had about reached the limit which it was capable of attaining. On moral philosophy in general my views have changed very considerably, but this change has not appreciably affected my views on punishment, nor even the more general views on ethics which I expressed in chapter 6 of the book. The changes represent an advance beyond rather than a correction of what I said in that chapter.

The three main changes are in very bare outline as follows. (The first two are of more interest to the academic philosopher than to the reader concerned only with punishment.)

(1) When I first wrote this book, I regarded ought (or right, whichever one calls fundamental) and good as both ultimate indefinable concepts, but in my *Definition of Good* (London & New York, 1947) I developed a theory according to which "good" was analysed in terms of "ought," "good" being "that toward which we ought to have a favourable attitude of some kind." But as long as I continue to hold that the things I pronounce good in themselves are things we ought to seek for their own sake there is no need for this to make any difference to my views as to practical questions about what ought to be done.

vii

(2) In 1929 and for many years afterwards I held with G. E. Moore that the objectivity of ethics, in which I firmly believed and still believe, requires the assumption that the ultimate ethical concepts (or concept) represent "non-natural" characteristics present in the real world. I now think that this way of talking is misleading because it assimilates moral and evaluative judgements to descriptive judgements, and it is not the function of these judgements to describe. I am now inclined to agree with the prescriptivist in holding that they express primarily a practical rather than a cognitive attitude; but I insist that they also claim the attitude to be justified and that as claiming this they are true or false in senses of these words by no means completely different from those in which other judgements are true or false; and further I still insist that what they assert is not merely something about the actual attitude of people, as the naturalist claims to be the case. My views are developed on these lines in *Second Thoughts in Moral Philosophy* (London & New York, 1959).

(3) While I was formerly inclined, though without committing myself to determinism, to think a determinist view could be adopted without serious damage to ethics and was more rational than an indeterminist view, I now definitely accept indeterminism. This change of view has not however been yet given expression in any published work. It is this third change which might seem highly relevant to one's view of punishment, but it does not seem to me that any of the arguments I used about punishment presupposed either indeterminism or determinism to be true. Most holders of the retributive theory in the sense in which I criticise it have been indeterminists, although I cannot see any relation of logical entailment between the two views either way; but the arguments I used against the retributive view are quite independent of any determinist assumptions, and it still seems to me just as reasonable to reject the view now that I have definitely become an indeterminist. On the other hand the non-retributive grounds for the infliction of punishment remain even if determinism is adopted. Determinism is, I now think, incapable of being rendered compatible with the application to

acts of the term "ought" in its moral sense, and this is why I reject it; but it is not incompatible with the admission that some acts are very harmful or even intrinsically evil, and that the infliction of punishment can be a useful means to lessening the frequency of such acts. It is not even incompatible with the appropriateness of blame; to blame a man is to say that he has chosen to do something bad or neglected to choose to do something good, and this is perfectly sensible even if a determinist view be assumed, provided only if it is granted that among the causes which determine action is choice. It is, further, even on a determinist view not only often true to say this but sometimes very useful since it can make repetition of similar acts less probable in the future.

Since I wrote my book, there has been a very disquieting increase in crime and violence generally, and in the western democracies at least there has also been a considerable decrease in the severity of punishments and a strengthening of the tendency toward a permissive society, though I do not feel able to dogmatise as to the relation between these different tendencies. The present situation certainly brings very much to the fore the question of punishment. Plainly, whatever may be our attitude to certain sexual questions, we cannot permit violence, fraud, and murder.

There is one question at least which most people would expect me to discuss in a book on punishment but which I omitted, namely the question of the death penalty. The reason for the omission was that I did not see any adequate philosophical grounds for a decision either way, and I did not think myself qualified to go into the empirical questions which have to be answered before we can decide whether or not to inflict a particular kind of punishment. I do not think one can say that the individual has an absolute right to life under all circumstances even where the granting of the right would carry a grave risk of his actions ending the lives of others, and I should therefore be prepared to support capital punishment if there were conclusive evidence that its deterrent effect was of much value in decreasing the number of murders; but it is very doubtful whether this is so, and the moral influence and other social repercussions of such a kind of punishment are undesirable. The revival of the death penalty would appear to me as in some degree a step in the direction of a lower kind of civilisation, but so does also a great increase in the number of murders, if this be indeed, which I very much doubt, the effect of its abolition. Whether it is so or not is an empirical question, and there is no doubt that at least a great deal of the agitation for it is emotional and not in any way based on a careful study of the empirical evidence as to the deterrent effect of the punishment. It must further be realised that there are a number of men whom in the interest of public safety it would never be reasonable to release from prison if there were no capital punishment, and some would argue that lifelong imprisonment is an even worse punishment than death, though this might be met by mitigations in conditions of imprisonment.

There is also a strong agitation in favour of corporal punishment. I have no a priori objection to it in its milder forms, but it does seem to me that for it to outweigh in its deterrent effects a long imprisonment sentence it would have to amount to real torture in order to make up for the enormous difference in the duration of the suffering involved, and the re-introduction of torture would be intolerable.

I should now emphasise still more the desirability of making punishments compensatory where possible by requiring the delinquent to work in his spare time for the benefit of the man he has injured or robbed, not only for the sake of the latter but because such a kind of punishment should strike even the delinquent as reasonable, and therefore much increase the chance of its being for his moral advantage.

In my book I have laid great stress on the conception of punishment as a kind of language, which expresses more emphatically the notion of blame or condemnation than mere words could do. At a time when most philosophers find it so specially helpful to look at every problem in linguistic terms, I should have thought this way of looking at punishment might have a wide appeal. I note that it also bulks large in the one book by a British philosopher devoted mainly or entirely to punishment that has appeared since I published mine, Sir Walter Moberly's *The Ethics of Punishment* (London, 1968), though I do not think the author can be classified as a "linguistic philosopher" any more than I can.

Punishment has two aspects. It is in the first place a kind of negative wage. There are some things which it is desirable for people to do, and therefore they are paid for doing them; there are others which it is undesirable that they should do, and therefore if they do them they are not paid but instead given something which they do not want. No doubt one can also give people a positive wage for abstaining from doing the undesirable things and a negative wage for not doing the desirable, and this, especially the latter, is sometimes done (e.g., penalties for refusing military service), but it would be obviously impracticable to make it a universal system if only because of the necessity of paying workers positively to give them their keep and the enormous cost of, for example, paying everybody a wage for not stealing sufficient to outweigh the gains of theft. This is the purely utilitarian aspect of punishment.

But as I insisted in my book, with perhaps even too much emphasis at times, punishment also has a moral aspect which is connected with its infliction being an expression of blame or condemnation. The possible therapeutic effect of this depends on the fact that crimes are normally committed not because the offender thinks they are right actions but because, though he is normally aware that they are wrong, this awareness fails to influence him or influence him enough at the time of temptation. The remedy for this is to make, if possible, his realisation of their wrongness stronger and more vivid, and this may be helped by impressing the wrongness of his action on him in such a forceful way as is done by a judicial punishment. I must emphasize the word "may" here; it is the business of one who writes on the ethics of punishment to mention the moral effects it may have, if successful, but not to talk as if it were always successful. Punishment for the reason I have just mentioned tends to lead in the direction of reform, but the many counteracting tendencies present in itself and its concomitants seem to cause it more often than not to fail in this purpose, at least in the case of state punishment. I have in my book (pp. 75–76, 123) given a list of the moral disadvantages which threaten to outweigh the moral advantages of punishment, and I have admitted (p. 123) that they were sufficient to lead me to the conclusion that if the sole object of punishment were the reform of the criminal, its success would be so problematic and the moral risks so great that it would probably be better for the state not to inflict it.

It is only, I think, because there are other reasons, chiefly deterrent and preventive, for state punishment that imprisonment, at any rate, ought to be inflicted at all. But once it has been inflicted, this is no reason why every effort should not be made to counteract its moral dangers and take advantage of the fact that the offender is by virtue of his imprisonment in a position in which he can have influences brought to bear on him which might not have access to him in his normal life. This is the usual aim of the prison reformers. They do not seek to reform the prisoner *by punishment* but only *while he is undergoing punishment.* Further, for various reasons the reformatory aim of punishment in education has a considerably better chance of being fulfilled. Though its place in education has been deplorably exaggerated in the past, I do not see how we can dispense altogether with punishment in some form.

The issue with which I was most concerned in my treatment of punishment was that between the retributive and the utilitarian views. Recent writers have contended that discussions of punishment have confused two questions, the question of the imposition of punishments based on an existing penal code, and the question what acts should be brought under the code and what penalties should be imposed by the code. The former question, it has been suggested, must be answered in a retributive fashion; the justification for the punishment must be found not in any consequences which showed the punishment to have been useful but in the mere fact that an offence had been committed which was included in the penal code and that the penalty fell within the limits prescribed by the law. On the other hand the question which wrong acts should be included in the penal code (they obviously could not all be) and what the legal penalties should be, could be decided only on utilitarian grounds. No doubt this is a distinction which I should have mentioned explicitly; there is a great difference between the function of the judge and the function of the legislator, and it may even be the duty of the judge sometimes to inflict punishments which he does not himself think just. If his disagreement with the laws he has to administer exceeds a certain degree he ought to resign his post as judge, but he cannot either overrule the law or resign for every minor difference. He administers the laws and does not make them; his private view cannot count as law. On the other hand it is impossible to keep the functions quite separate. The law may leave a good deal of discretion as regards the penalty to the judge, and then in deciding it he should be determined by the same kind of considerations as would be relevant to a legislator in fixing the law. And there remain the borderline cases where the law is so bad or the situation so different from what it was intended to cover that the judge has to consider whether it is not his duty somehow to evade the law in his decision. At any rate this distinction gives no support to the retributive view in the sense in which I attacked it. It does not show or even suggest that one should regard as an end in itself the pain inflicted in punishment. But it does help to explain the essential relation of punishment to the past, which worries the utilitarian. When we are drawing up penal laws, reference to the past does not play the same role because laws should not be retrospective.

The way of looking at punishment to which I have just been referring is an example of "rule-utilitarianism." The rule is justified by its consequences, but the attempt to regard all particular acts of the kind as justified by their particular consequences is abandoned. The question can then be asked, as with all rule-utilitarianism, why it should be right and even obligatory always to do something which is itself often likely to produce more harm than good just because in most cases of similar action more good than harm is produced. We should not think much of a doctor who gave penicillin to a patient known to be allergic to it on the ground that it was a good general rule to give penicillin to infected patients. Yet to punish an innocent man on utilitarian grounds is, if done deliberately, an action that arouses the greatest moral repugnance.

Part of the answer is that, while it is no doubt true that there are some cases in which more good would be done by punishing an innocent man, we cannot trust any human authority to decide when such cases occur so that it is much safer to stick to the general rule that innocent people should not be punished, but I do not think that this is a complete answer. That there is something intrinsically evil about punishing the innocent is an element in the retributive view which I can accept. But I am not so clear that there is something intrinsically good about punishing the guilty, and to this law I should be much more prepared to allow exceptions on utilitarian grounds.

—A. C. Ewing

*Jesus College, Cambridge*
*January 1970*

# FOREWORD

THE problem of the objects and the justification of punishment is such a crucial one in ethical theory that it is surprising that in this country, at all events, there seems to have been no recent attempt to make it the subject of a separate full-length inquiry. This gap in our literature Dr. Ewing has now filled. He has endeavoured in separate chapters to do justice to what truth there is in the two views that have in the main held the field, the retributive theory and the deterrent theory ; and has in a later chapter dealt with the views which emphasize the reformation of the offender and the education of the community as objects of punishment. His whole discussion of these views is commendably unprejudiced, and free alike from excessive faith in the effectiveness of punishment and from a too narrow view of the grounds of its justification. He has further seen that a theory of punishment requires as its complement a theory of reward, and has dealt, though more briefly, with this topic. And finally, since punishment cannot be adequately treated in isolation from more general problems of ethics, he has indicated his ethical standpoint briefly in his Introduction, and has dealt in a separate chapter with a problem that is somewhat neglected in most books on moral philosophy, the question of the nature of the thinking by which we decide what is right, and of the part which moral philosophy may play in helping us to the decision. Here again he shows a notable balance of judgment in claiming neither too much nor too little utility for ethical theory.

Dr. Ewing's treatment is philosophical throughout, but he has a keen eye for the practical considerations that should determine the nature and the amount of the punishment to be inflicted in different types of case ; not only students of philosophy but also teachers and those who are interested in the concrete problems of punishment by the state should find much food for thought in his book. A discussion so open-minded, so acute, and so clearly written will, it is to be hoped, receive wide attention as an original contribution to the study of a subject of great importance alike theoretical and practical.

W. D. Ross, M.A., LLD., F.B.A.,

*Fellow of Oriel College, late Deputy Professor of Moral Philosophy in the University of Oxford.*

# AUTHOR'S PREFACE

THIS book is based on a thesis which won the Green Prize
in Moral Philosophy at Oxford, but it has been thoroughly
revised since, and at the suggestion of the examiners a chapter
has been added sketching my views on general moral
philosophy. The content and purpose of the work are
sufficiently explained by the foreword of Dr. Ross, so the
briefer my preface the better. The original title was *The
Morality of Punishment and Reward*, but in the course of
revision I came to the conclusion that, while it was still very
desirable to include a chapter on reward, both on its own
account and also for the sidelight it throws on punishment,
this subject occupied too small a portion of the book to
justify mention on the title-page. It is naturally impracticable to give an exhaustive list of the books to which I am
indebted, including both attempts to deal with the practical
problems of punishment and general works on moral
philosophy, but I might mention especially the chapters on
punishment in Rashdall's *Theory of Good and Evil*,
McTaggart's *Studies in Hegelian Cosmology*, Bosanquet's
*Some Suggestions in Ethics*, and Green's *Principles of Political
Obligation*.

I take the opportunity of expressing my gratitude to Dr.
W. D. Ross for having done me the honour of writing a
foreword, and for his much-valued help and encouragement.
I am indebted to Dr. Ross himself, Prof. A. E. Heath, Dr.
R. I. Aaron and Mr. H. H. Price for having read portions
of the book, and to my mother for having carried out the
laborious work of proof-reading.

A. C. EWING.

University College, Swansea.
*July*, 1929.

# CONTENTS

# CONTENTS

# THE MORALITY OF PUNISHMENT

## CHAPTER I

### Introduction

PUNISHMENT and reward are certainly subjects which must at some time have touched all of us closely, at least in our childhood, and the former at any rate is one of those topics which may at times move to philosophic thought even the least speculatively inclined. For discussion as to the value of punishment is forced upon all who think either of the State's treatment of those who have offended against its laws or of the problems of the educator, topics which even the daily newspaper is continually bringing home to us. It is the business of Ethics as a science to do the same thing as " the man in the street " is doing when he wonders what is the use of punishment and whether it can make anyone better, only to do it systematically, thoroughly, precisely, without gratuitous assumptions, in a word " scientifically."

In the past there have been two main theories current as to punishment, the one that it was only by reference to its consequences that it could be justified and its amount fixed, the other, the so-called " retributive " view, that its primary justification was to be found not in its consequences but simply in the fact that it was deserved as the penalty for a wrong act committed in the past. The present book is among other things an attempt to reconcile these two theories in a way which will do justice to the elements of value in both.

But any part of Ethics brings one into touch with the whole, and though my treatment of punishment and reward should be intelligible without a previous study of philosophy, I have in Chapter VI tried to develop something of the nature of a general theory of ethical knowledge after dealing with the more specific problems of punishment and reward, and I must also in this introductory chapter make just a few, I fear, rather dry, but none the less necessary, remarks on Ethics in general before proceeding to the main subject.

About the problem before us, as about any or almost any ethical problem, there are two questions to be asked : (1) What good is done by punishment and reward ?  (2) When and how ought punishment to be inflicted and reward bestowed ?  The two are, however, so connected that the answer to the first is at least the most important datum required if the second is to be answered satisfactorily.  It is indeed natural and common to go further and say that the answer to the second is totally dependent on the answer to the first, that the amount of good produced ought to be the sole and sufficient premiss and criterion in determining what it is right to do.  It must be admitted that we may know (or be practically certain) that an act is right or our duty without being able first to sum up the good which it is likely to do and prove this to be greater than the good likely to be done by alternative courses of action ; but it is possible to admit this and still hold the only ultimate reason why it is our duty, the only ultimate justification for it to be that it is the act which will do the most good possible under the circumstances (including in " good " the diminution or averting of evil).  But whether the above view be accepted or not, in any case we seem bound to hold that it is part of the function of moral philosophy to tell us what kinds of good (and evil) are produced by punishment and reward.  Even if to know the good did not help in the least in deciding what we ought to do, a moral philosophy that ignored this first question would be shirking a large part of its work.

It seems quite incredible, however, that knowledge of the good likely to be produced by an act should not be at least a help in deciding what we ought to do.  That its consequences are the best possible under the circumstances may perhaps not be an adequate premiss from which straightway to infer the rightness of an act, but at any rate one of the chief points to be taken into account must be the goodness of the consequences.  The issue in dispute is not whether consideration of consequences should play any part at all in determining what is right, but whether it is the sole determining factor[1] or not.

Even Kant, who went to the extreme in his rejection of a

---

[1] I mean logically, not psychologically.  It is obvious that our moral decisions are not always psychologically determined by it alone, but it may still be the case that the sole and sufficient ground for an action being right or one's duty is that it will produce the best possible consequences (not only, of course, to oneself but to all concerned).

morality which depended on consequences, clearly did not mean that we ought never to take account of any consequences at all in deciding what we ought[1] to do. For he admits as a categorical imperative that we ought to relieve the distress and further the happiness of others, in so far as we can do so without violating another categorical imperative like—Thou shalt not lie, and if there are certain actions which we ought to perform simply because they will lessen the pain or increase the happiness of others, these must be actions the rightness and obligatoriness of which depend, at least partly, on their consequences. For example, to give an invalid medicine to cure him would clearly cease to be a right act if we had reason to think that the medicine would make him worse instead of better, *i.e.*, if the likely consequences were different. Similarly the Kantian imperative that I should develop my faculties commands, as a moral duty, acts the rightness of which depends on their consequences, *i.e.*, on the improvement of my faculties effected by them. What Kant did maintain uncompromisingly was that, while particular circumstances and consequences may have to be considered in determining *the means by which we are to carry out* a general

---

[1] The following note on terminology is perhaps necessary :—

*Right, ought and duty* are obviously closely allied terms, and it is of no importance to my argument how precisely they are distinguished. For our duty, or the action that we ought to do, cannot be different from the action that is right. Though it may be contended that some right acts, *i.e.*, those which are required merely by self-interest and do not conflict with the agent's desires, or those, if any, which are morally indifferent, are not " duties," this is not to say that an action different from the right one is ever our duty, but that there is in these cases an action which is right but no action at all which is our duty. A complication is indeed raised by the fact that " right " is used in two different senses : (1) as signifying the act which would really have been the best to choose, all things considered, (2) the act which we should choose if we judged rationally *according to the data at our disposal.* An act will be right in the second sense and wrong in the first if it turns out badly through consequences which I could not be expected to foresee ; it will be wrong in both senses if it turns out badly through an intellectual error on my part, though perhaps, if the error is not due to negligence or prejudice, not morally blameworthy. In deciding what is right we try to find (2), and hope that it is at the same time (1).

*Ethics and moral philosophy.* No clear distinction is usually drawn between the terms, and they are applied to the same branch of knowledge, so they are used in this book as synonymous except that, when I say " Ethics," I am thinking more of it as a study of what we ought to do, when I say " moral philosophy," as the investigation of the conceptions of good and right as such and as a branch of philosophy in general. This seems in accord with the current usage.

moral law, they must on no account be used to determine *the law itself*, still less to justify *exceptions to it.* This general position it is not within my province here to discuss ; but very few will deny that anyone who gives an account of punishment ought to consider, at any rate as part of his task, the consequences likely to be produced by it, the ways in which it may be useful to society, even though he holds that these advantageous consequences are not its only nor its main justification. For such consequences are in any case good, and, other things being equal, it is desirable that punishment should produce them.

As is now generally agreed, the science of Ethics cannot by itself tell us what to do in particular cases, and I at any rate shall make no attempt to provide this information. This does not mean that Ethics as a theoretical study is useless for practice, only that it is not all-important. If it could alone serve as a basis from which to deduce all our particular duties, it would both include in itself all other sciences and supplant all insight into individual cases by general rules. This it cannot do, but it may still be a valuable help and guide. In order to decide what is right we must take account of the consequences ; but it is not sufficient to predict these as matters of fact, we must also analyse them to see what good and evil they contain. It is this analysis of the good and evil in the consequences that is the most important function of Ethics in regard to practice. It is not possible to lay down general rules which will enable each particular case to be decided mechanically from them by a mere syllogism in Barbara ; but it is possible for Ethics as a science to give general considerations which will *help* us in deciding particulars, tell us what questions to ask and suggest the right intellectual attitude to practical problems.[1]  I do not claim to fix the rules for punishment or reward, but only to analyse the function of these institutions, the good and evil they produce, and so the ultimate principles on which decisions as to right and wrong in these matters should depend, *in so far* as they can be based on any general ethical principles at all. This is a part, though not the whole, of the work that is necessary before deciding how a particular offence should be punished, or a particular achievement rewarded, and it is all that Ethics can do. To complete the work is the function partly of immediate insight into the particular case, partly of

---

[1] In Chapter VII try to justify this view of ethical knowledge.

branches of knowledge other than Ethics which will tell us what consequences are likely to accrue.  The task of Ethics is not itself to decide alone but to supply an essential part of the knowledge for deciding.  This is the reason why my book is not more directly " practical," to make it so would require more special knowledge of certain (non-ethical) facts than I possess.  But Ethics may suggest principles which another science has to apply ; there must be some division of labour between the sciences.

The good produced by an act is not limited to its consequences.  It should be interpreted so as to include any intrinsic value[1] possessed by the act itself, for this may be an important factor in deciding what to do.  Consequently, the statement that punishment must be justified by the good produced is not itself incompatible with the retributive theory according to which punishment is an end-in-itself[2] as well as a means.  What our attitude to the theory shall be we must decide in the sequel ; but, *if* the infliction of punishment is an end-in-itself, this must be regarded as an additional reason for its infliction.  To the objection that this involves a vicious circle I reply in Chapter VI,[3] where I also attempt to justify some of the statements made here.

This book makes two fundamental assumptions about Ethics.  The first is that Utilitarianism,[4] or the doctrine that pleasure is the only good, is false.  To go into the arguments against this theory, which are stated in so many ethical works, would be tedious and futile when one is concerned with another topic, and I can only say here that the conception of duty seems to me to imply that moral action has a value of its own not reducible to the pleasure it causes, and that it seems clearly wrong not to distinguish between the intrinsic value of different *kinds* of pleasurable experiences.  It is assumed therefore that good character is of value not merely as a means to pleasure but as an end-in-itself.  This will not, however, make the practical difference to the argument which might be expected, for everybody is agreed in thinking that a good moral character is something valuable which ought to be furthered, whether they hold it to be good in itself or good merely as a means to another end.  Where

---

[1] " Intrinsically valuable " is, of course, just a synonym for " good in-itself."
[2] *v.* pp. 26-28.       [3] *v.* p. 171.
[4] I am not referring here to Rashdall's Ideal Utilitarianism, which admits other goods besides pleasure.

the adoption of the view that pleasure is the only good would affect the theory of punishment most is through its absolute incompatibility with the retributive view which makes pain an end-in-itself.

The second assumption is that in Ethics it is possible for us to have real knowledge[1] of what is good and right. If we do not assume this, we are not entitled to say that any one course of action is ever in any degree more rational or obligatory than any other. To sacrifice one's life for a friend would be no more laudable than to murder him for a trifling gain, universal happiness would be no whit better than universal misery.

It seems almost equally certain that we cannot prove the truth of any ethical judgments either by pure logic or by the methods of the natural sciences, or in general from any premises which are not themselves ethical. No attempt that has been made to do so has come anywhere near success, and even if successful sometime in the future, this would not alter the fact that people have for long enough possessed ethical knowledge without knowing about the proof of it which may be given in, say, a thousand years' time. Even if all true ethical propositions could be logically proved in the future, we have some ethical knowledge (however imperfect) *already* without knowing the proof, and, therefore, independently of it. We must rely in Ethics *partly* on our immediate moral insight,[2] though it does not follow from this that we need treat it as infallible.

On the other hand, we cannot possibly be justified in concluding that, because we need something of the nature of " intuition " in Ethics, we can dispense with reasoning. What function ethical reasoning fulfils and what the nature of it is I shall try to show in Chapter VI, but it will consist

---

[1] I do not mean to imply that ethical judgments are infallible, although they are often non-inferential. " Knowledge " is, therefore, I suppose, a term liable to objection, but the word " opinion " on the other hand, implies that they bear a more problematic character than I should be willing to admit. Many of these judgments seem to be at least as well entitled to the designation " knowledge " as the best-established of the non-mathematical parts of science or the ordinary psychological judgments about other people which we commonly say without hesitation we " know " to be true, though they are not absolutely certain ; others may perhaps be instances of knowledge in the fullest possible sense of the term. Whether there are any such and what the distinction between knowledge and opinion really signifies are questions which I do not feel called upon to discuss.

[2] For a defence of this against the charge of obscurantism, *v.* pp. 184-8.

largely in analysis of the good and evil produced by or involved in an act. In Chapters III to V we shall be mainly concerned with this analysis in regard to punishment and reward.

It is a presupposition of all rational action, all beliefs as to what is good or bad, right or wrong, that this process of inference and " intuition " is capable of yielding truth, though not necessarily infallible. In this sense we must hold ethical judgments to be " objectively valid," if we are to admit any such judgments as asserting what is true at all. We know that certain things are good and certain actions right, and we see what is meant by this sufficiently to make the judgment, (just as we see what is meant by any other simple term, though we may be in difficulties when it comes to a philosophical investigation of its properties). This is the irreducible minimum with which scientific or philosophic Ethics (..hichever you prefer to call it) must start. What particular things are good and what particular acts are right is still a problem, but we must at least admit that *some* are.

Ethics is not, therefore, subjective in the sense of being arbitrary. Good and right are real, though not physical, qualities cognisable by us. What is good or right is not made so merely by people thinking it good or right, that is no more possible than it is for a schoolboy to alter the multiplication table or the date of the Battle of Hastings by his blunders. An error is still an error even if all people are agreed on it. Unless we are prepared to admit that the sun went round[1] the earth till the time of Copernicus and that afterwards the earth started going round the sun for a change, or that the heart, not the brain, was the seat of intelligence as long as the ancients thought it was, neither must we suggest that religious intolerance was necessarily right as long as people believed it to be so, and is now wrong just because (and in so far as) people believe it to be wrong. When a man tries to find out whether an act is right or wrong, he is trying to discover what the act really is, not what people think about it, though he can only do so by thinking, and may perhaps accept the authority derived from other people's thinking. It is not his thinking it right that makes it right, but rather

---

[1] *i.e.*, in the " absolute " sense and not only in the sense suggested by some exponents of the " Relativity Theory," because our ancestors certainly believed its motion to be " absolute," and therefore, if the subjective doctrine applied in Ethics holds here, actually made it absolute.

*vice versa.* To say the contrary is to say that a judgment that something is good or right is either no judgment at all or a purely arbitrary one. If good merely means thinking something good, thinking it good is either a vicious circle or a mere illusion and prejudice. There are no doubt some senses in which ethical knowledge might legitimately be said to be " subjective," but, if we are to admit the truth of any ethical judgments at all, we cannot apply the term " subjective " in any sense which will ultimately reduce " good " and " right " to a mere fancy of ours or to the crude fact that we desire something.

A great deal less would have been heard about the subjectivity of Ethics if it had not been for certain ambiguities in the term. It is clear that right and (intrinsically) good, as known by us, are never attributes of inanimate things (with the possible exception of natural beauty),[1] but only of actions, experiences, minds (or at least these in conjunction with some objects external to them), and therefore, if " objectivity " means existence apart from any mind, they cannot be " objective." But this is not to deny that they are real qualities of these actions and experiences, or to assert that the latter are made good or right merely by thinking them so. We do not hold this to be the case with psychological properties, otherwise all theories in psychology would become true in fact as soon as they were accepted by anybody.

Secondly, it is often suggested that Ethics is subjective because in the same external situation the right act may be different for two different men. But the total circumstances must include the nature of the agent as well as other factors, and this may be so different as to justify the two in acting differently. It is, therefore, not a case of different acts being right under the same circumstances, but under different circumstances, and there is no contradiction in that whatever.

It is also true that the agent is often the only person capable of judging what it is right for him to do because he alone knows his own nature and how " he feels about it," as it is colloquially expressed, but this does not prove that his

---

[1] *If* this is a property of physical objects apart from any perceiving mind, it seems to me that it must have some intrinsic value, so that it would be an exception to the above generalisation. Whether it is such a property or not must be decided by considerations which fall outside the sphere of Ethics. Even if this question is answered in the negative, we have, however, no right to say that there are no values possible apart from conscious experience simply because we know of none such.

thinking the act right makes it right, unless the fact that I am the only person who can remember what I felt like on a certain occasion a year ago proves that my feelings at that time were caused by my remembering them now, a year afterwards.

Another argument used for the subjectivity of Ethics is that it is always a man's duty to do what he thinks right. One man may think it his duty to strike, another to stay at work and fight the strike ; in a case like this we cannot, if right is something objective, hold them to be both right, yet we say that neither is to blame, that they both did their duty, if they only acted conscientiously as they thought right. Is not this to say that what a man thinks right must be (for him) right ? The answer is that he incurs no *moral* blame in doing what he thinks right, but may have made a mistake in judging it right. *Granted that* he thinks A right, the least unsatisfactory action in his power may be to do A ; but if he has judged mistakenly, he has involuntarily done an action which is wrong, though not (unless the mistake is due to culpable negligence or prejudice on his part[1]) morally blame-worthy. If a man has made a mistake in judging what is right, he is not in a position where it is possible for him to perform the right action at all. To perform the action which in fact is externally right while thinking it wrong would make it a different action and not the right one. He has committed an intellectual fault by judging wrongly, but he is only held to have committed a moral fault in the specific sense of the term if he consciously does something which he. thinks to be wrong. It is on this ground that a man who does what he thinks right is commonly pronounced free from blame.[2] He had done wrong, but his wrongdoing is not the result of conscious sin. This makes no difference to the question which act he ought to have decided to be right. It would be a far simpler business than it is to decide this, if our deciding an act to be right really made it right, but in deciding we are clearly not in the position of making something but of trying to find out a truth, namely, what is right. If this be denied, there is no purpose left in our efforts at

[1] And even in that case it may be contended that he deserves moral blame for a previous act or acts, but not for the act in question.
[2] We should, however, blame him if the error consisted in having a wrong sense of values or a wrong ideal, *e.g.*, in supposing that material wealth was the most important aim of life, and I am not quite sure how far this distinction can be maintained rigidly.

decision.  In that case it could not matter what we decided to do, for whatever we decided would be *ipso facto* right.  And the same argument must apply to the judgments of society. Neither society nor the individual can therefore make, they can only discover the moral law.

The great diversity of ethical views is no proof of the subjectivity of Ethics.  There is a similar diversity in opinions as to matters of fact, yet we cannot maintain that the differences of historians as to whether a certain event occurred prove that it neither did nor did not occur in reality, or that it was made to occur by historians thinking it did, and not to occur by the other historians thinking it did not.  Then why hold the corresponding view in Ethics ?  It may be objected that Ethics is in a somewhat different position because it claims to be a matter of intuition, not of proof, and there is no way of deciding between these conflicting intuitions either by experience as in the natural sciences or by demonstration as in mathematics.  But " intuition " in the sense in which it must be admitted in Ethics only means cognition otherwise than by inference or by mere observation, and this must be admitted in any other branch of knowledge also.  For without " intuition " in this sense we could have no inference, since the connection between two successive stages in an inference must be immediately apprehended and cannot be mediately inferred by interpolating another stage, otherwise there is an infinite regress.  Again all reasoning of any kind presupposes a cognition that certain particulars are instances of a certain universal,[1] a cognition which cannot be itself either mere sense-perception or a mediate inference, and therefore is an " intuition " in the only sense of the term which need be admitted in Ethics.  There may be nothing more mysterious in our apprehension that something is an instance of good or right than in our apprehension that it is an instance of some other universal, and after all Ethics is far from being the only branch of knowledge where it is not possible to settle disputes with certainty.  I may add that the diversity of opinion is not nearly so great as would seem

[1] *e.g.*, that red is a colour, or that this particular act of mine is an instance of willing, or that this table is a piece of furniture.  We see these judgments to be true without being able to prove them by " inference," nor are they mere sense-perception, for our senses by themselves can only give us the particular, not the universal, to which it belongs. Yet all use of language presupposes this classification under universals, every word except proper names stands for a universal (whether a quality, a kind of thing or a relation).

to be the case, since in different states of society acts which are nominally the same may be quite different in reality because the circumstances in which they are performed are also so different. It may conceivably be the case that war and polygamy are right for certain savage tribes, though wrong for modern Europeans, but then they are only nominally the same, and really quite different acts, owing to the different stage of development and the different state of society.

This is not, however, the place for a complete defence of the " objectivity " of ethical knowledge. To me it is an adequate proof of this " objectivity " that it is presupposed in any ethical judgment we can make. It is true that we cannot prove the truth of Ethics by strict logic to a complete ethical sceptic, but neither can we refute by strict logic the complete theoretical sceptic. The man who refuses to admit in the theoretical sphere that any belief whatever is rational (*e.g.*, even the belief in the truth of the laws of logic or the existence of other human beings besides oneself, etc.) cannot be refuted,[1] strictly speaking, and neither can the man who refuses to admit that any one action is better or more rational than any other ; but there is no reason to regard the views of the second with any more respect than those of the first. But, if any ethical judgments are true at all, good and right must, it seems to me, be real qualities of certain experiences and acts, for good and right do not mean the same as " desired " or " thought good by society." We cannot, however, discuss the question in full here.

I have tried to assume as few controversial points as possible without explanation and defence, but it seems to me better to state something of my general outlook in Ethics frankly than to smuggle it through in the shape of unstated assumptions, as I should otherwise have to do. Disagreement with me on these points will not vitiate most of the arguments I have used in the book. After all, everybody, whether Kantian, utilitarian, or subjectivist, agrees in admitting that all the kinds of good mentioned (at any rate except mere retribution) ought to be produced by us. The main question for me here is what are the kinds of good (and evil) produced by punishment and reward, not how best are

---

[1] *i.e.*, provided he does not put forward any belief of his own, as in fact all sceptics inconsistently do. If he says that all beliefs are false he contradicts himself, but not if he, without positively denying, simply refuses to accept any belief.

they to be fitted into a general system of Ethics, nor what is meant by good as such.    But in any case, it seems better that the reader should know beforehand what my general preconceptions are than that he should have to guess them from my detailed argument.    But do not let him think that either those stated here or the more detailed discussions of Chapter VI are necessarily presupposed in my treatment of punishment and reward.    I have tried to avoid in any way resting my conclusion on disputable points of general moral theory.

# CHAPTER II

## The Retributive Theory

THE retributive theory of punishment involves two main conceptions : (1) that it is an end-in-itself that the guilty should suffer pain ; (2) that the primary justification of punishment is always to be found in the fact that an offence has been committed which " deserves " the punishment, not in any future advantages to be gained by its infliction, whether for society or for the offender as an individual. The second conception, it is argued, involves the first, for, if punishment is not an end-in-itself, it is justifiable only as a means to other ends, and, therefore, cannot be defended by simply referring to a past act, since the ends to be attained cannot now be attained in the past but only in the future. It is admitted by all parties that in general any future ends which a punishment may have can only be achieved if it is inflicted on " the guilty," *i.e.*, on those who deserve it, but this is not what the retributive theory means. It means that the punishment of the guilty is in itself something of value quite apart from the fact that it is a method of attaining other ends, like the deterrence or reformation of offenders. On that view even if society were to be dissolved to-morrow it would still be intrinsically right and good that the guilty should be duly punished, not for any ulterior reason but in and for itself alone. Its treatment of punishment as an end-in-itself and not merely as a means is both the essential characteristic which distinguishes the retributive theory and the chief target for the attacks of its opponents.[1]

Clearly the theory, thus defined, cannot be proved by any

---

[1] I should not classify as retributive any view which justifies punishment by its good social consequences. Thus Bosanquet seems rather misleading when he calls his own view " retributive," although he does not say that punishment is an end-in-itself, only that it has certain good consequences which cannot be fitted into the ordinary class of reformatory, deterrent and preventive and have, a special connection with the fact that a punishment is for past wrongdoing. (*Suggestions in Ethics*, see below, pp. 52, 113.) Such a doctrine is naturally not affected by the criticisms given in this chapter.

argument which shows only that punishment has good consequences of a certain order. To support punishment in this way is to justify it as a mere means and not as an end-in-itself. It is indeed no argument against punishment being good-in-itself,[1] since it is common enough for something to possess both " instrumental " value as a means and " intrinsic " value as an end-in-itself.[2] But it is clearly impossible to *prove* that anything is an end- or good-in-itself merely by showing that it is an effective means to some other end which commends itself to us as good. You cannot show that punishment ought to be inflicted for its own sake by showing that it is likely to have good consequences.

Nor can I see any other possible way of establishing the retributive theory except by an appeal to moral " intuition."[3]

This is not necessarily an argument against the theory, for, as we have admitted already,[4] if we mean by " intuition " " knowledge obtained otherwise than solely by inference or observation," we must accept the validity of some " intuitions "[5] as to what is good or right if we are to admit any ethical truths at all. Further it must not be denied that the natural man is usually intuitively convinced of something that is at any rate like the retributive theory. He certainly believes that there is a peculiar fitness in the bad man being punished and the good man rewarded quite apart from the consequences, that punishment should be given primarily because a man has done wrong and so *deserved* to be punished, that happiness and unhappiness ought ideally to be in

[1] By the expression, " good-in-itself," I mean only " good otherwise than merely as a means to something else." I do not mean that anything good-in-itself would necessarily remain good if other things were different (v. pp.164-6). " Intrinsically good " and " good-in-itself " are used as synonymous terms, and I make no distinction between them.

[2] It is not absolutely necessary to hold that " good-in-itself " and " end-in-itself " are convertible terms (v. p. 28), but whether we say that just punishment is intrinsically good and therefore to be inflicted for its own sake, or whether we say that we ought to inflict it irrespective of the question as to its intrinsic goodness, in neither case can we justify our position by an appeal to the good consequences of punishment.

[3] This does not mean that the " intuition " is attainable without some inference, explicit or implicit, for probably no intuition stands by itself quite alone, but only that without it no justification whatever can be given for the retributive view, either by an appeal to ethical principles not peculiar to the question at issue or by other means.

[4] v. p. 6.

[5] This does not necessarily make our ethical judgments less certain than others, for all inference in any sphere presupposes and involves non-inferential cognition, which is all I mean by " intuition " (v. pp. 186ff).

proportion to moral goodness and moral badness, that there is such a thing as " atoning " for crime by suffering, that " justice " should be sought for its own sake apart from expediency. To justify punishment merely by reference to its future consequences seems, *prima facie* at any rate, to take from the word " deserve " all its meaning. Such a widespread intuitive belief should at least receive serious consideration. In it lies the whole strength of the retributive theory.

This theory, although it has fallen on evil days in the last generation or two, seems to be supported by the authority of some of the greatest philosophers of modern times, especially Kant, and in a less extreme form Bradley and probably Hegel.[1] For Kant retribution seems to be the sole consideration in fixing not only whether the state has a right to punish a man, but also in determining the amount and kind of punishment. " Judicial punishment . . . can never serve merely as a means to further *another* good, whether for the offender himself or for society, but must always be inflicted on him for the sole reason that he *has committed a crime*. . . . The law of punishment is a categorical imperative, and woe to him who crawls through the serpentine windings of the happiness theory seeking to discover something which in virtue of the benefit it promises will release him from the duty of punishment or even from a fraction of its full severity."[2] In the next paragraph he says that the principle of likeness (Gleichheit) between punishment and offence provides the only legitimate and effective means of determining both the degree and the kind of penalty. This leads him into an obvious difficulty as to the possibility of fixing the right proportion between the guilt of the criminal and the pain[3] of the punishment, but he meets it by an appeal to the *lex talionis*. This virtually means an abandonment of any attempt at correlating the pain with the real inward guilt and the substitution of an external resemblance between the outward nature of the punishment and the injury done by the offender as our sole criterion, but it has at least the advantage of being a workable method. The injury done to the offender in punishment must then correspond quantita-

---

[1] Not, however, according to the interpretation given by, *e.g.*, McTaggart in his *Studies in Hegelian Cosmology, v.* below, p. 24-5.

[2] *Metaphysik der Sitten, Akademie Ausgabe* 331.

[3] The word " pain " is, of course, always used in this book to cover anything of the nature of mental distress or even displeasure, and not only physical suffering.

tively to the injury done by him ; it must not be diminished owing to utilitarian considerations even in a slight degree. Kant, however, insists even more that the punishment should correspond in quality.    In particular he argues that the only rightful punishment for murder is death, just because death is like no other punishment in kind.[1]  Even in cases where a punishment exactly equivalent to the crime cannot be inflicted, e.g., in sexual offences, a punishment must still be inflicted that is equivalent in principle, e.g., permanent deprivation of human rights as the penalty for a man who has committed offences that reduce him morally to the level of an animal.   " To fix *arbitrarily* punishments for them is in literal contradiction with the concept of a *punitive justice*. The only case in which the offender cannot complain that he is being treated unjustly is if his crime recoils upon himself and he suffers what he has inflicted on another, if not in the literal sense, at any rate according to the spirit of the law."[2] Kant thus differs from most advocates of the retributive theory in insisting on equivalence not only in quantity but also in quality.   " It is only *the right of requital* (jus talionis) which can fix definitely the quality and quantity of the punishment."[3]

It will further be noted that Kant makes retribution not only the chief but the sole consideration in fixing the punishment.   This agrees with his view that, if anything is commanded by a general law, the law must be such as to admit of no exceptions due to empirical circumstances and is not itself to be justified by any reference to consequences.   The principle that the State ought to inflict an adequate retributive punishment for crime seems to be put by him in the same position as universal laws like " Thou shalt not lie," though unfortunately he does not give a full deduction of the duty of punishment from his fundamental moral principles.   In the first passage referred to, however, Kant gives as his reason for the retributive theory that man should never be used merely as a means,[4] " for man can never be handled merely as a means to the purposes of another and included among

---

[1] *id.* 333.   Kant admits, however, that if the number of offenders involved is so large that the infliction of the death-penalty might be very dangerous socially, it may be justifiable to substitute some other penalty, but this is the only case in which he allows that punishment may be modified by utilitarian considerations, and even this admission seems irreconcilable with his main doctrine.

[2] *id.* 363.          [3] *id.* 332.          [4] 331.

the objects to which the laws of inanimate property apply "
(Gegenstände des Sachenrechts). Here Kant seems to be
basing his retributive doctrine on his second main principle
in morals, " So act as to treat humanity, both in your own
person and in the person of every other man, always as an
end, never merely as a means." But the conception that
the treatment of a man as an end-in-himself involves punishing him retributively for crime must itself be based on something of the nature of intuition. It seems quite incapable of
logical proof, and no such proof is attempted by Kant. It
may, indeed, be said that a theory which makes punishment
purely deterrent and preventive must involve the treatment
of the criminal merely as a means to the good of others, but
no theory which recognises also the reformatory purpose in
punishment can justly be charged with this. A theory which
admits that punishment ought to reform as well as to deter
and prevent is not treating the offender *only* as a means to
another's good. It may indeed be said, in a sense, to be
treating the offender " only as a means to the *purposes*
(Absichten) of others," these being Kant's actual words in the
passage quoted, for it is not usually the criminal's own
purpose to be reformed or at least to be reformed by punishment ; but the retributive theory also treats him only as a
means to the purposes of others, for neither is it his purpose
to be retributively punished, and of the two retributive
punishment seems to be more an infringement of his liberty
than punishment for his own good would be.[1] We can admit
that he ought to be treated as an end-in-himself and not as
a mere means, but that the retributive theory fulfils this
condition rather than the reformatory theory is not proved
by Kant. It may be true, but it is a view that depends only
on moral intuition for its support.[2]

In a case like this the decision must ultimately rest on what

[1] It is clear that Kant is using the argument to refute the reformatory as well as the deterrent view, for he says in the same sentence
that punishment must not be merely a means to another good " for the
criminal himself or for society." In other words, because a man must
not be made a mere means to the good of others, he must not be made a
means to his own ultimate advantage.

[2] *If* and in so far as these passages can be interpreted as an account
not of the duty to punish but of the intrinsic evil of crime, I should not
attack them, but in that case they would not support the retributive
theory. As this is not a book on Kant's ethics, it would be out of place
to go further into the question of interpretation, but it seems to me that
the passages quoted are, as definitely as anything could be, rules for the
infliction of punishment.

each individual really feels himself bound to think when he views the question calmly, abstracting from all irrelevant considerations as far as he possibly can. The issue here is— Is punishment to be inflicted only as an end-in-itself quite irrespective of consequences ? Now it seems to me that, instead of it being intuitively certain that punishment should be inflicted only as an end-in-itself without any consideration of consequences, the intuitive evidence is all the other way. The appeal to moral intuition may indeed legitimately be used to support the view that punishment ought to be pursued for its own sake as well as for its consequences, but it does not seem to support the view that punishment should be pursued for its own sake *only*. For it is clearly an important good that crime should be lessened, it is also clearly an important good that the criminal should be reformed, and this being so these goods ought to be taken into account in inflicting the punishment and not simply neglected. To see the issue plainly it is desirable to suppose a case in which the punishment required by retributive justice conflicted with that required by reformatory and deterrent considerations. (For the sake of the argument we will admit the possibility of fixing a punishment by retributive considerations alone, a possibility which, though essential to Kant's view, is very disputable and, some would even say, quite meaningless). Now suppose, that in a particular case the retributively just punishment were much worse in its consequences than an alternative punishment not as severe as that required by retributive justice. Suppose that by the infliction of a lighter punishment we could, without doing any social harm, reform the criminal so far as to make him a really good citizen, while if we inflicted the punishment required by retributive justice we should be much less likely to reform him. Surely in a case like that it would be our plain duty to inflict not the punishment that was retributively just but the other, milder punishment. It is surely far more desirable that the criminal should be reformed than that he should suffer the exact amount of pain which is retributively due to him. Retributive justice may be a very good thing, but the saving of souls is a much better thing, and to seek to achieve the first at all costs, even where it will probably involve the sacrifice of the second, seems to me not a moral duty but positively, and in a serious degree, wrong. Anyone who wishes to maintain the position that in punishment we ought *only* to consider the retributive principle must be prepared to admit that it

is our positive duty to inflict the punishment which is retributively just even in cases where the consequences are in the
highest degree harmful, that to try to reform the criminal
where the only or best way of reform involves the remission
of one jot of the retributively just penalty would be itself a
crime.   Even if the milder penalty would probably reform
those sentenced and remove a great social danger, while the
retributive punishment would irretrievably ruin their life
and character, he must hold that it would still be our duty
deliberately and with eyes open to inflict the latter punishment, knowing all the time the evil that would follow in its
wake and the great good, otherwise probably attainable with
ease, that we were throwing away by our insistence on strict
" justice."   Unless we are prepared to hold this, we cannot
accept the view that punishment is merely retributive but
must conclude that it has other ends which are more important.

The only alternative now left for the thoroughgoing
retributionist is to say that, although the retributive principle
will not always lead us aright, we shall be more often right
if we follow it always than if we rely sometimes on the calculation of consequences, which are notoriously uncertain.   I
shall try to refute this position later in the chapter by showing
that the retributive principle is quite useless as a practical
criterion, on any matter of detail at least, and, so far from
being a safer guide than other considerations, is, except as
regards one or two general negative rules, no guide at all.
Here I shall just point out that a man who takes up the
position suggested has already abandoned the view that
punishment is to be inflicted solely because it is an end-in-
itself in favour of the view that the retributive principle is
always the means by which we are most likely to attain the
end of punishment.

But we must not allow our argument to carry us too far.
We may have disposed of the view that punishment should be
exclusively and only retributive, but we have not disposed
of the view that *one* of the functions of punishment is to be
retributive.   Punishment ought not to be inflicted for its
own sake without regard to its consequences, but it does not
follow from this that it ought not to be inflicted for its own
sake as well as for its consequences.   Kant is on firmer
ground when he argues that punishment is retributive
because a man must first be found to be deserving of punishment before we have any right to ask what advantages could

be derived from the punishment for himself and others,[1] although this argument does not imply that punishment need be *only* retributive.    The theory agrees well with the fact that there seems to be a special intrinsic connection between punishment and crime, that the punishment has a backward as well as a forward reference, and it seems needed to express the meaning of words like " deserve," " justice," " responsibility."    By " deserving a punishment " we seem to mean something more than that the punishment is socially profitable because of advantages subsequently to be produced by it, by " justice " something more than expediency even in the highest sense of the term, by " responsibility " something more than agency *de facto*.

This is not quite enough for most advocates of the theory. Not content with maintaining that retribution is an end-in-itself, they maintain that it is the most important end to be sought in punishment, and here they seem to be going wrong. The only evidence they have on their side is ultimately our ordinary non-reflective moral consciousness, and this, as far as I can see, does not confirm but contradicts the view that retribution is to be sought in preference to social security and the reforming of character.    The same considerations which make it impossible to hold that retribution is the only end make it impossible to hold that it is the chief end.    That the punishment should be retributively just seems far less important than that it should reform.    It follows that retributive considerations should at the most play only a small part in fixing the rightful amount of punishment.    Where they conflict with other considerations they should in most cases be sacrificed, for we cannot be justified in seriously impairing the much more valuable ends of improvement of character and social order for their sake ;[2] where they do not conflict, the punishment can be fixed equally well by other considerations than retribution, since *ex hypothesi* the result will be the same.    It would be different if we could hold that it was much less doubtful whether a punishment was retributively just than whether its effects would be advantageous.    If that were so we might often have to prefer the lesser and more

---

[1] *Metaphysik der Sitten, Akademie Ausgabe*, 331.

[2] It is no doubt possible to argue that, since a very large amount of a lower good may be preferable to a very small amount of a higher good, we may sometimes be justified in sacrificing a small (or doubtful) amount of other advantages in order to make a punishment retributively just, but this could at the best only apply to exceptional instances.

certain good to the greater and less certain, but then it is at least as doubtful whether any particular punishment really corresponds to the moral guilt of the offender as it is whether its effects are likely to be the most satisfactory attainable. It is impossible to ascertain either with anything in the least degree approaching certainty, but the former seems even more doubtful than the latter. (If I am right in my contentions later in the chapter, it is not only a doubtful goal that we should be seeking, but an absolutely unattainable one). But the view of punishment as primarily retributive has one great merit. It does justice to the truth that punishment always presupposes guilt, and when we leave the retributive theory and search in other realms for a solution of our problem we must always remember this. Perhaps it may ultimately lead us back to a position in some respects not so far removed from the one we have now left. To say that a punishment ought to be fixed mainly by other than retributive considerations is *not* to say that it ought to be inflicted except *for* a bad act, and the latter is after all the chief point which most advocates of retribution have at heart. In this I agree with them, but we must first see whether an adequate place cannot be found for this principle in theories which are not in the ordinary sense retributive.

Hegel would found the retributive theory on the metaphysical nature of crime as " nichtig." " The nullity (*das Nichtige*) of crime consists in its having abrogated the right as right. The right, as being absolute, does not allow of being abrogated, is not to be cancelled, and, therefore, the external essence of crime is in itself a nullity, and this is the essence of its influence. But that which is null must manifest itself as such, *i.e.*, it must reveal itself as being itself violable. The criminal act is not a primary, positive thing to which the punishment would be added as a negation, but a negative, so that the punishment is only a negation of negation."[1] Hegel concludes that, because the crime, as a bad act, is ultimately " unreal," its unreality ought to be made manifest by a punishment which " negates " the wrong and so annuls it. He adds that the criminal in his crime is ultimately striking at his own will because his own will is really identical with the will of his victim, and the punishment may therefore be conceived as his own will returning upon himself. He holds that there is an immanent " dialectic " by which crime leads to punishment and punishment to amendment.

[1] *Philosophie des Rechts*, § 97.

In dealing with this view I am in a specially difficult position, and this for several reasons.   In the first place the view presupposes two far-reaching and important, but, as stated, very ambiguous, metaphysical doctrines—namely, the unreality, or relative unreality, of evil, and the ultimate identity of all selves; and it is impossible to do justice to these doctrines in a few pages of an ethical essay not mainly concerned with Hegel.   In the second place it is doubtful whether this passage is really meant as a defence of the retributive doctrine as I have defined it, namely the doctrine that punishment is an end-in-itself.   It is interpreted by, *e.g.*, McTaggart, in a way which would not imply this doctrine, but would make punishment valuable, primarily at least, as a means to moral improvement or a necessary stage in moral development.   Thirdly, it seems clear that the value and probably the actual purpose of Hegel's account is best realised if we read it not as a logical argument but as an account of moral experience in cases where punishment fulfils its proper function.

Since, however, it may be taken as a logical proof of the retributive theory, I must point out that, if regarded from this point of view, it has several flaws, even supposing we assume the truth of the metaphysical doctrines that I have mentioned.   In the first place, it would prove at the most that punishment must inevitably follow crime by virtue of its own inherent nature, not that the State ought to intervene to inflict an external punishment.   Nobody argues that, because the law of gravitation is universal and inevitable, the State ought to intervene to help in carrying it out. Secondly, the argument assumes that punishment annuls the evil in the way required and that reformation without punishment will not do so.   It would undoubtedly be a good thing if the past evil could really be annulled, but " annulling" cannot be meant literally because what is once done cannot be undone, and, if it is meant metaphorically, a further argument is needed to show that punishment conceived as retributive really does " annul " in the special metaphorical sense required, whatever that is.   It is, after all, reformation and not retribution that destroys the moral evil[1] in the character of the offender.   Thirdly, even if, as Hegel says,

---

[1] This, and not the evil of the past act, is what can be annulled, but, if it is said that punishment should be inflicted to annul this, the retributive view is abandoned in favour of a view which makes punishment primarily of value only as a means to reformation.

crime and punishment are both to be regarded as " negative," why should the addition of a second negative improve matters ? The metaphor breaks down, for, although the denial of a negative makes a positive, punishment is not the denial of the crime. It would be more appropriate to call it an affirmation of its gravity. Fourthly, the premises— all that is real is good, and punishment inevitably follows crime—can never prove that punishment is good-in-itself, for it might still be good only as a means. Either by " real " is meant everything that is, in which case it is obvious that some elements in the real are not good in themselves, but only, if at all, good as means ; or by " real " is meant everything that is good (its reality being in proportion to its goodness), in which case we cannot say that punishment is real till we have first shown that it is good, and the argument becomes a circle. Still less does it follow that it is a good of great importance or the chief good to be considered in dealing with offenders. The argument that, because something is real, it is intrinsically good, *i.e.*, good-in-itself, is either circular or would prove the intrinsic goodness of the crime as well as of the punishment. I do not wish to impugn the postulate that Reality is good, but I do not see how this postulate can be used to deduce what particular kinds of things are intrinsically (and not only instrumentally) good or what are the moral principles which should govern a particular class of actions.

The argument, however, is best regarded not as a strict logical proof but as a statement of what Hegel holds to be the inherent dialectic of experience, a dialectic that in order to convince must be lived. We may welcome the account of the way in which men come to realise the need for punishment and are amended through punishment, but our admiration for Hegel's account of the development of different phases of moral and spiritual life must not make us forget that he has not bridged the gap between the " is " and the " ought to be." We cannot prove that punishment is an end-in-itself by showing either that it leads to good consequences, or that wrongdoing in fact tends to bring its own punishment.

It is not, however, certain whether Hegel held that punishment was an end-in-itself, though *prima facie* it would seem so. What he did insist on, undoubtedly, was the essential connection between crime and punishment, but this might still owe its value to its good consequences, especially as punishment is for Hegel a necessary stage in amendment. He also repudiates the view that makes each punishment a

mere means to particular goods, but it is just possible that
he meant, not that punishment was justifiable apart from
consequences, but that, while it was justifiable only because
its consequences in general were good, we were still obliged,
as we often are in morals, to rely on the general law and not
to confuse ourselves by calculating what good can be produced in each particular instance. Nor does he altogether
rule out the consideration of consequences in determining
the specific nature of a punishment, though he does not think
that they should determine whether a man ought to be punished or not, only *how* he ought to be punished. However,
he seems to regard the retributive principle of correspondence
between crime and punishment as the chief criterion for
determining the quantity of punishment, though not, like
Kant, its quality.[1]

It is indeed possible to interpret Hegel in a sense which
excludes the strictly retributive notion. This is the course
adopted by, *e.g.*, McTaggart. According to the latter Hegel
holds that the justification of punishment lies only in the fact
that it is a necessary stage in the amendment of the criminal.
" What, then, is Hegel's theory ? It is, I think, briefly this.
In sin man rejects and defies the moral law. Punishment is
pain inflicted on him because he has done this, and in order
that he may, by the fact of his punishment, be forced into
recognising as valid the law which he rejected in sinning, and
so repent of his sin—really repent, and not merely be fright-
ened out of doing it again."[2] This seems very like the reformatory theory, but the advocates of the latter have generally
insisted, not, like Hegel, that punishment by the very fact
of punishment is reformatory, but only that we ought to use
other means to reform criminals while they are being punished.
" The reformatory theory wishes to pain criminals as little
as possible, and improve them as much as possible. Hegel's
theory says that it is the pain which will improve them, and,
therefore, although it looks on pain in itself as an evil, is by
no means anxious to spare it."[3] For Hegel crime and punish-

---

[1] *Philosphie des Rechts*, § 101, but this is difficult to reconcile with
§ 96.

[2] *Studies in Hegelian Cosmology*, p. 133.

[3] pp. 132–3. McTaggart argues that Hegel's view that in punishment
the criminal is to be treated as a moral being is incompatible with the
retributive view of punishment as an end-in-itself that should be
inflicted even if it does no good whatever, but I should have thought
rather that the second view presupposed the first, *i.e.*, those who hold
that punishment is an end-in-itself also hold that it should be inflicted

ment, on the one hand, and punishment as painful and reformation on the other, are essentially connected by virtue of
their inherent nature in a way in which they never are in the
merely utilitarian theories on the subject. Crime from the
nature of the case ought to be definitely and unequivocally
shown up as wrong both to the criminal himself and to others,
and this can only be done by the disgrace of punishment,
while on the other hand the beating down of the evil will by
pain is an essential stage in reformation and not merely
preventive or deterrent. For this reason McTaggart prefers
to apply the term " purifying " rather than " reformatory "
to this conception of punishment. It seems to me doubtful
whether it is possible to do away with the retributive element
in the statement of Hegel's doctrine, but at any rate the view
of punishment given in this interpretation is one of very great
importance to which we shall have to return later. Moreover, even if Hegel treats the punishment as primarily
retributive, to be inflicted just because the man has done
wrong, this does not imply that it is not of great value as a
means also, and this is borne out by the fact that in his
treatment of sin he makes punishment an essential, and not
merely an accidental, stage in amendment.

What is the punishment that crime implies as its necessary
consequence ? One would expect *prima facie* that it consisted in the offender being made worse. But this deterioration of character, though the natural result of sin, is certainly not a result that Hegel would desire the legislator
deliberately to bring about by punishment. It is, on the
contrary, a result against which it is our duty to fight.[1] But
this is not the meaning of Hegel's doctrine ; what he insists
on is not that crime makes the criminal worse, but that
eventually, if he goes on sinning long enough, he must become
disgusted with it, because sin and moral evil are essentially
" nichtig " and will not satisfy. Because Reality is essentially good, moral evil ultimately is self-contradictory and
destroys itself. This doctrine is a very valuable one,[2] but

just because the criminal has incurred moral guilt, which he could not
do if he were not a moral being at all. This is especially clear from a
consideration of Kant. (It does not follow necessarily that we can
reverse the argument and say that the view of man as a moral being
implies the retributive theory.)

[1] *v.* Princ. Moberly, *Proceedings of Aristotelian Association*, June, 1925.

[2] As will be seen later the debt I owe to it is very great, but it is clearly
not a proof that punishment is an end-in-itself, which is what we are
discussing here.

for the reasons above given I do not see how it can be used as a basis for the retributive theory. For the natural process indicated is primarily one of reformation, and though it must involve pain it does not follow that the pain is a good-in-itself (or even that the process will be quickened by the infliction of external pain, for to be reformed one must be disgusted with the sin itself and not merely with its painful consequences). The healing of a wound is a good thing, and pain is a necessary accompaniment of the process by which it heals, but it does not follow that we ought deliberately to inflict further pain on the wounded man for its own sake.

But, if it cannot be proved that punishment is an end-in-itself, can it either be disproved? Even if retribution is not the chief factor to be considered, it may be one of the factors; even if punishment must not be inflicted regardless of consequences, it may be that it ought to be inflicted for its own sake as well as for its consequences. Such a partially retributive view would seem to be the view that accords best with the feelings and moral intuitions of the average man about punishment. What can be said against it?

In the first place it is urged by, e.g., Rashdall[1] that the pain of punishment, being, like all pain, an evil, cannot be an end-in-itself. To inflict a painful punishment where it did not produce good consequences would be to bring into existence an additional evil without any compensating good, it would be useless cruelty. You cannot lessen an evil—here the bad moral state of the criminal and the harm done through the crime—by adding to it a second evil—the pain of the punishment, unless the second evil produces some good results. If it fails to produce them you have by your act made things worse than they were before, and you have, therefore, done wrong. "If the purpose of punishment be anything else besides the production of good effects on conscious beings, it seems to me wholly immoral and irrational," says Rashdall. The infliction of pain for pain's sake is what the retributive theory enjoins, yet the infliction of pain for pain's sake is just the definition of the worst type of cruelty. This kind of objection is perhaps the chief reason why the retributive theory seems so irrational to so many thinking people.

Rashdall's view is determined by the doctrine that the rightness of an act depends on it being the act which is likely

---

[1] *Theory of Good and Evil*, I, pp. 287.90.

to produce the greatest balance of good over evil possible under the circumstances (or the least possible balance of evil over good), but there are various ways of reconciling this view with retributive punishment, if the latter is accepted on other grounds. In the first place we might admit that the pain was not an end-in-itself and yet hold that, while the moral evil in the offender and the pain of the punishment were themselves both evils, it was yet intrinsically good that a certain relation between them should subsist or be established. It would then be a good-in-itself that the wicked should be punished without either their wickedness or the pain of the punishment being valuable in themselves. Or the intrinsic value might belong to the act of punishing. Rashdall objects that a mere abstract relation cannot be good in itself, not being a state of a conscious being, but the position does not seem to me impossible. In particular cases the end would still be not a mere abstraction but the establishment of a *particular* relation, *i.e.*, between *this* crime and the misery it deserves.

A second way of escape is provided by what Dr. Moore calls " the principle of organic unities."[1] According to this principle pain, though, if taken by itself, an evil, may under certain conditions actually make a complex state, of which it is a member, better and not worse by its presence. This seems paradoxical enough, but we are forced to admit its truth if we agree that, for instance, the state of a man who feels a painful sympathy in contemplating the dire misfortunes of others is intrinsically better than it would be if he viewed them with painless indifference. Similarly, as Dr. Moore suggests, although moral badness and pain are both evils when taken by themselves, the two combined might conceivably be a lesser evil than the first alone, which would be sufficient to justify retributive punishment.[2]

---

[1] *Principia Ethica*, pp. 27ff.   For my further account of this principle *v.* below, pp. 175-6.

[2] Rashdall himself admits this in the second edition of *The Theory of Good and Evil* (vol. I, pp. 294n–5n), and accepts the possibility that a bad state of mind plus pain may be better on the whole than it would have been without the pain, though not a positive good. He adds, however, " I should submit that the ground of our approbation is not the mere fact that the combined existence of two evils may yet constitute a lesser evil than would be constituted by the existence of either singly, but the tendency of pain to make the state of mind less opposed to the ideal of what it ought to be."   But what about cases where the tendency .is not realised ?   Suppose the case of a man who is not improved by his punishment.   Is it better that he should suffer punishment apart from

Thirdly, even if nothing can be of intrinsic value but states of conscious beings, it does not follow that nothing can be of intrinsic value but conscious states of these beings. Rashdall says that the only rational purpose of punishment is the production of good effects on conscious beings, but even if this is accepted it still may be the case that among these good effects is included the state of suffering a punishment which is deserved. This is still the state of a conscious being and so would come under the formula, even if the offender is not conscious of the justice of the punishment. The value of a man's state of mind is not constituted wholly by what is present to his consciousness. Thus we should certainly regard a man's state as more intrinsically valuable if he loved a person worthy of his love, or enjoyed a really beautiful object, than if he loved a person who was really unworthy, though he thought him worthy, or enjoyed æsthetically an object which he thought beautiful through lack of taste, but which was really ugly. Yet his conscious state would be the same in the two cases.

Neither is it impossible to challenge Rashdall's theory that the right action is always the action which produces, or, as far as could be judged at the time, was likely to produce, the greatest good. It may be argued that there are plenty of possible cases in which the act we should be convinced that we ought to do seems likely to produce less good than an alternative act which seems clearly wrong, e.g., we ought to pay a debt to a rich man known to be mean rather than give the money to a deserving charity. Again we should not consider it right to make two or three people utterly and irretrievably unhappy in order slightly to increase the good enjoyed by each of many thousands, even if we could be sure that by so doing we should greatly increase the total amount of good. But, however that may be, I think I have said enough to show that the advocate of retributive punishment can avoid direct refutation by Rashdall's argument.

The argument does, however, show that the retributive theory is not one which can easily be fitted into a coherent system of Ethics. It leaves it with a certain tinge of irrationality, and puts punishment in a position quite out of relation

its consequences to others ? If so, what of the objection to the retributive theory ? If not, what about Rashdall's admission that an evil state of mind which is punished may be less bad in itself than the evil state would be if not punished ?

to our other moral duties. In every other instance the deliberate infliction of pain is wrong, except where necessary as a means to happiness or ethical improvement, in every other instance our primary duty is to abstain from bringing evil on our fellow-men. In some cases it may conceivably be right or even our duty to produce a lesser good rather than the best possible under the circumstances, but nowhere else is it right deliberately to inflict evil as such. Yet here we are asked to inflict pain for pain's sake.[1] It seems strange that a kind of action which under ordinary conditions is regarded as the very extreme of moral depravity should become a virtue in the case of punishment. The duty of retributive punishment is incapable of being deduced from a wider ethical principle or of being brought into rational connection with our other ethical beliefs. If it is to be accepted on the strength of intuition, that intuition must stand by itself without the support that is gained by membership in a coherent system of ethical judgments. Indeed it must be regarded as a fatal obstacle to our attempts at the establishment of a truly coherent system. But it might be true for all that. This difficulty of fitting it into a system is not the same as self-contradictoriness or logical impossibility. Even if all ethical truths must constitute a perfect system, we are a long way from having achieved such an ideal, and though we may suspect a moral judgment we cannot absolutely reject it because it does not conform to this demand. Even a Bradleian will admit that, for us at least, comprehensiveness is needed as a criterion besides coherence, and we have perhaps no more right to reject a perception of value because it will not fit into our system than the scientist has to reject a perception of fact for a similar reason. It would be different if we held that pleasure was the only good and the only end-in-itself, for the retributive theory definitely contradicts this utilitarianism. But, as it is, we are not entitled altogether to reject the retributive view, at least till we have produced another theory which will still leave some meaning in the word " deserve " and which will justify our conviction that punishment must be inflicted, not only as a means to future good, but as a reply to past wrongdoing. On the other hand we must remember, if the sole basis of the retributive

[1] Whichever of the above ways of escape is adopted, they all imply that the pain of the bad or the infliction of pain on the bad is an end that should be pursued for its own sake. Without this doctrine the strictly retributive element would disappear.

theory is an unproved moral intuition,[1] that, however great
the respect which philosophy must pay to such intuitions,
it cannot be maintained that we are always bound to accept
them without criticism as they stand. We may find that
it is possible to do substantial justice to the demands which
the retributive theory meets in a form which is somewhat
different from but more rational than that in which they
first present themselves to our moral sense. In the mean-
time, unless we can discover any further convincing arguments against it, we must leave as an open possibility the
partially, though not the exclusively, retributive view.

Another objection brought by Rashdall against retributive
punishment is that it cannot be reconciled with the duty of
forgiveness.[2] If the retributive theory were true, he says, it
would always be wrong to forgive till the crime had been completely expiated by punishment. The natural reply to this
is that forgiveness consists primarily in a right state of feeling
and a right mental disposition towards the man who has
wronged you, especially in the laying aside of personal
resentment, and that this subjective condition is quite recon-
cilable with the infliction of the retributively just punishment.
Rashdall, however, thinks this sense of forgiveness by itself
too indefinite. He admits, indeed, that " it is true that in
its essence the duty of forgiveness is the duty of laying aside
*private* or personal resentment—of resenting the wrong
because it is a wrong and not because I am the victim of it,"
but he adds, " What Bishop Butler[3] has missed is the fact
that vengeance often loses its moral effect just because the
avenger of the wrong is its victim, while forgiveness often
touches the heart just because the man who forgives is the
man who suffered by the wrong, *i.e.*, the man for whom it is
hardest to forgive." That forgiveness may have this effect
is certainly both true and important. Further, it would be
a valid argument against a theory which was exclusively
retributive. If it is our duty in punishing to consider nothing
but the requirements of the retributive principle, it must be
wrong to remit any part of the punishment, even if that be
the only way of securing the salvation of the offender. But
anybody who makes retribution only *one* of the points to be

[1] The argument that all other reasonably satisfactory theories of
punishment presuppose the retributive view cannot well be discussed
till we have turned to the non-retributive theories.
[2] *Theory of Good and Evil*, I, pp. 306 *ff.*
[3] *v.* Butler, *Sermons* 8 and 9.

considered can easily admit that there are cases in which it should be sacrificed for the sake of the offender's moral good.

Further Rashdall himself is faced with a similar difficulty, for it certainly must be wrong on his own view to remit any part of a really just punishment, *i.e.*, of that punishment which is, all things considered, likely to produce the best effects possible. Hence forgiveness must either be wrong, if it means remission of the just punishment, or be identical in its outward expression with justice. But this is hardly a very serious difficulty. What forgiveness consists in is being as well-disposed to the man who has wronged you as if it had not been *you* that he had wronged, and not treating him less kindly for that personal reason, *e.g.*, resisting the temptation to make his punishment severer than it ought to be. It does not consist in making the punishment less than it ought to be. As applied to the actual penalty, forgiveness cannot, in so far as it is desirable, be anything different from the highest justice, but it may still be distinguished from justice because it consists in acting justly in face of one particular kind of temptation, *i.e.*, resentment against enemies, as opposed to acting justly in face of other temptations, *e.g.*, of pecuniary gain. It might be said that there is rarely any difficulty in reconciling the duty of forgiveness and the duty of punishment, because the private individual cannot, strictly speaking, punish his enemy, unless he happens to be acting for the State in an official capacity, while the duty of forgiveness does not apply to magistrates who deal not with their personal enemies but with offenders against the State, though the duty of " mercy " does, in so far as compatible with the best interests of the offender himself and of society. We may, however, fairly speak of a conflict between the two requirements where (1) the individual has to decide whether it is his duty to take legal action against a man who has wronged him ; (2) where he has the chance by perfectly lawful proceedings of inflicting an injury on the reputation or social position of his enemy, which may be construed either as an act of purely vindictive anger or as an attempt to assert a moral principle for the common good. For his acquaintances to express their moral disapproval of a man's actions is undoubtedly to punish that man, yet one cannot rule out the possibility of such a proceeding being sometimes justified, in fact if rightly used it might be a very valuable means for the diffusion and improvement of moral ideas. But, even where it is desirable that this disapproval should be definitely expressed, it is undoubtedly better that the man who is primarily wronged should, if possible, "keep a back seat in the proceedings," especially as, if he does so, their moral effect is less likely to be spoilt by the offender regarding them as simply an act of vengeance or personal pique. Enough, however, has been said to give some ground for holding that the duty of forgiveness need not be inconsistent with the retributive principle, provided the latter is not regarded as the only principle which should determine punishment.

If retribution is one good, but not the only good to be sought in punishing, we might even say that it is easier to state and justify the antithesis between strict justice on the one hand and mercy or forgiveness on the other than it is if a non-retributive view is adopted, because then we can say that the virtue of forgiveness may be shown in sacrificing the good that we happen to desire most strongly at the moment (retributive justice) for a good that appeals to us less but is, in some cases at least, intrinsically more valuable. The retributionist need not make retributive justice an absolutely unconditional duty. He would, however, be bound to admit that, where a man is forgiven and thus reformed without retributive punishment, we ought to feel that there is some-thing lost, *i.e.*, justice, though it is less than what is gained, as we feel when, *e.g.*, a man gives up intellectual pursuits for a great social service ; and this might be questioned.

Other objections against the retributive theory are taken from its association with revenge. Revenge as the outcome of a mere desire "to have one's own back" is obviously a non-moral principle, and the retributive motive in punishment is often held by its opponents to be just a modification of this desire, of no more moral value than anger at a personal injury. "The retributive theory is apt to seem not so much a rational justification of punishment as the refusal to reason about the matter at all. It seems to be a wilful substitution of passion for reason as a guide of conduct, and of a kind of passion which, in the form of private revenge, civilised society has agreed to condemn."[1] But, as the writer of this passage admits directly, this view does not do the retributive theory justice. It cannot be dismissed lightly as merely an expression of our natural but non-moral (if not immoral) feeling of resentment at those who offend us. It is not right to speak as though the retributive view meant that the only justification of punish-

[1] Princ. Moberly, *Proceedings of Aristotelian Society*, June, 1915.

ment was that it satisfied the desire for revenge. It is as open for a retributionist as for anybody else to say that punishment should be inflicted not merely because we desire to inflict it but because we think it to be right, right because the offender has done wrong and not because we feel angry at him having done wrong. Even if punishment ought to be an end *per se*, our feeling of anger need not be either the criterion or the sole motive of our action in punishing. We still ought to inflict the punishment, whether we feel resentment or not, and inflict it only if, and because, it is just.

The advocate of retributive punishment will admit that the disposition to punish is closely connected with some form of " righteous indignation." But to say that a certain desire is very closely connected with a certain kind of right action is not to say that the action should be exclusively determined by that desire without regard to any other considerations. Any kind of virtue can be shown to be connected with specific desires or feelings that impel on the whole to actions exemplifying that virtue, *e.g.*, benevolence is connected with natural sympathy, courage with natural pugnacity or dislike of appearing weak, and so on, but it does not follow in the least from this that it would be right to allow these desires and feelings exclusive control of any action. It obviously would not. So it is with retributive punishment ; " righteous indignation " may be a help in making it easier to carry out the duty of punishment, but it obviously should not be the only determining factor in fixing the penalty, and this for two reasons. In the first place the good of retribution, even if it be a good, sometimes has to be sacrificed to other goods. In the second place, even if retributive justice were the only end to be considered in a given instance, it would not follow that we ought to be entirely governed by any passion or desire rather than by reason in deciding what punishment was retributively just. Passions and desires are notoriously not clear-sighted guides in matters like these.

Further, the supporters of the view often maintain that the anger expressed in true retributive punishment, if it can, strictly speaking, be called anger at all, is at any rate radically different from anger at injuries as injuries to oneself. It is impartial and not personal, an anger aroused by moral evil as such, not by one's private suffering or loss. Aversion to evil is a necessary concomitant of attraction to the good, and this may take the form of a righteous indignation expressible in retributive punishment. This kind of indignation may be held to be a valuable emotion both in its consequences and in itself, and to be inseparably connected with the idea of just punishment. It may also be urged that the impulse to private revenge is a passion that forms the groundwork on which the loftier emotion of " righteous indignation " is built up, that the latter emotion is only attained by what the " new psychology " would call the " sublimation " of the former. As being impartial and impersonal, it is free from the defects of anger with one's private enemies. Its adherents would admit that it should be anger at the sin rather than at the sinner, though unfortunately it can only vent itself on the person of the sinner. While pointing out—and this is undoubtedly historically true—the development of punishment from the desire for private vengeance, they are free to emphasise the differences that have arisen in the course of development. Green, while insisting on these differences against some advocates of the retributive theory, yet declares : " Such indignation is inseparable from the interest in social well-being, and along with it is the chief agent in the establishment and maintenance of legal punishment."[1] Yet he is no retributionist.

But we must remember that the question of the motives which actually lead to punishment is purely psychological. Even if indignation at wrong is the chief motive which leads to its infliction this does not prove that punishment is really of value in itself, only that we (or many of us) desire it for its own sake, at least for other people. The fact that a thing is very widely desired may be taken as an indication that it, or something closely connected with it, is generally of value either in itself or as a means, but this leaves open the possibility that it may be not punishment itself but something closely connected with it which is of intrinsic value, or that punishment is of value but only as a means. " *Righteous* indignation " as an emotion is certainly much less strong[2] than the desire for security which provides the deterrent motive, and benevolence which, in the main, provides the reformatory motive. Further, it seems to me very questionable whether it is a mark of goodness to desire the punishment of sinners just for the sake of hurting them. Righteous indignation, if it is to be righteous, must be based on the aversion to moral evil, but it would seem that a genuine aversion to moral evil ought to lead one rather to try to des-

---

[1] *Principles of Political Obligation*, Sec. 183.
[2] And, we may add, much less valuable as a means to other goods.

troy it by reforming the sinner than to avenge it by retributive punishment. It is natural and, at least in the present state of human nature, quite excusable sometimes to feel a desire that a man who has committed a particularly atrocious crime should be made to suffer, should be " paid out " ; but, whether this anger, this desire that pain should be inflicted would be felt by an ideal man, seems to me at least very doubtful, however much the ideal man realised the necessity for the punishment as a means. Nor should we think the better of a man who indulged this " righteous indignation " so far as to dwell frequently with pleasure on the sufferings of criminals, however well deserved they might be. Aversion to evil is a necessary element in a good character, but this aversion need not take the form of a desire to inflict pain for its own sake. It would be a strangely perverted impulse if its main aim were not to remove the evil that is there, but to add to it what is always *per se* a fresh evil, pain, and to rejoice in the infliction of this pain. Righteous indignation, in so far as it has value, is rather a sentiment determining action than an emotion. The associated desire that pain should be inflicted cannot with safety be developed much for fear that it should turn into unrighteous anger, and, though it may be very useful as a means without which the amount of punishment socially necessary would not be inflicted, its intrinsic value seems very small. A right attitude to evil must be admitted to be of the greatest importance and value (indeed the chief aim of punishment is to secure it), but the same cannot be said of the desire to inflict pain even on criminals, except in so far as this desire is useful as a psychological incentive without which justice would not be so effectively done.[1] Even if one of the objects of punishment is to cultivate some form of " righteous indignation," this does not make punishment an end-in-itself but only adds another end to which punishment is a means.

Another popular objection against the retributive theory is that it presupposes an irrational indeterminism. It certainly presupposes freedom in that sense of the word (whatever it is) in which freedom is a necessary presupposition of moral action, but the same must apply to any ethical theory. Whether freedom in the sense of undetermined ($=$uncaused)

---

[1] It must, however, be admitted that one of the advantages of punishment is that it sometimes provides a legitimate outlet for a popular indignation which might otherwise lead to harmful results, *e.g.*, lynching, *v.* p. 71.

action is presupposed by morality is another question. In popular discussion the indeterminist is too apt to assume that freedom has only one sense, namely, his sense, and to jump too hastily from the true premiss that morality presupposes freedom to the somewhat more doubtful conclusion that he has been right in his analysis of freedom. If morality does imply indeterminism, this is no special objection against the retributive theory ; if it does not, why is it necessary that the retributive theory should ? The proposition that the pain of those guilty of a crime should be treated as an end-in-itself does not necessarily presuppose anything more than that the commission of the crime is morally bad, not only bad in the same way as physical disease, but this must be accepted by any tolerable theory of punishment. It must be admitted, however, that the retributive view appears more rational, to most people at any rate, when associated with one particular theory of freedom, namely the theory that free acts are undetermined. This is mainly because indeterminism is commonly supposed to be the only way of making a man responsible for his acts. But there are other theories which claim to give a man freedom, besides the theory of indeterminism or uncaused action. The ordinary " scientific " conception of causality requires remodelling when applied to a human agent, and to me this rather than indeterminism seems to provide the best hope of a solution of the problem. There are conceptions of " self-determination " which do not require the exclusive one-sided determination of the present by the past that is the chief bugbear feared by the " indeterminist." But, if so, the retributive theory might be associated with these rather than with indeterminism.[1]

But the advocate of retributive punishment has still to face the difficult question of proportioning punishments to the moral guilt of the offender. It seems to me quite possible to maintain the view that punishment is an end-in-itself in spite of the objections I have mentioned (provided we recognise that its value as an end-in-itself is not the only or the chief thing that should be taken into account in determining whether and how to inflict it) ; but I shall now argue that this view, as interpreted retributively, is altogether inapplicable in practice, at least as regards criminal law and State punishment.[2]

[1] Neither Kant nor Hegel were indeterminists.
[2] I shall, in a later chapter, show how it is possible to regard punishment as an end-in-itself and yet avoid the drawbacks of the retributive theory.

The object of retributive punishment is to make the pain of the offender correspond to his guilt.[1] Now it is difficult enough to see how there can be such a thing as a right proportion between pain and moral guilt ; but, waiving this difficulty, it is harder still to see how we are to determine the right proportion in particular cases. In the first place, in order to find the degree of wickedness involved in the commission of the offence, the offender's exact state of mind at the time would have to be ascertained, and how that could be done, even very roughly, without introspective knowledge of the criminal, I cannot see. But this introspective knowledge can only be possessed by one man, the criminal himself, and he would not be likely to tell the truth about it. Even if he would, he could hardly do so to much effect. That a man cannot properly estimate even his own motives is a platitude, and a man about to commit a crime is not likely to be introspecting carefully at the moment. In the second place not only his state of mind at the time of committing the offence, but also a great deal of his previous psychological development, would have to be ascertained in order to estimate the moral guilt even of the particular act by itself, for we must know how much or how little excuse he had, and this knowledge could only be acquired by examining a psychological process lasting over years. For instance, how far was the abnormal difficulty he had in resisting a particular kind of temptation congenital, and how far was it due to his having formerly yielded to that temptation when resistance would have been as easy as it is for the average man ? How far was his mental outlook at the moment when he committed the crime due to bad education ?

But, in the third place, surely it could not be retributively just to punish the offender for the moral guilt involved in one act without taking into account his whole character. That would be to judge a man by his worst acts only.[2] What is the use of attempting to achieve the end of bringing happiness and misery into proportion to merit and guilt, if you only consider a few exceptional actions ? But what chance is there of a law-court or any outsiders forming a fair estimate

[1] For a criticism of the form of retributive theory which renounces this idea v. pp. 40-43.
[2] If the punishment is to be proportionate only to the badness of the particular crime and not to the man's whole character, we should have to punish habitual offenders more lightly because their will is weakened by habit, and perhaps finally let them off altogether.

of the man's whole character and moral worth so far as to know that he deserves such a degree of punishment and no other? Can a man determine with the least accuracy and certainty the degree of his own deserts, let alone that of somebody he has only met for a few hours in the criminal court?

Besides, fourthly, we should have to settle how far, if at all, we were to regard the criminal as responsible for innate tendencies and how we were to separate innate and acquired characteristics. Finally within any acquired characteristic itself we should have to distinguish what was forced or almost forced on him by external circumstances, and what was due to his own culpable perversity.

Fifthly, granted that the degree of moral guilt and the degree of pain that ought to correspond were fixed, we should still have to ascertain what punishment would cause the requisite amount of pain, and this could only be done by considering the criminal's individual peculiarities and susceptibilities to an extent which seems quite impracticable.

But, lastly, how are we to fix the right proportion between guilt and pain by the retributive principle, how are we to say what amount of guilt deserves a certain amount of pain and what another, different amount? We have no doubt an intuitive conviction in extreme cases that a punishment is too severe or too lenient, e.g., we certainly feel that torture on the rack would be too severe a punishment for an angry word, or that a fine of sixpence would be too light a punishment for a murder, and this conviction seems to be quite independent of utilitarian considerations, at least as far as conscious reasoning goes. But this does not help us to fix an exact proportion between punishment and guilt. More detailed intuitions, such as the number of years of imprisonment a particular theft deserves, seem to be wholly lacking.[1]

Thus anybody who wishes to apply the retributive theory in practice is confronted with very serious difficulties. This is not only the case if he holds an exclusively retributive view, but if he holds any view according to which the amount of punishment must be fixed even partially by retributive considerations. The difficulty is not only that we must take account of other factors besides retribution, but that the retributive principle can give us no help at all beyond provid-

---

[1] We cannot settle the question, as Kant did, by the "lex talionis," unless we suppose that the moral badness of an act corresponds to the amount of external damage caused by it, an assumption which, as Kant himself would be the first to admit, is quite impossible.

ing the general rule that a greater offence should be punished more severely than a lesser one, and forbidding certain ridiculously small and atrociously severe punishments, which would probably be rejected on other grounds in any case. Its sphere of possible application thus becomes very limited. The practical difficulties would be less fatal, though still serious enough, if it were a question of applying the retributive principle in the education of children, for here the person who inflicts the punishment has more intimate knowledge of the offender than is the case in the ordinary administration of criminal law, but then even the advocates of retributive punishment are loth to apply their principle except to the adult. It may be retorted that there are great practical difficulties involved in carrying out any theory of punishment, and that any theory must proceed by general rules at the expense of being sometimes unfair to individuals, but the deterrent and reformatory theories, especially the first, seem to be in a considerably better position in this respect than the retributive.

But worse is to follow. An examination of these difficulties shows not only that the retributive theory cannot be applied with anything like success, but also that it is wrong even to attempt to apply it. It shows not only that the retributive principle cannot tell us the exact degree of the punishment, but that it could not justify us in inflicting any punishment whatever. The object of the retributionist is that the punishment should be just, and every excess over the just amount must be in the same ethical position as punishment of " the innocent," an injustice which seems much worse than non-punishment of the guilty. Yet it is certain that either this injustice or the opposite one of inflicting too slight a penalty will be perpetrated in nine cases out of ten, nay in 999 out of a thousand, so great are the difficulties in the way of securing the right proportion between the punishment and the guilt of the offender. If failure is so likely or, rather, almost certain, ought the State to inflict punishment for the sake of retribution at all ? If the object of punishment is to prevent future crimes and reform criminals, it is clearly the duty of the State to try to fulfil this essential function, even at the risk of failure, at least if it tries it will be more likely to succeed than if it does nothing at all in the matter. But, if and in so far as the object of punishment by the State is to do retributive justice, then the case is different. Here, if the State interferes, it is on retributive standards more likely actually to make things worse than to make them better.  For, owing to the impossibility of estimating the moral guilt of the offender and the degree of punishment proportionate to it, and owing to the serious consequences for some innocent persons that his punishment is almost sure to involve, we may be certain that, if and in so far as justice consists in a retributive proportion to guilt, almost all punishments will be unjust.  But to do injustice seems worse than to do nothing at all, at least in so far as injustice consists in punishment of the innocent, and, according to the view we are discussing, punishment of the guilty beyond the retributively just amount must be in the same category, ethically, as punishment of the completely innocent.  Ought the State to aim at retributive justice, if the overwhelming probability is that each time it tries to inflict it it will do serious retributive *injustice* ?[1]  The injustice is greatly enhanced if it is true that criminality is in the majority of cases associated with special weakness of will and intellect, though this must not be taken as eliminating, only diminishing, the responsibility of the criminal.

But the case against retribution has not yet been stated in its full strength.   It is bad enough to know that we are almost certain to go wrong in assessing the guilt of the offender and the punishment which should correspond, but some further considerations make the position much worse.   I shall, however, reserve these till we have discussed a way of escape from our objections which is now commonly advocated.

The difficulties involved in fixing the proportion between punishment and guilt have led most present supporters of the retributive principle to say that it can only be invoked to settle which people are to be punished, not to fix the amount of their penalty.  For example, Bradley, in his *Ethical Studies*, says :—" Having once the right to punish, we may modify the punishment according to the useful and the pleasant, but these are external to the matter ; they cannot give us a right to punish, and nothing can do that but criminal desert."  According to that view we ought then to decide who is to be punished by means of retributive considerations alone, but having decided that we may fix the amount of the punishment by other standards.

The advocates of this view have certainly put their finger

---

[1] I mean what the retributionist, according to his own principles, ought to consider serious injustice.

on the weak spot in most non-retributive doctrines of punishment, namely, the failure to do justice to the truth that punishment should be inflicted for a past offence as well as to secure a future end, a failure which obliterates the vital distinction between a penalty paid by the guilty and suffering inflicted on the innocent as means to a supposed greater good. At present, however, I must confine myself to bringing certain criticisms against the view as an attempt to avoid the practical difficulties of the retributive theory without abandoning its central doctrine.

In the first place, the doctrine that retributive considerations and retributive considerations alone give one the right and impose on one the duty of punishing seems incompatible with the admission that the amount of punishment should be determined by other criteria. If we can and ought to fix the amount of punishment by non-retributive considerations, this seems almost equivalent to saying that we may also fix by these considerations whether we are or are not to punish at all. For, if we could not remit the penalty altogether, we should yet be justified on that view in inflicting one so small as to be practically, though not quite, no punishment at all. It makes very little difference whether we admit that, if utilitarian considerations ever required it, we ought to let off a murderer, or deny this, but admit that we might for those reasons lower his penalty to any extent, say, to a fine of one shilling.

Also it may be urged that, *if* the punishment as such can only be justified by retributive considerations, it is difficult to resist the conclusion that each part of it can only be so justified. For each part of the punishment is itself a punishment. If the retributive principle can only be used to decide *when* and not *how much* we are to punish, there will be no distinction between different degrees of desert. Yet, if we are sure that a crime deserves a punishment just because it is a crime, we are equally sure that a decidedly worse crime deserves a severer punishment just because it is worse. We are no surer that " Justice " requires the punishment of a brutal murder than we are that it requires the infliction of a severer punishment for this than for a petty assault committed under dire provocation, and this conviction as much as the other seems independent of utilitarian considerations.

If we are justified in increasing the punishment of the guilty as much as expediency bids and again in reducing it till it is hardly any punishment at all, what is left of the retributive view ? Practically nothing except the injunction not to punish the innocent on any account whatever, even if expediency seems to require it. But unfortunately even this meagre remnant is not secure against the critic. We are involved in difficulties as soon as we ask either what " punish" or what " innocent " means. For if " punish " means " inflict pain or harm," it is hard to defend the doctrine that the innocent ought never for any reason to be put to the slightest discomfort, or caused the slightest harm, against their will. If, on the other hand, it means " inflict pain *for* the commission of a crime," the command not to punish the innocent becomes little more than a tautology, since they have *ex hypothesi* not committed a crime. This criticism may appear purely verbal ; and there is no doubt that the injunction in question does stand for a very important ethical principle, however hard it may be to express it adequately, and however necessary it may be to admit occasional exceptions to the law, so I shall lay stress rather on the second difficulty, which may be expressed by the question—Who are innocent ?

If we decide whom the State ought to punish from retributive considerations, I should have thought the logical conclusion would be that it ought to punish everybody, because everybody has sinned in some way or other. This clearly will not do. It would make the principle that the innocent ought not to be punished quite senseless, because nobody would be " innocent." What does " innocent " mean then ? Those who have not interfered with the rights of others, or those who have not offended against Society ? But practically all wrong-doing interferes, directly or indirectly, with the rights of others, and is an offence against Society. Therefore, again, the State either ought, or at any rate has the right, to punish everybody. Again the principle—Thou shalt not punish the innocent—becomes, for human beings at least, meaningless. What the retributive theory is asked to justify is the punishment of those who have offended against certain definite laws ; but which kinds of offences are to be made punishable by law and which not, is a question that can be answered by considerations of the public good, but not by considerations of retributive justice. What the principle is reduced to now is—Do not punish anyone except for an offence which has been, prior to his committing it, prohibited by law. This is a sound maxim, but it does not tell us either how severe any punishment ought to be, or even what offences ought to be punished by the State. These questions cannot be decided by retributive considerations. If thinkers who hold the view under discussion are content with their principle in this diluted form and not inclined to claim anything further, well and good, but it is difficult to imagine that they will be.

This raises a further difficulty for all retributive views. What about the fairness of singling out some men for punishment by the State when everybody has sinned in a greater or lesser degree ? Is that retributively just ? Even if everybody outside prison were better than everybody within, which can hardly be maintained, it would still be on retributive principles very unjust to punish some men severely, while others who, even if they are not as bad as the " criminals," have very considerable moral defects, are not punished at all. It is obviously impracticable for the State to inflict pain (or bestow pleasure) on everybody in accordance with their faults (or virtuous actions) ; but, if the State cannot do that, whenever it punishes a criminal it is surely committing what must be regarded as an injustice from the retributive point of view. It is inflicting a very severe penalty on a very small fraction of its subjects while letting all the rest go scot free. There may be other reasons in defence of this practice, but it cannot be defended by an appeal to retributive justice. Further, it is obvious that in most cases the punishment of an offender brings suffering on his family and those closely connected with him, though they are innocent of the offence in question. A retributively just punishment for one person, if such a thing be possible at all, would thus involve a retributively unjust punishment for several. Thirdly, we have seen that it is quite chimerical to attempt to proportion the punishment to the guilt of the offender. It follows from all these reasons that the State cannot seek retributive justice without doing an injustice that outweighs the justice according to retributive standards. Therefore the retributive principle can never supply a legitimate reason for State action, since to apply it must frustrate its own ends. As far as this principle is concerned the State ought not to punish at all ; punishment can only be justified, if at all, on other grounds.

To sum up this chapter, the view that pain ought to be inflicted for its own sake in proportion to guilt is based not on argument but on " intuition." It is possible to maintain this view against the objections that pain cannot be an end-in-itself, and that it is our duty to forgive as well as to punish, and against those based on the association of retribution with anger and vengeance ; but it must be admitted that this is at any rate not the sole or the chief reason for punishment, since retribution, even if it is a good, is of much less importance than some of the other goods secured by it.  Further, there are such insuperable difficulties in the way of the practical application of the principle that we seem forced to banish the retributive aim from punishment as applied by the State.  A correct proportion between pain and wickedness may be an end-in-itself, but at any rate it is not an end which the State is justified in pursuing.

Nevertheless, the conviction on which the retributive theory is based is strong, genuine, and almost universal, so that it would be very rash to ignore it as a mere fallacy.  I may appear to have been somewhat over-critical of the theory, but I shall close the chapter by enumerating what seem to be its strong points.

1.  Punishment implies guilt and must be retrospective, in so far as it is inflicted because of a past offence.  This is not accidental but essential to the nature of punishment.  There is a vital difference between punishment for a wrong act and the infliction of non-penal suffering as a means to a future good, e.g., through a surgical operation.

2.  We must not in considering the nature of punishment talk as though the man punished were a mere " thing," like a tool which needed repair.  Punishment derives its specific nature from the assumption that the criminal is a moral being, otherwise he could not have incurred guilt.  It is for this reason that Hegel calls punishment " the criminal's right," and in a sense even an honour to him, because it implies that he is a being capable of moral action.

3.  Psychologically the chief motive which has led to the infliction of punishment in the past is the retributive one.  The historical development of State punishment from private vengeance and the fact that the desire for retribution makes it much easier to see justice carried out must be recognised by us.

4.  While the retributive theory seems to break down in practice, certain general principles for which it stands are of very great importance and value.  It condemns the punishment of the innocent, i.e., of those who have not deliberately committed offences against definite laws in force prior to their commission ; it demands that a lighter offence should not be punished more severely than a much graver one ; it

insists that considerations of expediency, or apparent expediency, should not be easily allowed to outweigh the general rule that the guilty are to be punished. These principles, however they may be justified, must be recognised as of great ethical importance. The retributive theory, though it is often stigmatised as " brutal," should defend the criminal against an excessive severity as unjust, and is far easier to reconcile with our horror at the deliberate infliction of punishment on the innocent for reasons of expediency than any merely utilitarian theory.

5. The ideas of desert, of " justice " as a good-in-itself, and even of proportion between guilt and penalty, are too deeply rooted in our ethical thought to be dismissed lightly, however hard they may be to rationalise.

6. True reformation presupposes condemnation of the crime, and some process involving suffering, at least the inward suffering of repentance. It presupposes a " beating down " of the evil will, and not merely an intellectual or emotional education.

It is important to note that most of the difficulties of the retributive theory spring from either its refusal to take adequate account of consequences or its excessive emphasis on the pain of the punishment as pain. If we avoid these mistakes, we may attain a view that includes its strong points without including its difficulties. The retributive theory insists that punishment ought to be for a past offence, utilitarianism that it ought to be for a future good, but may it not be for both ? Perhaps it can only play the latter *rôle* effectively by first playing the former, and perhaps by playing the former *rôle* it *ipso facto* plays the latter. The retributive theory in its extreme forms must be rejected, but we shall see later that no solution can stand which does not satisfy the essential purpose of this theory.

## CHAPTER III

## The Utility of Punishment
## (especially as a deterrent)

WHATEVER view of punishment we hold, whether we think of it as primarily the expurgation of a stain incurred by a past act or as only a means to the prevention of social evils, whether we think that its essence and only justification is retribution, or whether we refuse to allow any argument for it that could not be accepted by the strictest utilitarian, we still must in any case admit that it may subserve many purposes, and may have many different consequences which are advantageous to society. Even though there may also be corresponding drawbacks, a reasonable system of punishment certainly does further some goods, does lead to some future gain. Now it would be part of the function of moral philosophy to enumerate and examine the goods producible by punishment, even if they had no share in determining the rightness of its infliction. After what I have said in the last two chapters I shall, however, assume that, in order to determine whether any particular punishment is right we must examine its consequences, and that its rightness depends, if not entirely, at least to a very great extent, on the goodness of its consequences. In this chapter I shall, therefore, consider the advantages which may be attained by punishment, the ends for which punishment may be used as a means. Whether punishment is good as an end-in-itself, or not, it is, if wisely inflicted, at any rate good as a means to some end other than itself. There is no difficulty about something being valuable both as an end-in-itself and as a means to the realisation of other ends ; and we are now to discuss the value of punishment as a means.

What are the advantages attainable by punishment, the reasons for which punishment appears socially necessary or expedient ? These advantages have been roughly classified as deterrent, reformatory and preventive ; but we may take first as more fundamental than any of these the fact that punishment is needed for the self-defence of society against crime, just as physical force may be needed for the self-defence of the individual or the State when assailed from outside. The existence of society, or at any rate of the State, depends on laws, and a law that is not enforced by punishment, if necessary, will not be regarded as a law in the present stage of moral development. A " moral law," indeed, does not depend on punishment for its binding force, it is binding simply because we *ought* to obey it ; but a law in the political sense is neither the same as a moral law (although its content may be the same), nor is it merely an expression of the opinion of the governing body about a moral law, it is something " enforced " and the enforcing of it involves a penalty for those who do not obey it. We can, indeed, imagine an ideal society in which laws would never have to be enforced by punishment but would always be obeyed without punishment ; but in an imperfect society where some people are likely to disobey laws, law implies coercion, and coercion implies some form of punishment.

Coercion may, indeed, be effected by simply using physical force to prevent a man doing something, and this does not by itself involve punishment. To tear the pistol from the hand of a murderer is coercion, perhaps, but not punishment. Such coercion has a place in the State and is illustrated, *e.g.*, by confiscation of arms, confinement of lunatics, etc. But the coercion that can be effected in this way would clearly not be sufficient by itself to maintain the laws in effective operation against those who wish to break them. To make coercion effective we must not only use physical force in the literal sense, but also the psychological resources at our command. We must work on offenders or possible offenders by implanting in them a new motive that will make against the motives prompting to crime, and this is done by punishment, or rather the threat of punishment. Punishment is not, indeed, in the strictest sense of the term, coercion to keep the laws, for the literal coercion involved in punishment comes after, not before, the crime. A man is not literally compelled to abstain from committing a crime because he knows that he will be sentenced to imprisonment or death if he commits it, even if the sentence were absolutely certain, for it is still perfectly open to him to choose to die or be imprisoned rather than abstain from the act. Punishment is not coercion in the literal sense, but it coerces in the sense that it forces a man to choose between acting as the State desires and suffering an alternative which is intended altogether to outweigh any loss that the individual may incur by obeying the State's desires.

As legal obligations imply penalties, so do legal rights, since legal rights must be protected against violation. As Green says, the right to free life " on the part of associated men implies the right on their part to prevent such actions as interfere with the possibility of free action contributory to social good. This constitutes the right of punishment, the right so far to use force upon a person (to treat him as an animal or a thing) as may be necessary to save others from this interference."[1] Punishment is a necessary incident in the carrying out of a law, for it would not be a law if its violation were passively tolerated. Psychologically it is an instance of the wider principle by which a being reacts against whatever impedes it, and[2] historically it is derived from ordinary retaliation, though it does not follow from this that punishment ought to approximate to the conduct suggested by the primitive impulses naturally associated with retaliation as such. A society is indeed conceivable in which the only penalty necessary was censure, but in the present state of society this is clearly not enough.

The root of punishment is thus the necessity for self-defence ; let us now go through its specialised functions one by one.

## Punishment as Preventive

Of the preventive function of punishment I need say little. It is too obvious to need elucidation that certain punishments, especially imprisonment, prevent a man from committing crimes during a given period in which he is undergoing the punishment. The direct preventive effect of punishment is, however, limited in time (except in the case of lifelong imprisonment and death), and has the drawback that it prevents the offender from doing good as well as from doing evil. I say " direct " preventive effect because to deter is *indirectly* to prevent crime. Direct prevention, however, obviously involves a much more serious restraint on liberty than mere deterrence, since it not only takes away a man's freedom to do illegal acts, but also his freedom to do many legitimate acts. A fairly innocuous kind of prevention is,

[1] *Political Obligation*, Section 176.
[2] *v*. Prof. Alexander, *Moral Order and Progress*, pp. 328 *ff*.

however, provided by the prohibition to stand in a position of trust which an offender has misused, *e.g.*, guardianship.

Now prevention in the direct sense is rather an external advantage than a necessary consequence of punishment as such. Certain kinds of punishment prevent from crime, but that is not an effect of the punishment *qua* punishment, but an effect of it *qua* imprisonment or *qua* deprivation of office. Imprisonment, even if it were pleasant and were regarded as a reward, would still prevent a man from committing crimes while in prison. Imprisonment is a punishment and also prevents ; it does not prevent because it is a punishment. The confinement of suspected persons before trial is intended to prevent them from escaping ; but, since they have not yet been found guilty, it is not a punishment. Certain kinds of preventive measures, *e.g.*, the prohibition of carrying fire-arms or entering military areas without special leave, may be imposed on everybody, whether suspected of any offence or not, and therefore can still less be described as punishments. If a man desires to commit an offence, it must always be more or less unpleasant for him to be prevented by external force, for it is at any rate a thwarting of his desires ; but this does not make it a punishment, for he is restrained neither for the sake of the unpleasantness nor because he has already done wrong.

## Punishment as Deterrent

By the deterrent effect of punishment is meant its effect on others than the man punished in making them abstain from wrong acts simply for fear of the penalty. For this end to be achieved it is necessary, in the first place, that punishment should be at least likely to follow the crime. However severe punishments were, their deterrent effect would be comparatively slight if an offender had, say, a ten-to-one chance of escaping conviction, and, in general, if it is to deter effectively, punishment must be increased in proportion to the chance of escape. Secondly, it is not sufficient that the punishment should just counterbalance the gain secured by the crime, for in that case it would be to the criminal's apparent material advantage to commit crimes, because if not caught he would gain, and even if he were caught he would be no worse off than he was before. It would not, for instance, be a sufficient deterrent to make a thief restore what he had taken and give him no other punish-

ment beyond that.   The penalty, in order to fulfil the require-
ment of deterrence, must, therefore, exceed the gain of the
crime, and exceed it in so palpable a fashion as to impress the
imagination of would-be criminals and make it quite clear
that if caught they will lose far more then they gained by
the crime, and even than they would gain if not caught.
Further considerations increase the amount of punishment
required if it is to deter.   Since punishment can never be
quite certain, the offender will always be able to turn his
thoughts to the chance of escaping scot-free and dwell on
that.   People are notoriously ready to think of the chance
favourable to themselves and ignore the opposite possibility,
and this would be especially so with the adventurous,
irresponsible, and desire-controlled types which to a large
extent make up the criminal class.   So in fixing punishment
for deterrent reasons we should have to take into account
not merely the real probability of escape, but the probability
as it is likely to be felt by the offender.   Similarly, the
punishment must exceed not only the real gain[1] of the crime,
which may be *nil* or a minus quantity, even if the crime is
successful, but the gain of the crime as likely to be viewed by
a man when tempted to commit it.   There may be no real
gain in horsewhipping one's enemy, but the apparent gain to
the man who is about to do it in a fit of passion may be very
considerable indeed.

How useful punishments are as deterrents may be disputed,
that they are in some considerable degree useful can hardly
be denied.   They provide a new motive to make men abstain
from crime.   The motive is indeed a " low " one, but a motive
of material expediency is needed to counteract the like
motives of material expediency that prompt a man to crime ;
and, even if the man who abstains because he fears punishment
is not made any better by abstaining, he is at any rate usually
not made any worse than he would have been if he had not
abstained, while the community clearly gains by his abstention.

It has been objected to the deterrent view that it treats
the individual not as an end-in-himself but as a means.   No
doubt it does treat the offender as a means, since it inflicts
pain on him for the welfare of others, but this is not necess-

---

[1] In saying that the punishment should exceed the gain of the crime,
I am not saying that it should necessarily exceed the harm done.   When
a man injures another severely by physical violence, he cannot even
think that he gains nearly as much as the injured man loses.

arily immoral unless it involves treating him *merely* as a means. But that it treats the criminal *merely* as a means is a charge which could only be brought against a theory which made punishment purely deterrent, not against a theory which recognised deterrence as one object among others of punishment. It is wrong to treat even a criminal as though he were not capable of being an end-in-himself and as though his good were of no account ; but that is no reason why we should go to the opposite extreme and sacrifice society to him. The other members of society are at any rate more numerous than the criminals and not less deserving of consideration. To refuse to society the protection afforded by deterrence is to wrong the innocent for the sake of the guilty. It does not follow from this, however, that deterrence is the only point to be considered. In any case the criminal must be treated as a human being throughout, as an end-in-himself ; but the necessity of treating him in this way must not lead us to the other extreme and make us sacrifice to his good the good of society. For this is what we are doing if out of tenderness to the criminal we fail to realise the importance of making punishment deterrent.

On the other hand, I admit that there does seem to be something distasteful and even perhaps morally repugnant in inflicting suffering upon a man against his will not for his own sake but for the sake of others, to be an example to them. It is one of those most difficult of all problems where we have to choose not only between pain and moral evil, but between courses both of which involve moral evil. It is a moral evil that a criminal should be treated in this way, but it is also one that the State should connive at crime, and of the two the latter generally is the worse. The necessity of making this choice is a mark and consequence of the imperfection of society ; but it is sometimes unavoidable, society being what it is. Of course, if we identify doing what involves moral evil with doing what is wrong, it can from definition never be right to do what involves this kind of evil ; but then it seems clear that, since two moral goods may conflict, the only alternative courses possible may all bring with them this evil, and in that case it must still be right to adopt one of the alternatives, since one may still be preferable to the others and it is impossible to adopt none. Since progress generally carries with it a loss somewhere, there are many other actions which must include among their effects some that are morally evil, while being in general good, *e.g.*, they may spoil a man's character in certain points while improving it in most.

But let us see what are the effects of the deterrent principle *per se*.   It must be admitted that, if other considerations are altogether ignored, punishments inflicted for the sake of deterrence will tend in the direction of gross cruelty.   For the more painful it is, the more deterrent is a punishment likely to be, and, since no punishment succeeds in deterring everybody from the commission of a crime, there is always a ground for making it still more severe in order to increase the number deterred by it, an argument which seems to open up a prospect of tortures without limit if our theory of punishment is to be merely deterrent.

Further, it would seem to follow from the deterrent principle taken alone that the severity of the punishment ought not to be decreased because the temptation was strong, but on the contrary increased, since the stronger the temptation the greater must be the punishment needed to deter.   So far from punishing a man less because he did not act of " malice aforethought " but under the influence of passion, ought we not on deterrent principles to punish him more, since a much more powerful reason for fear is needed to curb a man in a fit of passion than in a calm and deliberate mood ?   Are not so-called " extenuating circumstances " on deterrent principles a ground not for less but for more severity, because they make the temptation harder to resist and therefore require a stronger motive of fear to counterbalance the increased temptation ?   Would it not follow that the crime of a starving man who stole a loaf of bread ought to be punished by the most cruel tortures, for nothing short of this could produce a fear strong enough to counterbalance the fear of starvation ?   Ought not the punishment in general to be increased in proportion to the difficulty of abstaining from the crime, and not *vice versa* ?   The retributionist can say :—the stronger the temptation the less the moral guilt, and therefore the less the punishment deserved—but from the deterrent point of view this line of argument is not possible.

We may distinguish two principal charges.   The first is that the deterrent view would logically lead to the infliction of the most cruel and barbarous punishments, these being the most effective deterrents ; the second that it is inconsistent with the duty of lessening the punishment in case of extenuating circumstances and would make it our duty on the contrary to increase it in proportion to the strength of the temptation. Anybody who regards punishment as in the main deterrent has to deal with the principle expounded by Bentham as a consistent advocate of the importance of this function :—" The strength of the temptation (*ceteris paribus*) is as the profit of the offence : the quantum of the punishment must rise with the profit of the offence : *ceteris paribus*, it must therefore rise with the strength of the temptation."[1]

Bentham, while giving great weight to this, adds indeed the opposite consideration that the stronger the temptation, the less the indication afforded of depravity of character, and hence, *ceteris paribus*, the less the danger to be apprehended from the culprit. How far can this ground be regarded as justifying allowance for extenuating circumstances and over-ruling the principle that, the greater the temptation is, the greater will be the punishment needed to deter ? If a man commits an offence through passion, this does not prove him to be as bad as the same crime would if he had committed it of " malice aforethought." But it seems doubtful whether it shows him to be less likely to commit future crimes, because he will be liable to be again carried away by passion. He will be less likely to commit crimes of malice aforethought than a more deliberate offender would be, but then, just as a crime committed in passion does not show its perpetrator to be liable to commit crimes of malice afore-thought, so a deliberate crime does not show its perpetrator to be liable to be carried away by passion. Further, a man who acts under the influence of passion is less likely to be deterred than a man who acts in a more calculating spirit. (The fact that one man is less bad than another does not prove that he can be more easily *deterred* from committing crimes than the other.) It might be argued indeed that those who, *e.g.*, steal under strong temptation are likely to commit fewer thefts than those who commit them under slight temptation, but this is counterbalanced by the fact that the former class must be much more numerous. So the deterrent principle does not seem to agree with the view that the punishment should be less severe if the motives which prompt the crime are less bad or the temptation more difficult to resist, but on the whole implies the contrary proposition, namely, the stronger the temptation or the harder to abstain from the crime, the greater the punishment. Yet few would be prepared to accept this latter principle as morally binding.

---

[1] *Principles of Morals and Legislation*, Ch. 16, 9.

Indeed it seems to me that it would be a logical conclusion from the deterrent principle taken alone that carelessness should be punished as severely as though the damage had been done deliberately.  Since the total damage done by carelessness in the shape of accidents is much greater than the damage done by crime, it might be said that carelessness is more dangerous to society than criminal propensities (being much more widespread than the latter) and ought to be punished accordingly.  It would, however, be just possible to meet this argument by replying that to punish so severely for carelessness would make people nervous and so increase the risk of accidents as much as it would diminish it by frightening people into carefulness, or that the natural penalties of carelessness may be such as to cast doubt on the use of adding a further deterrent.  But, however that may be, the argument has at least shown up the fact that the deterrent principle cannot justify the radical distinction of kind as regards punishment that we feel bound to draw between mere carelessness and deliberate offences.

It would indeed be difficult on purely deterrent principles to condemn the punishment of an innocent man[1] if he were only popularly supposed to be guilty, for it would deter others as much as if he were really guilty.  It is difficult to refute Bentham when from the deterrent principle he draws the following conclusion.  " In point of utility apparent justice is everything, real justice, abstractedly from apparent justice, is a useless abstraction, not worth pursuing, and, supposing it contrary to apparent justice, such as ought not to be pursued. . . . From apparent justice flow all the good effects of real justice—from real justice, if different from apparent, none."[2] Or, if we cannot lay hands on the guilty man, why not punish his relatives ?  It might be effective as a deterrent.  Our moral horror at such proceedings is not adequately explained by the principle of deterrence.

Even if it could be shown that in all these cases the harm done in other ways would be likely to exceed the good done by increased deterrence, this still would not establish any essential connection between punishment and guilt.  It would still be *per se* as satisfactory to punish the innocent as the guilty, and only *incidentally* unsatisfactory because it would in most cases happen to produce a balance of pain over

---

[1] He might not suffer more than the guilty man would, and it might be impossible to lay hands on the latter.

[2] *Principles of Judicial Procedure*, Ch. 3 *ad fin.*

pleasure or some other evil. There would be nothing intrinsically bad either in punishing a slight offence far more severely than a grave one, or even in punishing an innocent man, only it would usually happen to be inexpedient. If it could be proved by psychologists that it would have as good a deterrent effect to inflict punishments beforehand on those who were thought most likely to commit crimes, it would be right to do so. For punishment on the deterrent view does not imply that the man punished has done wrong, only that it is desired to prevent future wrongdoing.

To sum up, then, a purely deterrent theory of punishment not supplemented by other considerations would involve the following drawbacks or paradoxes :—(1) as long as there are any criminals left undeterred, punishments should be made as severe as they can possibly be ; (2) there is no special connection between guilt and punishment ; (3) if in any case the punishment of the innocent should deter as much as a punishment of the guilty which would cause equal pain, it would be equally justifiable ; (4) the presumption is not that the morally worse act should be punished more severely, but rather the opposite.[1] How it ought to be supplemented will be considered later, but the present seems the most favourable opportunity for giving the reasons which make a system of very severe punishments undesirable although somewhat more deterrent than lighter punishments.

In the first place, there is the effect of the punishment on the offenders and those connected with them. The pain inflicted on the offender and his relatives is an evil to be weighed against any good done by the punishment, and as the punishment increases in severity the pain may increase to such an extent as to outweigh the good done in the way of deterring. But, further, the severest punishments rule out the chance of the man who suffers them being of any more use in the world.

Secondly, while it must be admitted that in general, other things being equal, a severe punishment will deter more than a milder one, it is very easy to exaggerate both the extent to which deterrence is possible at all and the extent to which it can be made more effective by greater severity. Thirdly, the bad moral effects on society of a very severe penal system have to be considered. The case against severe punishments

---

[1] Because the less the temptation to do wrong, the less the strength of the deterring motive needed to prevent it, yet the worse the act.

is well stated by Prof. Hobhouse in a passage which I shall quote at length.[1]    " The general right to punish may be derived from the right of society to protect itself.    This principle taken by itself might be held to justify the barbarities of the old law, had not experience shown that extreme severity was not in reality an effective instrument of discipline while it undoubtedly tended to harden manners and accustom people to witness suffering with indifference.    Its dealings with the criminal mark, one may say, the zero point in the scale of treatment which society conceives to be the due of its various members.    If we raise this point, we raise the standard all along the scale.    The pauper may justly expect something better than the criminal, the self-supporting poor man or woman than the pauper.    Thus if it is the aim of good civilisation to raise the general standard of life, this is a tendency which a savage criminal law will hinder and a humane one assist.    Moreover, the old rigour, so far as it rested on reason at all, was based on a very crude psychology.    People are not deterred from murder by the sight of the murderer dangling from a gibbet.    On the contrary, what there is in them of lust for blood is tickled and excited, their sensuality or ferocity is aroused, and the counteracting impulses, the aversion to bloodshed, the compunction for suffering are arrested.    Fear, on which the principle of severity wholly relies, is a master motive only with the weak, and only while it is  very present.    As soon as there is a chance of escaping detection it evaporates, and, it would seem, the more completely in proportion as the very magnitude of the penalty makes it difficult for a man really to imagine himself as the central figure in so terrible a drama.    Finally, the infliction of heavy penalties for secondary crimes may induce a reckless despair, and the saying about the sheep and the lamb was but too apt a comment on the working of the criminal law at the time."    We may compare the failure of the doctrine of eternal punishment as a deterrent from wrongdoing.

It would be quite wrong to suppose that the deterrent effect increases in the same degree as the severity of the punishment.    Any sentence of imprisonment appeals to the imagination of most men as a fairly formidable deterrent, but this effect is not likely to be very much increased by even doubling the sentence.    An additional length of time in

---

[1] *Morals in Evolution*, I, pp. 113–4.

prison will probably make little impression on the mind beforehand compared to the prospect of being imprisoned at all, especially as any addition to the usual sentence will not have to be served immediately after conviction, but will be further away in time and therefore less terrifying.   Provided a punishment is sufficient to give a potential offender the general sense that it would be a very serious misfortune to incur it, it is doubtful how far its deterrent effect will be increased by any addition to its severity.   If it were certain that an additional year of punishment would deter as much as the first year, it might be as well worth inflicting ; but then it is certain that it will on the whole deter very much less and perhaps so much less that the harm it inevitably does outbalances the good involved in the additional deterrence. The disgrace is a very powerful deterrent to most men, but the disgrace of punishment is not appreciably increased by making punishments in general more severe.   As for the death penalty and savage corporal punishments, it may be pointed out that the risk of death and physical suffering must be a much less powerful deterrent than one would suppose *a priori* ; otherwise it would not be the case that so many men (probably the large majority in most semi-civilised communities of the past) have positively wished to fight in battle for its own sake, and not only because they thought it their duty or their interest to do so.   The frequency of reckless driving would suggest the same conclusion.   Even those criminals who calculate probabilities carefully would not be nearly so much influenced by an increase in the severity of punishments as they would by an increase in the likelihood of them being inflicted.   It is so easy for them to persuade themselves that they will escape detection.   If they were purely intellectual beings, the extent to which they were deterred by a punishment would indeed be in proportion to its severity ; but then this is not what any of us feel in relation to threatened misfortunes, our feelings are not exactly in proportion to what we think is the real magnitude of the disaster, and we must expect that the feelings of criminals would be still less likely to be conformable to reason in that way.   As a class they are specially free from the liability to be affected in their conduct by fear of consequences.   Further, where the established system of punishments is a severe one, we must allow for the effect of custom in blunting the fear of them.   Beccaria[1] says : " The more cruel punishments

[1] *Dei Delittie della Pene*, Ch. 15.

become, the more human minds harden, adjusting themselves, like fluids, to the level of objects around them ; and the ever living force of the passions brings it about that, after a hundred years of cruel punishments, the wheel frightens men only just as much as at first did the punishment of prison." It must be remembered that this hardening of the mind, besides making punishment less deterrent, is in itself a moral evil and a factor which makes a man less likely to be restrained from crime by ethical considerations or by sympathy with the victim.

We need not deny that on the whole and for most people concerned a severe punishment is in some degree a stronger deterrent than a milder one, but only that the difference is sufficiently large to outweigh the bad moral effects of a system of very severe punishments, together with its other drawbacks. These considerations also explain why there is not a large increase in crime whenever punishments become milder. The best way of deterring is not by severity but by making conviction almost certain. It is largely for this reason that in Britain we are much more secure against crime nowadays than our forefathers were in the days of very severe punishments. Where detection is not very likely, the danger of punishment may in many cases become rather an incentive than a deterrent. " It is a quality of our imagination, that difficulties, if they are not insurmountable nor too difficult relatively to the mental energy of the particular person, excite the imagination more vividly and place the object desired in larger perspective, for they serve, as it were, as so many barriers to prevent an erratic and flighty fancy from quitting hold of its object, and, while they compel the imagination to consider the latter in all its bearings, it attaches itself more closely to the pleasant side, to which our mind most naturally inclines, than to the painful side, which it places at a distance."[1] Beccaria seems to exaggerate somewhat the extent and importance of this tendency as far as concerns the fear of punishment, but it well may be that the spirit of adventure is in many cases aroused rather than quelled by a danger of severe punishment. We often see this in the conduct of schoolboys, to take a non-criminal instance. Further, the severer the punishment, the more inclined on the whole will the offender be to think of the matter not in moral terms but in terms of force as a struggle between himself and the

[1] *Beccaria*, Ch. 36.

State for victory, and other people too will share in this tendency.

This is at the root of the objection to corporal punishment as corporal in so far as that objection is well founded. A physical punishment more than any other suggests the idea that it is merely a question of brute force and so probably tends more than any other to arouse in the offender not repentance but the quite different attitude called forth by what is regarded as mere violence. On the other hand, while very sensitive about the infliction of physical pain, we are far more apt to be callous about even severer mental pain. We should cry out in horror at the idea of physically torturing a murderer for even a few minutes before death, yet we do not shrink from allowing him to wait three weeks before his execution, an ordeal which, owing to its length, is surely likely to cause him far greater mental than the other would bodily suffering.

There must be added the further drawback that the extreme severity of a penal code may easily make people unwilling to co-operate in carrying it out, so that the deterrent effect of the extra severity is quite outweighed by the increased hope of impunity. The various evil effects of this are stated in a single sentence by Bentham, when, referring to the frequent use of the death penalty, he says[1] that because of its unpopularity—" In the first place it relaxes prosecution in criminal matters ; and in the next place foments three vicious principles : 1. It makes perjury appear meritorious by founding it on humanity ; 2. It produces contempt for the laws by rendering it notorious that they are not executed ; 3. It renders convictions arbitrary and pardons necessary."

We may class as another bad consequence of a very severe system the harmful moral effect it is likely to have on all who are in any way concerned with the administration of the penal laws.

Finally, its effect will be not to make people condemn the crime, but to make them sympathise with the criminal, and the bitterness it arouses in the latter will be an almost insuperable obstacle to any hope that he may be reformed by it. In general it will deprive the laws of their moral authority by substituting a reign of terror for a reign of justice ; and once this is done the resultant moral evil will inevitably diffuse itself in a multitude of different ways over the community.

[1] *Principles of Penal Law*, II, 12, 4.

It follows from all this that deterrence can only be admitted as the main end of State punishment if qualifications are laid down so as to avoid the evils which flow from great severity. The charge that the deterrent principle does not admit of a real connection between punishment and guilt cannot be disposed of so easily. It is this failure which is at the root of the practical difficulties we encountered in reconciling the deterrent principle with certain fundamental moral ideas about the injustice of punishing the innocent and of punishing a worse crime less and not more ; and it suggests that thinkers influenced by utilitarianism may have been over-hasty in rooting out as barbarous every vestige of the retributive conception. Those who take this line may be humbled somewhat if they remember that a purely deterrent theory, if indeed it presupposes a " moral " standpoint at all, presupposes a decidedly lower moral standpoint than the " barbarous " retributive theory itself.

For deterrence presupposes only susceptibility to pain and the power to consider consequences ; the retributive theory presupposes that the criminal has acted immorally (and not only harmfully), and therefore that he is a being capable of morality. Now a theory which does not take account of the moral side of punishment can hardly be right or at least complete, for an essential feature of crime is that it is morally wrong and a theory of punishment which is wholly expressed in terms of pain can hardly be adequate to the moral issue involved. To deter men by pain or fear of pain from doing a certain act is not the same as condemning the act as morally wrong ; nor is it equivalent to bringing people to abstain from it for moral motives, and not only out of fear or for the sake of expediency. It is true that fear of punishment though itself non-moral may prove a means towards moral development ; but the deterrent theory proper speaks not of the moral improvement but only of the fear and the outward act, and therefore is a theory that could be applied to beings who were not moral at all, provided they were susceptible to pain and had a certain amount of prudence. Since this is not the last word about the nature of man, since man is not incapable of true morality, it is hardly likely that a theory of punishment can be in all respects sufficient if it says nothing of moral wrong or moral reformation.

Further it must be added that in many cases the deterrence itself owes half its effectiveness to the fact that punishments are something more than merely deterrent. For it is, often at least, rather the disgrace than the actual judicially inflicted penalty which deters, and the disgrace can only arise because punishment is imposed for an act rightly or wrongly held by society to be evil.   The infliction of a fine is regarded as a very much worse penalty than the loss of the same amount of money by accident would be, a short sentence of imprisonment as very much worse than the suffering of equivalent inconvenience through other causes, execution as very much worse than death in battle, although the former is nowadays made almost painless.   This cannot be explained merely by the fact that punishment is an infliction of pain in order to outweigh any supposed advantage from certain acts and to frighten people into abstaining from these acts.   It is only regarded merely as that if the government is not treated by the offender as having any moral authority in the matter, because he has no sense of wrong in regard to the act punished, or actually thinks it a duty (as sometimes in the case of penalties imposed by a hostile army of occupation for military offences, or with religious persecution).   It might be inexpedient to risk incurring a purely deterrent punishment (unless obliged by duty) ;  but that would not make it a disgrace.   To be a disgrace punishment must be essentially a condemnation of a wrong act as well as a means of preventing like acts in the future by pain and fear of pain.   If our punishments were merely deterrent and not also disgraces, they would not do even their deterring work adequately.   We shall return to this later ;  at present let us just note that even the deterrent function requires that punishment should be a moral condemnation of a wrong act, and not merely deterrent.

It has been urged in favour of a *mainly* deterrent view that the State is limited to the sphere of external behaviour and external constraint (at least as regards punishment) ;  but the only or chief argument for this is that the State would do more harm than good by attempting to promote morality as such and therefore had better let it alone altogether in its penal system.   But unfortunately the State has already interfered with private morality by punishing at all.   It cannot repudiate responsibility for the moral consequences of its acts, and it is certainly a fact that punishments inflicted primarily to deter sometimes have very harmful consequences on the moral character of those punished and on the people as a whole.   But, if so, it is surely the duty of the State to try and remedy these consequences ;  to do so is not necessarily to interfere in matters of morality more than it already has done, it is to interfere in a rational and deliberate instead of a haphazard way. It is not a question here of interfering more, of imposing penalties for new kinds of actions, but of rightly adjusting the penalties which on general grounds it is in any case clearly desirable to inflict. If punishment cannot do moral good, it may at least do moral harm ; those who refuse to admit that punishment may make a man morally better on the ground that force and fear cannot improve motives insist, at the same time, that it may and very probably will, make him worse. The reason they give against the State trying to promote morality as such by punishment is that constraint by means of punishment tends to destroy the disinterestedness and spontaneity on which morality depends, *i.e.*, affects men for the worse morally. But, if punishment is likely to have bad moral consequences, it is the duty of the State to consider these and try to mitigate them or, if possible, turn them into good. If the State cannot prevent punishment having a bad moral effect on the whole, this very much limits the extent to which deterrence is justifiable ; if it can prevent it, it ought to do so. Nor can I agree with T. H. Green[1] that the State ought to pursue the reformatory purpose only as a means to improving the offender's outward behaviour towards others, and not as an end-in-itself. Good character has an intrinsic value, as Green would be the first to admit, but if so, surely it is obligatory on the State to pursue it for its own sake, in so far as this is possible. It cannot be right to neglect the attainment of anything that is admittedly of value, unless other values are sacrificed thereby, nor to treat merely as a means what you know to be an end-in-itself, *i.e.*, the improvement of the offender.

The situation would, I think, be different if the only object of punishment were the reformatory one. Later consideration[2] will reveal so many dangers and drawbacks in the use of punishment by the State that it would be hard to justify its infliction by the reformatory effects alone, *i.e.*, effects on the character of the offender himself. But, once granted that punishment is justified by reasons other than the reformatory purpose, these drawbacks are no objection against modifying it in order to reform the offender. To inflict punishment simply for the sake of improving the man punished, if there were no other reason for it, might be to create fresh moral

[1] *Principles of Political Obligation*, Section 204.
[2] *v.* pp. 85-7, 121-2.

harm and dangers which outweighed any moral good attained thereby ; but that would be no reason for refusing to modify for this purpose a punishment justified on other grounds. To do so would not cause fresh moral harm or dangers, but only lessen those which would in any case naturally follow from the punishment. Nor do these objections apply with nearly so much force to the use of reformatory punishment in education or to censure without further penalty.

Even if State punishment were only or mainly deterrent, this would not mean that all punishment was so. In education also punishment is commonly applied, and here it is generally admitted that it is the business of the parents or teachers to try to improve the moral character of a child, not merely to deter the child from violating the rights of other people. Deterrence does play a part in education : where the child is punished in order to break a habit that is not bad in itself but sufficiently dangerous to make it more important that the child should abstain from the act than that he should abstain with the best motives and in the best spirit, punishment may rightly be governed primarily, though not altogether, by deterrent considerations, e.g., with throwing stones where there is a risk of hitting someone, playing with fire, etc. This is, however, not quite analogous to deterrence as usually understood in the theory of State punishment, since the object of punishment there is not, as here, to deter the offender from repeating the act, so much as to deter others from imitating him. The term " deterrent " is usually applied to cover only the effects on persons other than the offender, not on the offender himself, the latter effects falling under the heading of " reformatory." But many of the punishments inflicted on children in a class may be deterrent in the same sense as State punishment is. Especially is this so where a master, confronted with a serious breakdown of discipline and unable to deal with all the offenders, selects one or two of the worst and " makes an example of them," rather for the sake of the discipline of the class as a whole than for their own sake. But it must be admitted that punishment with children should in general have the object of educating them (reformatory), and not merely of keeping them well-behaved because they are afraid of being punished (deterrent). Even as regards external actions a deterrent theory will not work here, for, if a child abstains from behaving in a certain way merely because he is afraid of punishment, he will (unless his desires have changed) start behaving in that way once he is grown up and need not fear being punished for it.    If he does not behave like that, it will not be because he is deterred, since there is now nothing to deter him.    Punishment can only deter when there is reason to fear it, and therefore the deterrent effect cannot extend to the period when the child is grown up and is not subject to punishment by teachers or parents.    If the punishments have so changed the child as to make him unwilling to commit the act even when he has no fear of punishment, then he is not " deterred " but " reformed."    If we were logical in applying to education a purely deterrent theory of punishment, we should only aim at making the children behave themselves while they were children, not as a training for when they are grown up (when they can no longer be deterred by us), but merely as an end in itself.

So, even if for practical reasons the State ought in its penal system to pursue mainly the deterrent rather than the reformatory end, it must be admitted that the deterrent view of punishment is not wholly an adequate one.    But perhaps the practical argument itself is not quite so cogent as it sounds.    It depends on the assertion that the deterrent effects are (a) less uncertain, (b) more extensive than the reformatory effects, and therefore should be sought in preference to the latter.    But, to take the first point, what is certain about the deterrent effect?    That crime will be less if criminals are usually punished than if they are not may be taken as practically certain ; but an advocate of the reformatory theory need not wish to abolish punishments altogether.    If they were abolished, they could not be used to reform.    Where the reformatory and deterrent views come into conflict is over the specific nature of particular punishments, and here the deterrent theory can no longer speak with certainty. Which of two particular methods of punishment will deter more is often very disputable ; and even where this is certain owing to the great difference of degree between two punish-ments, we have seen that there are other factors which may more than counterbalance the value of an increased deterrent effect and make it doubtful whether the severer punishment is ultimately for the real good of society, even if we do not consider the reformatory effect at all.

It no doubt is very uncertain also whether any particular offender will be reformed ; but it seems about as uncertain whether any particular man who would have otherwise com-mitted a crime will be deterred by punishment.    We can only say that the deterrent effect is fairly certain because we know that the total number of offenders is rendered considerably less by the fear of punishment, though we do not know what *particular* offenders will be deterred by it from a crime that they would otherwise have committed. Similarly we may say that recent measures to make imprisonment reformatory are at the least very likely to leave a large number of prisoners in a considerably better moral and mental state than the old system, though we do not know beforehand which particular prisoners they will be. But we must not compare the uncertainty of reformatory methods with the certainty that some potential criminals will be deterred by punishment, but with the very doubtful question whether a particular modification suggested for reformatory ends will make the punishment do appreciably less good as a deterrent. We have seen that there is every reason to suppose that, as the severity of punishments increases, their deterrent effect does not increase in anything like the same proportion, and there is no means of computing with any precision what the effect of a particular modification will be, or whether it will produce any deterrent effect sufficient to counterbalance the harm involved in making the punishment severer. In fact we labour under at least as much uncertainty in regard to the influence of these comparatively minor modifications on the deterrent effect of a punishment as in regard to their reformatory results. Some advocates of the deterrent theory talk as though they could attain something like certainty in these matters by the use of statistics, but this seems quite a vain hope, for there are always many different causes besides the fear of punishment which affect the number of criminals. The fundamental difficulty which a statistical method has to face is due to the distinction between sequence and causation ; that the number of crimes of a particular kind has increased or decreased since the institution of a new system of punishment does not prove that the increase or decrease was caused by the new system, and still less does it show what particular element or elements in the new system caused it. This difficulty could only be really overcome if we could by experiment isolate certain causes from all others to the same degree as we can in, *e.g.*, chemistry,[1] but that is clearly impossible in a matter of this sort. Hence inference from statistics, though perhaps useful, can hardly give anything at all like certainty,

---

[1] Metaphysically speaking, the isolation even there is only relative.

especially in regard to comparatively detailed modifications in punishment, for it is in regard to such detailed modifications, if anywhere, that there is likely to be a conflict between reformatory and deterrent ideas. As a matter of fact, statistics show a large decrease,[1] not an increase, of crime during the period of 30 years or so since reformatory methods began to be adopted to a large extent, even though these methods have certainly made imprisonment somewhat less unpleasant and so less of a deterrent.[2] But, while it cannot be shown by statistical evidence that reformatory methods have increased the number of fresh convictions by making imprisonment less deterrent, there is some evidence[3] that these methods very considerably diminish the chance of reconviction for those to whom they have been applied. The giving of special privileges for good conduct, the mitigation of severity as regards solitary confinement and the supply of books for educative purposes must tend in the direction of making imprisonment slightly less deterrent ; but this may be altogether outweighed by the reformatory effect of these measures. They still fail with very many prisoners, but at least they lead to more being reformed than would have been the case either if the men had been left in their old environment without punishment or if we had continued the old prison methods.

" But surely you ought to consider the good of society more than the good of the criminal," it may be retorted. " Surely you ought to prefer the good of the many to the good of the few ; to sacrifice the deterrent effect in any degree for the sake of reforming criminals is always to sacrifice the many innocent to the few guilty, and is therefore always wrong."

But we must set against the greater extensiveness of deterrent effects the greater magnitude of reformatory effects. In a sense the deterrent effect of a punishment concerns everybody who is either liable to commit a crime or to become the victim of a crime, while the reformatory effect only concerns the criminal reformed and those who come into relation with him ; but it is the penal system as a whole which deters, and not the punishment of a single offender, and if the total num-

---

[1] At any rate proportionately to the population. This is apart from the abnormal decline in crime due to war conditions.

[2] Even in cases where an increase in crime can be attributed to the introduction of milder punishments, it would have to be shown that it was not merely temporary till offenders became used to the new scale.

[3] Though not as much as is frequently maintained.

ber of men deterred from crime could be divided by the total number of convictions, we should hardly find that each conviction on an average deterred many men as its share in the total contribution to this end by punishment. The question, however, is not whether any particular offender should be convicted or reformed without conviction or punishment, but whether he should be punished in a way that makes for reformation even though it may deter slightly less. The deterrent effect lost by a reformatory modification would in most cases either be *nil* or only a small fraction of the total deterrent effect of the punishment. Also, if punishment, when it deters, lessens crime not only in those punished but in others, so it does when it reforms, because the criminal then ceases to have a bad influence on others. A reformed criminal may benefit society in many positive ways, while a man merely deterred from crime will very possibly, without coming under the criminal law, do even more harm than he would have done if he had not been deterred.

We must, therefore, consider in practice the reformatory end also and not only the deterrent. We are certainly not justified in saying offhand that one end ought always to be sacrificed to the other. Where they conflict we shall have to choose sometimes the one, sometimes the other, taking into account, (1) the intrinsic value of the ends not in the abstract but as realisable in the particular case, *e.g.*, not improvement of character in general but improvement in industry or whatever other particular quality the measure suggested would, if successful, develop ; (2) the extent to which such values are expected to be realised, the quantitative, as opposed to the qualitative, difference between the two conflicting ends ; (3) the relative probability of their attainment. This is a very meagre and unprofitable rule for practical purposes, but it is the most moral philosophy *as such* can say, an inability which is not peculiar to this subject but extends to every sphere of conduct.[1] At any rate, as soon as we consider details, we pass from moral philosophy to other sciences which require for their application not so much general ethical principles as special empirical knowledge combined with practical insight in particular cases. As an instance of the factors to be considered in deciding we might take the conclusion that the requirements of industrial training for the

[1] This does not make moral philosophy useless, but only, when taken by itself, incomplete, *v.* pp. 194ff.

time after release and the restoration of a sense of self-respect and honour to criminals make it worth while giving more responsible work to well-behaved prisoners after a sufficient lapse of time, although this may make imprisonment slightly less deterrent, for the following reasons : (1) This improvement of character is intrinsically of greater value than mere deterrence (intrinsic value of ends) ; (2) Experience shows that a marked improvement may be produced by means like these, while the diminution of deterrent effect is hardly appreciable (quantitative extent to which end is realised) ; (3) These means are more likely to improve a considerable number of criminals than they are to prevent a considerable number being deterred from crime (relative probability).[1]

The difficulty of the problem, overwhelming as it is, is much lessened by the fact that in many cases the good sought in one direction is definite and fairly likely of achievement, while the harm is very problematical. It must be remembered always that slight differences in the severity of a punishment are likely to produce a change in the deterrent effect that is much slighter still and therefore often hardly worth considering at all. Even large changes are, considering the psychology of deterrence, likely to make only a small fraction of the difference that the presence or absence of the punishment as a whole would make, provided only they do not destroy the sense that to incur the punishment would really be a serious misfortune. For these changes to make very much difference criminals would have to be a great deal more calculating than they usually are, and if they were so calculating they would need a much smaller punishment to deter them from crime. It would be very unreasonable to suppose that the deterrent effect increases *pari passu* with the severity of the punishment—unless criminals indeed approach far more closely to being purely rational beings than do the majority of law-abiding citizens !

On the other hand it is a prime condition of punishment that it should be to some considerable extent unpleasant, and it is frequently not practicable to make allowance for cases in which even the minimum unpleasantness necessary if it is to be at all an effective deterrent seems on the whole undesir-

---

[1] This is not meant as a statement how far I consider the measure practicable (that requires more detailed knowledge than I possess), but only as a possible instance. Under the Borstal system the best behaved inmates are towards the close of their period of confinement employed in positions of trust.

able for reformatory purposes. Here the deterrent effect is the less uncertain. In the case of serious crimes of passion by men who are genuinely sorry for them afterwards judicial punishment often seems unnecessary for reformatory ends, but is held to be necessary as a deterrent for others. Speaking generally, we might say that punishment should be definitely and clearly unpleasant,[1] so that a man, if he has any sense at all, must realise in his calm moments that it is not to his material advantage to incur the risk of it, for otherwise the deterrent purpose will not be secured,[2] and that within these limits we should make punishment as reformatory as we can. That certainty and speediness of punishment are excellent substitutes for severity in increasing the deterrent effect is a principle now generally accepted. But deterrence remains one of the most important objects of State punishment ; nor ought we to despise it as aiming at low ends. For although deterrence does not further the higher life directly, it does so indirectly, since public order and security from crime are most important conditions for the realisation of this life.

## Punishment as a means to Vindictive Satisfaction.

This brings us to the function of punishment as reformatory and educative ; but before we pass on to this question, which requires a separate chapter, we must deal with minor advantages, or supposed advantages, of punishment. There is another alleged good gained by punishment, namely, the feeling of pleasure experienced by individuals at the thought that the criminal has been brought to justice, and especially by the victim of the crime. If it is admitted that pleasure is a good, it must be admitted that any pleasure gained in this way is as pleasure a good, though its value may be and frequently is more than counterbalanced by the moral evil involved in the state of mind of the man who enjoys it.

Some people have attached great importance to this pleasure, and Lotze, if we are to take his words literally, would seem to have even gone so far as to make it the chief justification of punishment. This view must not be confused with the ordinary retributive view, because it maintains not that

---

[1] There is some real danger that as the result of reformatory measures prison may eventually appear more agreeable than the life of the poorer classes outside it to a man who has little sense of the shame involved.

[2] We must add a reservation excluding cases of extreme want. Here we could only deter, if at all, by a punishment so severe that it would be most undesirable to inflict it.

punishment is an end-in-itself, but that it is valuable as a means to the realisation of another end, namely, vindictive pleasure. It is quite compatible even with hedonistic utilitarianism to recognise this pleasure as one of the ends of punishment, and it is maintained as such by Bentham, who says of it :—" Produced without expense, a clear gain resulting from an operation necessary on other accounts, it is an enjoyment to be cultivated like any other."[1] Those who recognise the importance of a difference of quality in " pleasures " (pleasant experiences) as determining their value may be more doubtful as to the desirability of cultivating what as pleasure (pleasantness of feeling) is no doubt *per se* a good, but is almost inextricably associated with an attitude of mind that, though often excusable enough, is still, in general at least, morally unworthy.

But, even *if* it is right to feel pleasure at the just punishment of the wicked, this pleasure certainly cannot be approved if it is very intense, and, as Bentham wisely says, it cannot serve as a justification for the increase of a punishment, still less for its infliction where it would not otherwise be justified. It surely cannot be maintained that anybody normally constituted would on account of the infliction of a year's more imprisonment or half a dozen more strokes of the lash feel a pleasure that could possibly merit comparison with the victim's pain. For the increase of punishment to be justified as a means to the production of this vindictive pleasure the latter would have to be at least equal to the pain caused by the additional punishment to the victim and his connections, and that is certainly not the case with any person who is not quite insanely vindictive! Even if anybody were found so vindictive, it would not be good that his desires should be satisfied, any more than a drunkard's desire for drink, for, whatever its value in moderation, there can be no two opinions about the badness of the desire when carried to such an extremity. The production of this pleasure cannot, therefore, from the nature of the case, justify the increase of a punishment or the infliction of one where it would not be desirable on other grounds.[2] It might still in some cases be made an

---

[1] *Principles of Morals and Legislation*, p. 171.

[2] Other people than the victim of the crime may feel it, but against that must be set the pain of sympathy, which in a normal person not specially concerned is at least as natural and likely a feeling, and will probably be far more intense in any friends and connections of the offender than will be the vindictive pleasure felt by the friends and connections of the man injured by the original crime.

argument for altering the form of the punishment ; but in view of the enormous social dangers to which vindictiveness leads, in view of the fact that the great majority of people are too much rather than too little inclined in that direction, and in view of doubts as to the moral worth of any state of mind in which that pleasure is an important ingredient even this cannot be admitted. Indeed, in face of these considerations, it seems rather an argument against than for any change that it increases the vindictive pleasure.

But there is a sense in which the conception of punishment as a means of satisfying the vindictive desires has not altogether missed the mark. The desires in question ought to be satisfied to some extent by State punishment, not because the vindictive pleasure is an end-in-itself, but in order to avert the satisfaction of these desires by illegal means in the absence of legal. State punishment was only able to take the place of private vengeance because it satisfied to a certain extent the desire of a man wronged that the person who had wronged him should suffer. This desire is not a highly laudable one, but it had to be satisfied, at least partially, if private vengeance was to be avoided. And, even nowadays, if the law did not usually do its punishing work adequately, private vengeance and mob violence would be far more common than they are. However, as long as some punishment is regularly inflicted, the actual penalties may no doubt be changed and moderated very considerably indeed without running much risk in this direction, though that might not have been so when the vindictive impulse was more strong and men were less accustomed to the authority of the laws. So I do not think that the principle can nowadays be rationally used to fix penalties, though it certainly provides an important instance of the harm averted by the existence of a penal system. Punishment, besides helping to stop crime, helps to stop lawless replies to crime. We must make the two further admissions, that (1) vindictiveness is in practice an important ally of the law, since without it it would be more difficult to induce people to take action against crime, unless money were used, which would lead to the drawbacks usually associated with a system of paid informers ; (2) in the past the anger felt at a particular class of crimes has had a very important part to play when it came to fixing the penalty. These seem to be facts, though perhaps deplorable ones. In the present penal code the great difference between the penalties for murder and for attempted murder, and between the treatment of an assault accidentally leading to fatal consequences and an ordinary assault, can only be explained by the fact that popular indignation at a fatal injury is naturally much greater than at a non-fatal one. Unless we can justify them by saying that, if the penal system lags too much behind popular indignation, harmful results will follow, these distinctions between acts morally on a par seem irrational and incapable of being defended. Whether it is possible to justify them adequately in this way I leave to the judgment of the reader ; to me it seems decidedly doubtful.

Another possible advantage of punishment is its *compensatory effect*. A punishment may be such as to compensate the victim of the offence for the harm he has suffered, just as the payment of damages in a civil case may be incidentally penal. Clearly the victim ought to be compensated by the offender if possible, and it is both fairer to the latter and more economical to treat the payment of compensation as part of the punishment. Similarly all fines might be regarded as compensatory when they are inflicted for offences against the community as such, except where they are penalties not for damage done but for damage attempted ; but in cases where the damage bears no proportion to the fine this would be rather far-fetched. Some non-pecuniary punishments might also be made compensatory. It would be possible, for instance, to punish a man by making him work for the benefit of his victim, and it has been suggested that this should be done in prison. Another example of a compensatory punishment would be the penalty suggested by Bentham for a deliberate insult, namely, that the man guilty of it should himself receive in public the insult he had given, or, I think better, should acknowledge publicly that his insulting statement had been declared by the court to be untrue. This would not only be an instance of a punishment which well served the purpose of producing vindictive pleasure, but it would also be compensatory in the stricter sense since it would remove the mortification felt by the victim of the insult. Legislators, however, have usually not given much consideration to this end in devising punishments, and in cases of bodily injury and theft have neglected the need of compensating the victim of the crime to a most surprising and deplorable extent.

# CHAPTER IV

## Punishment as a Moral Education

By the reformatory effects of punishment are generally understood any good effects punishment has on the moral character and outward habits of the man punished himself in abstraction from its effects on individuals other than the offender. These reformatory effects may be understood to include the deterrence of the offender punished from future crimes as opposed to the deterrence of others, but they need not be limited to deterrence of any kind.

Now we must carefully distinguish two ways in which punishment can be conducive to reform. In the first place a punishment may produce this effect indirectly not because it *qua* punishment is reformatory, but because it alone makes it possible for other reformatory agencies to be brought to bear on the offender. This is the case when a man is helped by the ministrations of the prison chaplain or by education given him in prison. It is there not imprisonment itself as a punishment which reforms him, but other educative influences that are not of the nature of punishments. It is of these latter, not of the punishment *qua* punishment, that advocates of the " reformatory " theory are generally thinking. The education a criminal receives in prison is not inflicted in order to give pain like the real punishment. It may indeed happen to be distasteful, but that would be an undesirable accident ; its primary purpose would be to train and not to be distasteful, and it would be a sign that it had failed if the prisoner took it as merely a part of his punishment.

In the second place, however, it may be conceived that the offender is reformed by the pain[1] of the punishment itself as a penalty for wrongdoing inflicted by a recognised authority. In that case it is the punishment *qua* punishment, not something else rendered possible by the punishment, that does the

---

[1] It must be remembered that, as before, I am referring throughout to mental and not only to physical pain, though of course the same applies to both.

work of reformation. This is according to McTaggart the distinction between the Hegelian doctrine of punishment and the ordinary reformatory view. " The reformatory theory says that we ought to reform our criminals *while* we are punishing them, Hegel says that punishment as such tends to reform them."[1] " Reformatory punishment " has been so often treated in theory as though it meant reforming without punishment, that McTaggart shrinks from using the term to indicate his own view and substitutes for " reformatory " " purifying " when he is describing the ethical effects of punishment *qua* punishment. Whether we follow him in this terminology is a question of practical convenience, but it is important to bear in mind that the end, moral reformation, is still the same as it is for those who stress means of reformation that are incidental and not essentially bound up with punishment. In order to distinguish between the two kinds of reformatory effect it is useful to ask—Would, for instance, the imprisonment which enables a criminal to be educated secure this effect equally if it were a reward? If the answer is in the affirmative, it is clear that the reformatory effect cannot be due to the punishment as punitive but to some other aspect or some incidental consequence of it, here to the facilities which imprisonment gives for compulsory education or re-education. For constraint to be a punishment constraint must not only be unpleasant but must be inflicted for wrongdoing *because* it is unpleasant. To make a boy learn a lesson that he dislikes is not necessarily to punish him, though the lesson may possibly be more unpleasant to him than many punishments. It is obvious that while being punished an offender may be reformed by other means, at least in the case of imprisonment ; but has the punishment *per se* any reformatory effect? Can pain inflicted for wrongdoing reform *because* it is painful? In dealing with the reformatory view we have to consider both the effect of the punishment in opening the door to other influences not themselves punishments, and, secondly, the direct effect it has on the criminal just because it is a punishment.

To take the first point, the advantages in question here, though not direct effects of the punishment as such, can in most cases only be secured by the punishment, for the con-

[1] *Studies in Hegelian Cosmology*, p. 133. On this interpretation Hegel's doctrine would be not retributive but genuinely reformatory, though not in the sense meant by most advocates of " reformatory punishment."

straint and supervision required would hardly be possible without confining the offender.    It is, therefore, legitimate to class these among the good effects which punishment should be devised to produce. . Undoubtedly, if reformation can be achieved, it will be an effect of the greatest value. The doubts are rather as to how far it can be achieved ; but it is at any rate clear that reformatory efforts have not been wholly unsuccessful, that the good in question has been realised to some extent, however much we may regret that it has not been realised more completely.

If we exclude any reformatory effect that may be produced by punishment *qua* punishment, what are the means conducive to reformation which can be brought to bear upon the occupants of prisons ?    They seem to fall mainly under the following headings—educational training, a right " moral atmosphere," appeal to " the sense of honour " where possible and a system of material rewards.    These measures would be more successful than they are if it were not for the fact that a prison system entails grave moral drawbacks which impede any attempt at reform, and recent reformatory efforts cannot be understood except in the light of these obstacles against which it was necessary to fight.    Here is a catalogue of some of the chief of them :—

1. The disgrace of imprisonment, once sustained, loses most of its terror for the future so that a second sentence is usually not dreaded nearly so much as the first, while the consequent destruction of self-respect lessens the offender's " moral stamina."

2. Imprisonment makes men definitely think of themselves as members of a separate criminal class, and so by suggestion tends to make them act like members of that class.

3. The association with other criminals[1] must exercise a harmful influence, yet the only alternative is a silence or a solitude[2] which, despite the favourable opinion of early prison reformers, especially the Pennsylvanian Quakers, seems more likely to brutalise or make morbid than to improve.

---

[1] Lombroso compares imprisonment without separation to confining a rich man in his club (*Criminology*, Eng. transl., p. 206 *f*.).

[2] This difficulty is mitigated but not removed by the fact that the solitude or silence need not be and is not complete, only debarring conversation with other prisoners, and is broken by educational instruction, etc., even in the first few months of complete separation.

4. The system of giving prisoners a definite sentence beforehand has been compared to a system according to which all smallpox patients would be released after so many weeks, whether cured or not. On the other hand, if prisoners are to be discharged when and only when they are found to be reformed, we are confronted with the great difficulty of deciding when they are reformed. It has been said that the criminals who relapse worst afterwards generally make the greatest protestations of reform, and in any case it is quite impossible to be certain whether a man is really or only outwardly better, or whether, if really improved for the time, he will not relapse under the renewed influence of temptation.

5. The difficulties in the way of giving a convicted prisoner a fresh start that will enable him to keep himself when released are obviously very serious.

6. A large number of the prisoners require special treatment as mentally deficient. It was said that at Sing Sing of 608 convicts consecutively admitted 59% were so obviously abnormal as to be readily detected.[1] That criminals are usually below the average in intelligence is the general testimony of those who have concerned themselves with prisons. This does not take away their responsibility for their crimes, since it does not mean that they are incapable of better things, only that they find them more difficult than the average man ; but it clearly lessens it and suggests that many of them are cases for the mental doctor. A man who is abnormal and mentally weak may still deserve blame and punishment for his acts,[2] but he deserves *less* blame and may need quite special mental treatment such as is outside the purview even of a reformed prison.

7. There are throughout the general difficulties of making imprisonment sufficiently penal to deter without being brutal, and of accommodating general rules to the widely varying individual cases.

It is hardly my province to dwell at length on the question of the detailed measures best suited to cope with these difficulties, so I shall just give a list of some of the main recognised principles of prison reform. (It is not for me to

---

[1] H. E. Barnes, *The Repression of Crime*, p. 256.
[2] *i.e.*, he may have been able to prevent them, but only with greater difficulty than is the case with a normal man, so that on the one hand he is still responsible, and on the other *less* subject to blame than the ordinary man would be for like acts.

specify to what extent these measures are actually carried out in prisons.)

1. Classification is now regarded as essential both to prevent contamination of the better by the worse, or the first offender by the hardened criminal, and in order that promotion to a higher grade may operate as a reward for good behaviour.

2. The start is made very unpleasant mainly for deterrent reasons, but afterwards conditions improve by stages in case of ordinarily good conduct.

3. Those below 21 are now always subjected to separate treatment if sent to prison at all, and, where possible, either sent to a Borstal institute or put on probation. It is recognised that effort must be to a considerable extent concentrated on this class as the most hopeful object of reformatory endeavours.

4. A real attempt is made by lectures, books and even sometimes debates among the prisoners to arouse new intellectual interests that will provide them with more food for thought and make it easier for them to realise that life is not merely a matter of trying to gratify sensual desires.

5. There is now a possibility for all long-sentence prisoners of a gradual advance in freedom and position during the prison period, thus restoring their shattered self-respect by degrees. The reward of promotion to a higher grade with a badge or special dress is intended to appeal not only to material interests but to " the sense of honour " ; and in classes for instruction or lectures prisoners are frequently " trusted " to keep order. The system involves somewhat of an approximation to the conditions of free life in the later stages of imprisonment. Both in regard to the Borstal lads and in regard to even the most hardened class of criminals, namely, those who are sentenced to " preventive detention," it is said " that the motive power used is in the appeal to the sense of honour. This appeal is conducted primarily, and necessarily, through the natural instincts which desire comfort and rewards in ordinary human beings. They are simple enough, but in their simplicity is their value, because they teach the homely lesson, which the older criminal may have forgotten, and the younger not yet learned, viz. : that by good behaviour and industry, and a proved effort to profit by the encouragement they receive, they may pass from a lower to a higher grade, with increasing privileges and comfort, until in the ultimate stages they are placed entirely upon their honour, employed

in positions of trust, free from supervision, and even outside the walls of the establishment. In this way the re-entry into free life is facilitated : semi-liberty precedes full liberty, and by breaking the abruptness of the change, rehabilitation or re-settlement under normal conditions of life is achieved."[1]

6. As a stimulus to good conduct hope is now used to a very large extent to replace fear.

7. Corporal punishment is in England now only allowed as a last resort in exceptional cases.

8. While extremely long sentences are much rarer than they used to be, it is coming to be realised that very short sentences of imprisonment are of no reformatory value and have the drawback of lessening a man's self-respect and of making prison less deterrent for him in the future. It is proposed by reformers that this should be avoided not by lengthening the sentences but by a much more extensive use of probation. The evil is already considerably lessened by the Borstal system and by measures greatly diminishing the number of people who are sent to prison through inability or unwillingness to pay a fine.

9. The indeterminate sentence and the system of release under supervision after prolonged good conduct are gaining ground.

10. The prisoners are kept fully occupied by work which is intended, where possible, to be useful for after life both as developing habits of hard work and good order and as an industrial training.

11. The connection of mental defectiveness and crime is more clearly kept in mind.

12. We must add a humaner attitude towards prisoners in general and the insistence on more individual treatment.

It must not be assumed that the humaner and more reasonable outlook here indicated has yet won the day, or that all is well even with reformed prisons ; but these are the main principles by which whatever progress there is in this respect has been achieved.

From a philosophical point of view the chief thing to be noted here is perhaps the substitution of rewards for punishments. It must be admitted that it is no more moral to behave well merely for the sake of reward than it is to do so merely for fear of punishment ; but it is generally agreed that

---

[1] Sir Evelyn Ruggles-Brise (Chairman of Prison Commission), *English Prison System*, p. 11.

reward is a better instrument than punishment where it is not a question of guarding against the commission of particular, definite offences, but of securing a steady course of positively good behaviour. Further, rewards during prison life help men to recover their shattered self-respect, while a system of punishments tends to lower it still further. Imprisonment itself must be a punishment in the real sense of the term, but that leaves room for a system of rewards during imprisonment, since the ordinary privileges of free life, once taken away at a stroke as a penalty for the original crime, may be given back one by one as rewards for good conduct. Material rewards, admittedly, do not appeal to very high motives, but it would be unreasonable on that account to reject them with scorn when applied to men who are presumably among the weakest or least adequately developed morally, considering that our whole social system by making income, as a general rule, dependent on work[1] assumes their necessity for normal men. The rewards given, however, are carefully devised so as to appeal to " the sense of honour," since the material rewards themselves (including under this heading any external advantages which make prison less unpleasant) depend on promotion to a higher grade, *i.e.*, on something which enhances self-respect and moral status, so that most rewards are primarily themselves " honours " in so far as that term can be applied to the treatment of convicted criminals. This makes them much more likely to be a help to real reformation, since the sense of honour is much more closely allied to the moral sense than are the material desires and the craving for pleasure (or relief from boredom) partially satisfied by other rewards and is much more likely to tend against the repetition of crime. The sense of honour that depends merely on approval by others will not on the whole help and may even prevent a man from rising much above the ordinary moral level ; but for people who have fallen or are inclined to fall below this level it is an invaluable specific, because here the popular standard on which it depends is at least less wrong than that of the sinning individual.

If, however, a man is reformed by measures like these, he is not reformed by his punishment as such, but by something else. Hence these reformatory schemes, however important they may be in practice, hardly belong to the theory of punish-

[1] Even socialistic systems do this, or else substitute the fear of punishment if a man will not work.

ment in the strict sense. For they do not show how punishment can be reformatory, but how other measures applied to a man who is already undergoing punishment can be. We must now ask the further question—Can the punishment itself reform *qua* punishment (or just because it is a punishment) ?

A negative answer is supported by the argument that pain or fear of pain, being a non-moral motive, cannot bring about moral improvement. If the offender abstains from future crimes because he has suffered for them in the past, his motive is not a moral one but merely fear of suffering and therefore his character is essentially unchanged. He would do the wrong he has done before quite as readily again except for a mere selfish fear that is no more commendable than the desire for selfish gain or whatever it was that prompted him to crime in the first instance. This is the antinomy with which anyone who makes the reformatory element predominant in punishment is faced—if punishment does not reform through being painful, you are not reforming the criminal by punishment but by something else ; if punishent does reform through being painful, you have to explain how a purely selfish fear of pain may lead to moral improvement.

But we need not be afraid to embrace the second horn of the dilemma, though we must admit that the reform of a criminal is not often achieved in this way. We cannot argue that, because a given instinct, fear of pain, is not moral itself, it cannot tend to produce moral results. Those who use the argument are apparently influenced by two main considerations. The first is an *a priori* idea about causation, that a cause cannot produce any effect which is not already contained in itself ; but, if this view were carried to its logical conclusion, it would be incompatible with any change whatever. The effect must be contained *potentially* in the cause, no doubt, if by this is meant simply that the cause must be capable of producing its effect, but this tautology does not prove anything about the degree of community required between cause and effect. Besides, when the morality of a man is affected by non-moral factors, it is not right to make these the whole cause, for his moral state just before they acted on him must also be viewed as an essential part of the cause. Even if it is impossible for a moral being to be brought into existence by purely non-moral causes, it does not follow by any means that, given a being with some moral attributes, his morality may not be affected by causes themselves non-moral, any more than it follows that, because he is a living being, he cannot be affected by inanimate matter.

The second consideration is that morality implies a moral motive and that, therefore, in so far as a man is influenced by non-moral motives, he is not acting morally at all. There is a certain, within its limits, quite legitimate and indeed necessary standpoint in Ethics from which the conclusion that a man's morality cannot be affected in the least by external circumstances or helped by non-moral motives seems difficult to avoid. But, once drawn, it involves consequences that few are ready to admit. For it would follow not only that punishment cannot help to make a man morally better, but that no external circumstances whatever can, that adversity has never in any case helped morally to improve a man, and the same would be true of all education of any description, except perhaps moral exhortations and examples appealing to the Kantian " good will."

But we may reply that, even if fear of punishment makes no difference to a man's morality in regard to the particular act from which he is deterred, it may make a difference to his morality in regard to future acts. Even if we accept a sharp separation between the will as capable of morality and all other factors in our nature, we have no right to say that non-moral factors cannot causally affect the will so as to make it better capable of morality, only at the most that they cannot be the motive of a moral will. For everything that causally affects the will is not necessarily its motive ;[1] our will is affected by many past events which we have altogether forgotten or which we remember without desiring their recurrence. If our will on the present occasion is affected by our previous abstention through fear of punishment, it does not follow that our motive now is only to avoid punishment, any more than it follows that our motive in doing a good act is desire of food, because, if we had not had enough food, we might not have had strength to resist the temptation to shirk it. Even if we take an indeterminist position, we must admit that, although what is not " determined " by causes in a man's character may have *special* value, still what is determined has *some* value, which is worth securing. Further, even if it is denied that causes may affect morality positively, it must be admitted that they may affect morality in the negative sense of removing obstacles to the exercise of free

---

[1] This distinction ought to be remembered by psycho-analysts.

will, or of lessening the force of the desires which tempt a man to exercise his free will in an immoral fashion.    Even an indeterminist must admit that there are conditions under which a man is more likely to make a moral use of free will than he would be under others, and it would surely be irrational not to try, *ceteris paribus*, to place him in these conditions.    The traditional indeterminist way of looking at the matter, however, seems to me to involve an impossible separation between the free will and the rest of a man's nature. But we cannot at any rate deny *a priori* that punishment may affect morality without also denying it of all external circumstances and all non-moral desires, also of almost all education.

It is a long step from this to saying that punishment *must* reform, and it obviously does not do so in all cases, but at least it *may*, and there are some reasons which make it likely that it should have a tendency[1] in this direction.    An enumeration of these will also help us to overcome the difficulty as to how the appeal to non-moral desires may in some cases ultimately further morality.

In the first place, even if a man abstains from a wrong act through purely selfish motives, that abstention may at least be the beginning of a habit of external action in conformity to law, and this habit once set up may easily pave the way for a disposition which does not abstain merely from fear of consequences.    At least it may be plausibly contended that a habit of refraining from crime for non-moral motives is much more likely to develop into a habit of refraining from it for moral motives than is the contrary habit of committing crimes for equally non-moral motives.    If a man starts a good habit from bad or indifferent reasons, may he not still, once he has started it, find it worth practising for its own sake ?    He may only not value it for its own sake because he has not tried it ; and if that is so and if it is something which ought to be valued for its own sake, surely he may be the better and may even thank one later for being made to try it. If a child only goes to school because he is compelled, it does not, therefore, follow that he will necessarily never come to care at all for education for its own sake.    Aristotle's whole theory of moral training seems to rest on the assumption we have made, for he holds that the natural process by which we come to do really good actions is by starting to perform actions

[1] That there are counterbalancing moral drawbacks and dangers I admit freely (*v.* pp. 85-7, 121-2.).

which are right externally but are not done from the best motive. Further, if moral motives are later aroused in the man, they are certainly more likely to take effect if he has already, for whatever reason, overcome the tendency to perform those external acts which are most violently in conflict with the line of action suggested by them.

Or the man's moral sense may have been so clouded and obscured by desire that it could only be freed by the counteracting influence of another desire of the same " material " order. As long as he is wholly dominated by a particular desire, he may simply not realise the moral iniquity of the deeds he does in order to satisfy this craving, but as soon as it is weakened by conflict with another counteracting desire, his mind may be set free to realise the badness of his behaviour. A similar effect, *mutatis mutandis*, may be produced by reward, though in itself the desire for reward may be no more laudable than the motives which lead a man to crime.

If punishment and reward could have no moral influence, the well-known maxim that each surrender to a temptation tends to make it harder to resist it in future, and that each performance of a good act tends to make it easier to do it again, would be altogether false and unfounded. If it is true, it must follow that the adoption of what is externally the right course will tend to make it easier to adopt it under similar circumstances in future.

But we have not yet really freed ourselves from the deterrent point of view. It was Bentham's mistake that he limited the reformatory effects of punishment *qua* punishment to the deterrent influence of pain on the man who has met with punishment. It is not only pain that is characteristic of punishment ; it is pain inflicted because of wrong done and after a judicial decision involving moral condemnation by an organ representing society. It is not only that the man suffers pain, but that he suffers it as a consequence and sign of the condemnation of his act by society as immoral and pernicious. Now this surely is a striking way of bringing home to him, so far as external symbols can, the wickedness of his conduct. It is generally admitted that recognition of one's sin in some form or other is a necessary condition of real moral regeneration, and the formal and impressive condemnation by society involved in punishment is an important means towards bringing about this recognition on the part of the offender. " The pain and coercion involved in punishment present the law with much greater impressiveness than can, for the mass of people, be gained by a mere admission that the law is binding.  On the other hand, the fact that the pain coincides with that intellectual recognition on the part of the offender that the law is binding prevents the punishment having a merely intimidating effect, and makes it a possible stage in a moral advance."[1]

For the offender to be reformed he must realise the badness of what he has been doing, and since his previous actions make it very doubtful whether he will do so of his own accord, this badness must be " brought home to him " and the consciousness of it stamped on his mind by suffering.  The infliction of pain is society's way of impressing on him that he has done wrong.   No doubt if he refuses to recognise the authority of society and believes that he is in the right and society in the wrong, then the punishment will not produce the desired effect.  On the contrary, except in so far as he is deterred by fear, it will make him more and not less determined to pursue his own course, it will probably add to his other motives anger at what he considers unjust treatment and a desire for revenge.  He will tend to view himself as a martyr for the cause of right.  But this is not the normal case.  Usually the offender is himself conscious that he has been acting wrongly, and for him to be reformed this consciousness must become predominant.[2]  Anything that emphasises his guilt will tend, other things being equal, in this direction, and no more striking emphasis can be given to his guilt than by public condemnation and punishment.

It is here, if anywhere, that we may find the moral, educative function of punishment *qua* punishment both in regard to the offender and in regard to others.  Punishment may reform by rendering possible the application of other educative influences, it may reform by deterring through the sheer painfulness of it ;  but if it is to produce a moral effect as punishment and not merely as a preventive safeguard, a convenient means for securing a compulsory training or a natural pain, it must reform by calling attention to the badness of the act.  Pain that merely happens to follow wrongdoing does not impress on the offender's mind that his act was bad ;  pain inflicted deliberately for wrongdoing after a considered judgment by an impartial authority is much more likely to do so.   I said " in regard to others " as well as " in regard to the offender," for this official branding of certain acts as

---

[1] McTaggart, *Studies in Hegelian Cosmology*, 145.

[2] By this is meant not a morbid dwelling on past sins, but simply the recognition by the agent that his act must not be repeated.

crimes is not a factor to be overlooked in the moral education of the community, but of this I shall speak later.   We are now talking of the reformation of the offender himself.

Here common sense will eye any eulogy of punishment with suspicion, even if unable to point out any definite reasons why it should not have that effect.   *If* the criminal is such a man as to look on his punishment as a moral lesson, he will be reformed by it ; but is he likely to look on it in this way ? Or, if he does so occasionally, only in his best moments, is this likely to have any considerable effect on his life ?   No doubt there are some instances of criminals being thus reformed, but few would venture to claim that they are very numerous.   Yet this is the only way in which punishment *qua* punishment can reform.   The reformatory effects of a train- ing received in prison do not constitute reformation by the punishment itself, but reformation by non-punitive means the application of which the punishment renders possible.   In practice far more prisoners are no doubt reformed by these than by the punishment itself, but our subject of discussion is not the effect of training on those receiving punishment, it is the effect of the punishment.   By all means let every effort be employed to devise the best method of improving criminals when in prison, only let us not call this reforming by punish- ment.   If I dismiss the ordinary " reformatory " methods with only the brief comment I have already given, it must not be supposed that this is because I am inclined to minimise their importance, far from it, but because we are not con- cerned here with moral education as a whole, only with the part of moral education constituted by punishment.   It is not the chief part of education, more can be done by other means ; but, even though a minor part of education, it is worth discussion by us.

It is reasonable to suppose that punishment, as implying the moral condemnation of a practice by the community as a whole and as, so to speak, branding this moral condemnation into the consciousness of the offender, may work some moral good, may tend in the direction of reform.   But we must not exaggerate the extent of the good it will do, and the use of punishment for this end has many serious counterbalancing drawbacks.   In the first place the infliction of punishment is very likely to turn the offender's attention from the wrong he has done to the pain he suffers, so that he only thinks of the latter, not the former.   If, as often, the offender is genuinely sorry for what he has done shortly after having done it, the punishment may actually counteract the good effects of this by making him feel sorry for himself instead.    Further, if he thinks the punishment at all excessive—and most people think it excessive in their own case—it arouses resentment and bitterness, and it may even make him feel that it is quite excusable to go on turning his hand against a society that has treated him in this way.    The reply to force by force, however justified, naturally arouses in a man, and not by any means only the most depraved of men, a desire to " hit back " and a tendency to remain in thought on the low plane in which might is right.    In any case this anger, this tendency to consider the punishment as though it were only an exercise of mere arbitrary force, this desire to " hit back " constitutes an additional difficulty, an additional temptation for the offender to overcome, and one that is directly due to the punishment itself.

Secondly, the disgrace and loss of self-respect inseparable from criminal punishments are serious and obvious obstacles in the path of reform, both intrinsically because of the admitted close connection between virtue and self-respect, and incidentally in that they make it much more difficult to gain a fresh start in life.    Difficulties of this kind seem quite inseparable from criminal punishment for serious offences, although they may be greatly mitigated by wise treatment. One of the chief advantages of recent prison reforms is the increase of self-respect they bring to prisoners who behave well.

Finally there is the danger that both the offenders themselves and others may be led to think of the punishment as the only reason for not doing the wrong act.    This is, indeed, the worst danger in the use of punishment in education, though it may be greatly lessened there by means of various kinds which make the punishment seem the natural sequence to the act and especially by showing the child first just how the act is wrong.    Also, where punishments are very infrequent and only inflicted as a last resort, a child will clearly be much less likely to look on all wrong acts as being wrong merely because they are punished.    But the danger becomes very serious indeed with the old-fashioned system of constant punishments.

The difficulties in the way of reformatory punishment are, therefore, serious enough.    The fact that punishment has a *tendency* to make the offender realise the wrong he has done by impressing upon him the disapproval of society is not altered by the existence of drawbacks and counteracting tendencies ; but it is true that this tendency by itself would not justify the infliction of punishment by the State, since it is seldom that a criminal is reformed in this way, and since punishments are in other respects detrimental to moral progress. As one of the functions of State punishment it must be noted, but it could not justify it if it were the only one. There seems to be much more chance of reforming criminals by means other than punishment, such as those advocated by the prison reformers, than by the penalty itself ; but the success of these too will always be seriously hindered by the drawbacks of punishment just mentioned as well as the difficulty for the offender of making a fresh start in life and the other numerous dangers involved in imprisonment. On the other hand, while lamenting the large number of prisoners who are not reformed, we must remember that, supposing they remained at large in their original environment, the chances would also be against reform. To estimate the success of the system we should compare the number of prisoners reformed not only with their total number, but with the number that would have been likely to be reformed if they had not been sent to prison or punished at all. This second method of comparison makes the results appear very different.

The following objections have been brought against any view that insists on the reformatory function without making punishment primarily retributive :—

1. That it really denies the value of punishment by making penal suffering only an incidental and not an essential moment in the process of reform ;

2. That it is a degrading insult to the man punished because it involves treating him as a non-moral being ;

3. That, to be successful, it presupposes the recognition by the offender that the punishment is retributively just, and therefore really implies the retributive theory ;

4. That the reformatory theory denies any essential connection between guilt and punishment, and therefore, if logically developed, would contradict the principle that we must only punish the guilty, and would lead to an intolerable tyranny in which the State claimed the right of reforming by punishment any man who it thought needed it.

The first objection is valid against those advocates of the view who deny or ignore the possible reformatory effects of the punishment *qua* punishment and only attend to methods of reform which are essentially other than punishment, though only rendered possible by the punishment. It is urged against the reformatory view that it really provides no reason at all why punishment should be painful, why you should not reform by means of pleasures instead of pain. But this objection may be met without admitting that punishment is an end-in-itself, if we simply recognise that a reformatory effect may be exercised by punishment *qua* punishment in addition to the reformatory advantages of any further educational treatment. This admission certainly does not imply the truth of the view that punishment is an end-in-itself, and yet it shows why it must be painful in order adequately to fulfil its moral function. A pleasure " inflicted " as a punishment would serve neither as a mark of social disapproval nor as a motive against repeating the action for which it was " inflicted." Pleasures may undoubtedly help to reform, *e.g.*, when used as rewards, but they do not help in the specific way in which punishment does, but in another way peculiar to them. We must not recompense a crime with pleasures because pleasure would have the opposite effect to that required, it would encourage repetition and not deter, it would convey approval and not disapproval, it would arouse not repentance but self-satisfaction. In order to justify the principle that punishments should be painful we need not show that the pain is an end-in-itself, only that it is a necessary means if they are to achieve their object. The term, punishment, does not cover reformation by any and every means, but reformation by pain deliberately inflicted for wrong done, and this pain has a peculiar reformatory tendency of its own just because it is painful.

Secondly, the argument that the reformatory view is an insult to the criminal and disregards his potential moral nature is valid against the doctrine that crime is merely disease, but this doctrine is not at all presupposed when we say that punishment should be reformatory. Historically the reformatory theory has been very much influenced by it, but logically it does not in the least depend on it. The more seriously we think of moral evil, the more we regard it as something worse than involuntary disease, surely the more we should emphasise the importance of curing it. The fact that crime involves a bad will and not merely a diseased mind does not remove the necessity for applying curative measures ; it only leads to the conclusion that the curative measures used should be those suitable for a bad will. Other methods of cure are suitable for involuntary defects, but for a bad will the method of cure involves censure of the sin (or moral evil) in some form or other, and often the most effective form to give it is judicial punishment.    The view that such external intervention is a violation of the rights of humanity could only be sustained either from a position of the extremest individualism, which ignores the importance of the criminal's reform not only for himself but for the rest of society, or from a position which repudiates all use of force and would therefore be equally irreconcilable with the retributive theory. *If* the State has a right to interfere with the individual by force so as to do retributive justice,[1] it has also the right to interfere with the individual by force so as to do him moral good, provided only—and here comes the reason why the State must not try to reform by indiscriminate punishment irrespective of guilt—it is likely to do more good than harm by the policy of interference.    I fail to see how the reformatory purpose can be described as " cruel."[2]    On the contrary, whether in ordinary education or in the treatment of criminals, it requires the avoidance even of the appearance of excessive severity, both because this is likely to arouse a resentment which will exclude contrition and because of its depressing and dehumanising effects on the offender.    The necessity of checking crime by deterrents may prevent our going as far as we should like in the direction of leniency, but, since everyone is apt to think his own punishment excessive, even without good ground, it is much better from the reformatory point of view to err on the side of mildness than on the side of severity.

Further, if there is any justification for the right to punish, *i.e.*, to put into a situation which is generally in some respects demoralising, surely it is also our duty to counteract these demoralising factors in so far as in us lies.    Otherwise we should have the right to put the criminal into a demoralising situation but not into a moralising one.    Reformatory punishment implies not that the offender is a mere animal incapable of morality, but on the contrary that he has moral potentialities, otherwise it would be useless to try to reform him.    It implies that he is immoral, not that he is non-moral.    It is a disgrace for a man to have to realise that he has acted so badly as to require special *retributive* punishment by the State.

---

[1] Or to deter others.    As far as respect for the criminal and his rights is concerned the reformatory is preferable also to the deterrent view.
[2] As it is by Bosanquet, *Some Suggestions in Ethics*, Ch. VIII.

The external disgrace is in fact needed to impress on his mind that he has done wrong. As McTaggart points out, it is futile to dismiss a punishment as degrading because it is disgraceful ; " degrading " means " making morally worse," and disgrace need not make a man morally worse; on the contrary, if its object is fulfilled, it will rather bring home to him that he has acted badly and by this means pave the way to reform. " A man is disgraced by being made conscious of a moral defect. And to become conscious of a defect is not to incur a new one. It is rather the most hopeful chance of escaping from the old one. It can scarcely be seriously maintained that, if a fault has been committed, the offender is further degraded by becoming ashamed of it."[1] The reformatory view should be least and not most open to the charge of treating the man punished as a mere thing, for it alone is concerned to develop his moral nature.

The third objection depends on the admission generally made that a necessary condition of reform is the recognition that the punishment is deserved. This admission seems to lead to the conclusion that the reformatory theory involves a vicious circle, for, if reform depends on the recognition that the punishment is deserved or just, we cannot say that the punishment is just because it reforms (or that its reformatory effects are the criterion of its justice). Is not the retributive theory still implied by the idea of a punishment being deserved ?

This objection is a more formidable one, and indicates the necessity of what may without unduly stretching the sense of the words be called a retributive element, if punishment is to be in the highest sense reformatory. But a good deal turns on the meaning of the word " just." The only sense in which the recognition that the punishment was " just " can be rightly said to be a necessary presupposition of the reformation of the offender is the sense in which it simply means a recognition that the act which brought punishment on his head was very bad, not because it was punished, but because it was wrong. He must recognise that it deserved, *i.e.*, called for, the social disapproval expressed in punishment, that it was sufficiently bad to need this emphatic condemnation. In admitting that his punishment was " just " or " deserved " he does not mean that the degree of pain he suffered was in proportion to the magnitude of his offence, he could never

[1] *Studies in Hegelian Cosmology*, 151.

be certain of that.   His admission is only a recognition of the badness of his act, for, if it had not been bad, it would not have been a fitting object for the social disapproval expressed in punishment.

So the reformation of the offender may still be one of the chief objects of the punishment, but the latter must be just, not only in the sense of being reformatory, but in the sense of being an expression of rightful disapproval, in the sense that it is inflicted for a really bad act.   This is a necessary condition if its reformatory function is to be adequately fulfilled, but it does not follow that the main purpose of punishment is not to reform, or even that " justice " is an end-in-itself.   For all we have seen yet is that, if punishments are to serve as a means of reform, they ought to be just, and not that this justice is of value *per se*.   We must not say, indeed, that the punishment is only " just " because it reforms, but we still might say that it is only justified or only right because it reforms.   To be right it would have to be just, *i.e.*, deserved, but that might only be because it would not have good consequences unless it were just.   Justice is not synonymous with rightness (as applied to punishments), but at most a necessary condition of rightness, since other circumstances besides justice have to be taken into account by us.

This point becomes somewhat clearer when we consider the fourth objection, which was that the reformatory theory recognised no distinction between the guilty and the innocent and would justify the State in punishing anybody who it was. thought might be improved by punishment.   If the pain of punishment is educative, why not inflict it on the innocent ? The answer is :—Because it is educative only for the guilty. Pain is needed for the reformatory purpose, because, first, it should deter the man from repeating the act as a consequence of which it is inflicted, and, secondly, it is often the most effective way of expressing social disapproval of a man's past conduct.   But, if he has not committed an offence, it would be futile or harmful to deter him from repeating what he has done, and by expressing disapproval of what is *ex hypothesi* right you will never " reform " but may only corrupt him.

It is said that, if you once allow the State the right to reform a man by pain, you cannot on principle lay down any limits to the use of that right.   Either the State has the right to improve any citizen it thinks fit by inflicting pain, or it has no right to inflict pain for the sake of improvement at all.

But we may well reply that a quite sufficient reason why the State ought not to try to improve by pain other people besides those who are guilty of a definite crime is that such action would be likely to do far more moral harm than good and is therefore undesirable. The State ought to refrain from trying its hand at indiscriminate reform by means of pain, not because it has no right to promote individual morality as such, but because it cannot effectively promote it in this way, that is, because interference beyond certain limits would do a harm that outbalanced the good, though within these limits it may be beneficial. Further the retributive principle is in no better case itself, since, as we have seen already,[1] it cannot possibly tell us which offences the State ought to make punishable by law. According to it all moral offences of any kind *deserve* punishment, and the fact that the State ought not to punish them all can only be explained by reasons of expediency or other principles distinct from[2] retribution.

If its reformatory function were the only reason for punishment it would be more doubtful whether the State ought to inflict it, but then this is not the case. The function in question can be exercised much more effectively in ordinary education than it can in the State treatment of criminals. *If* a criminal is reformed by punishment *qua* punishment, he is reformed in some way like this, but we must admit also that the criminals who are benefited by punishment *qua* punishment are likely to be few in number. Consequently, in considering the general utility of State punishments and for one who has to make practical decisions in the matter, the deterrent effect and the reformatory treatment by means other than punishment *qua* punishment deserve more attention as being more likely to lessen crime. But they do not reveal the special nature of punishment to the same extent as the function we have just been considering.

In the education of the young the situation is different. It would be generally admitted, I think, that the main object of punishment as applied to children is not retributive or deterrent, but rather, as put colloquially, " to get them into good habits." There are two ways in which it may achieve this object. In the first place, the end may be secured by making them abstain from bad acts through fear of consequences till they eventually come to abstain even when the fear of

---

[1] *v.* above pp. 42-3.
[2] I do not say necessarily incompatible with.

punishment is absent, and till they through habit have ceased to wish to act otherwise. But, secondly, it may also be secured if we make them regard the act as wrong by associating it with the emphatic condemnation of a teacher or parent whose authority they respect. The second is the better way, since it appeals to moral motives, and here the chief thing is to make the child see that the act is wrong. This may be done by various means—by verbal representation, by experience of the natural effects of the act, and by punishment in the strict sense. Unfortunately offenders frequently do not pay attention to words unsupported by anything more solid and palpable, and since the second way is impracticable in most cases, punishment is sometimes needed " to din the words in." Children may tend to feel that an act is not sufficiently bad to matter much, if it is not sufficiently bad to be punished as well as merely blamed ; and this necessity for a lesson more impressive than can be given by words alone is, I suppose, the ultimate reason for the use of punishment in education. It is difficult to state the point without giving some slight impression that one is inculcating a morbid habit of introspection, but nothing more self-conscious is needed than the simple reflection on the part of the child that he must not " repeat it." It is in the education of the young that punishment may most easily fulfil this function, for the habitual tendency of a young child to regard those who bring him up as almost infallible gives to their moral authority, whether expressed in encouragement and advice or blame and punishment, a weight very much greater than would be ascribed to the authority of the State by adult citizens. This view does not make punishment a very important part of education, or imply that the educator should rely on severity. Rather the contrary, for it makes the advantage of the punishment consist not in the fact that it is unpleasant *per se* but in the fact that it is an expression of disapproval. In the majority of cases verbal disapproval is enough without further punishment, and, even where it is needed, the punishment should not exceed the absolute minimum required, both because pain is an evil in itself and because of the bad moral effects of severity.

We have seen that punishment may exercise a reformatory effect by acting as a vehicle of moral disapproval, but hitherto we have spoken as though this reformatory effect were limited to the man actually punished. We have now to ask whether the moral influence of punishment does not extend a good deal further. May not the moral disapproval expressed in it serve other purposes too? Need it be limited in its good effects to those who have already become criminals? May it not serve as an important part of the education not only of the individual but of the community as a whole? Here from the nature of the case we are concerned rather with State punishment than with punishment in education, since the former provides an example not only for some individuals but for the whole community.

Now the existence of a penal law is an impressive condemnation of the practice prohibited by it. But surely this solemn, public condemnation on behalf of the community will have some effect not only on those actually punished but on others also. If it may help the offender to realise the badness of his action, may it not help others to realise this badness before they have committed the kind of act in question at all? This must not be confused with a purely deterrent effect. A man who abstains from crime just because he is deterred abstains through fear of suffering and not because he thinks it wicked ; a man who abstains because the condemnation of the crime by society and the State has brought its wickedness home to him abstains from moral motives and not merely from fear of unpleasant consequences to himself. The existence of the punishment was one of the causes which led to the rise of these moral sentiments, but once they had arisen it could not be said to provide his motive. The same distinction occurs in the case of reformation of criminals. A criminal is reformed as far as external habits go, if one experience of punishment has made him feel afraid of a second experience and so unwilling to repeat the crime, not because it is wrong but because it is dangerous for himself, but he is reformed in a truer sense if his experience of punishment has brought him to realise the badness of the crime more than he did before, and if it is for this reason that he abstains. The two elements, the deterrent and the truly moral, may be very much intermingled in practice—mixed motives are a commonplace—but they are nevertheless essentially different.

What we have now to consider, however, is the moral effect of punishment not on the offender but on the community as a whole. As we saw earlier, punishment is often a necessity of self-defence. The community must defend itself against the violation of its laws, otherwise they would not be laws. When a law is broken the governing body cannot sit still and do nothing, for such inaction would definitely encourage and in a sense even sanction other crimes.  So it is easy to see that the neglect to punish will have consequences that are morally harmful.  It will tend to make some people think that lawlessness does not matter, it will render the laws and government despicable in the eyes of many, and the moral judgments of those who represent and rule the State, being not carried out in action, will cease to be taken seriously at all.  It is not merely that people will commit crimes when they have no fear of punishment, but that they will tend to think more lightly of the gravity of crimes, not only of the unpleasantness of their consequences.  This is what will happen, *ceteris paribus*, where crimes go unpunished ; and, if punishment averts these evils, it is clear that it will have a good moral effect on the community, though an effect which cannot be summed up wholly by saying that it deters potential and reforms actual offenders.  In particular, to punish an act implies a declaration that the act is bad, and the declarations of the State as to certain acts being bad enough to call for more or less punishment must have an effect on the moral standard of the community.

This very same factor, we have seen, is presupposed if punishment is to do its deterrent work in the most effective manner, for it is not merely the actual punishment that deters but the disgrace associated therewith.  Punishments would deter less if they were looked on as mere natural calamities and did not imply the condemnation of a wrong act.

We have also seen that it is presupposed in the reformatory function ; if a punishment is to reform it must come to be viewed by the offender as a moral condemnation of his action.  Again it is this feature of punishment which has tempted thinkers to regard it as primarily retributive.  We seem to have at last found in this what must be the central point of any sound theory on the subject ; we have also, as we shall see later, found the basis of a possible treaty of reconciliation between the different views.

But, to return, it may be replied that crimes are so obviously wrong that we do not need the State to tell us that they are wrong, but this argument mistakenly limits the alternatives.  It is not that the plain man does not know a crime to be wrong unless he knows it to be punished by the State, but that he does not realise its wrongfulness so fully.  Men are apt to put wrong acts into two classes.  In one are acts that are really wrong but still excusable, acts that they will commit themselves under considerable temptation, though perhaps not under very slight temptation, and that they will not be *very* sorry for having committed, though they will admit them to be wrong.  A man may treat in this manner, say, unkind remarks made in anger or certain " somewhat doubtful " practices in business.  But there is a second class of acts which are regarded as not only wrong but *very* wrong *indeed*, so wrong that " they simply must not be done on any account whatever," and that the consciousness that oneself or anybody one loved had committed them would be a really great grief.  I do not contend that this is ideal morality, but it represents roughly the general practical stand-point, and it is this standpoint and the standpoint of those morally below the normal that we have to consider in applying punishments.  Now the removal of an act from the first class to the second class, provided it is really wrong, does represent a moral improvement, at least if lived up to in practice.  But, by branding an act as a crime subject to fairly stringent punishment, the State definitely places it in the second class, the class of acts which " simply must not be done."  It is not that men only think theft and murder wrong because these acts are punished, but that they think them " more wrong " than they otherwise would.  In many cases this increased realisation of their wrongness may be enough to hold back from crime a man who would otherwise have succumbed to the temptation to commit it.  It is not correct to say in a case like this that he merely abstains from crime because he is afraid of unpleasant consequences for  himself. That would not be true at all.  He abstains from crime not because owing to the existence of the penal system he thinks it less advantageous for himself, but because owing to this he thinks it more evil than he otherwise would.  The fact that theft is punished by imprisonment surely makes people in general think of it as a worse offence, not because they are afraid of the punishment but because they think the crime must be bad to deserve such a punishment.  Facts like these must have exercised an important unconscious influence on most of us as we formed our ideas of morality, even on the best.  But the criminal code should not be expected to be of much moral help to the best ; it is from the nature of the case intended for the weaker brethren, for those who are hovering on the borderland of crime, and it is difficult to oppose the view that the added realisation of the wrongness of certain acts which is facilitated by the fact that they are declared worthy of special punishment must prevent a great number of people from falling into criminal habits who would otherwise do so, and this quite apart from any deterrent effect.    There is no name in general use for the function of punishment now under discussion, since " reformatory " is used of the effects on the man punished, not on others, so I shall employ the term " educative."

As Rashdall says—" There are many offences which the State can do little to check by the directly deterrent effects of punishment, but which it can do much to prevent by simply making them punishable.    Since a few persons with good coats have actually been sent to prison for bribery at elections, the respectable public have really begun to suspect that there may be something wrong in the practice.    A very little reflection upon the different estimates that are formed of those forms of immorality or dishonesty for which people go to prison, and of those for which they do not go to prison, will show at once the enormous importance of the criminal law in promoting the moral education of the public mind."[1]    The mere living in a society where certain acts are subjected to severe penal condemnation must, in the absence of strong counteracting influences, develop the habit of regarding these acts as " very wrong indeed," as " out of the question for respectable people."

Not only does this habit prevent men from committing acts which have been stigmatised as crimes ; it prevents most men from even seriously considering whether they shall commit them.    This is not to remove the need and chance of fighting temptations and so deprive them of the moral strength which comes from this ; it is to free their energy so that they may combat other and less elementary temptations.    The effects of punishment have been well compared to the effects of physical habit in making certain acts automatic.    Our physical capacity with practice to do mechanically and half-consciously certain things which required conscious effort at first has the great advantage that it enables us to attend to other matters and so saves time and energy ; similarly the fact that certain acts are branded as crimes makes it " a matter of course " for most people that they will not commit them,[2] and therefore liberates attention and energy which

[1] *Theory of Good and Evil*, Vol. I, pp. 296–7.
[2] Punishment is only one of the agencies that achieves this.    The individual may do it for himself, or it may be done by social disapproval not expressed in the form of punishment, or by education.

would otherwise in many cases be needed to fight the temptation to do these acts. If legal punishment extended to every kind of wrong act it would indeed eliminate the moral struggle and tend to make men automata ; but, where it is a question only of some particularly bad and harmful acts being punished, it does not put an end to the struggle, it only transfers it to another sphere, and that a somewhat higher one. If a man is freed from any need of combating the temptation to some of the worst class of acts, he will be able to turn his energy to meeting other temptations to acts which, though not quite so bad, are still morally blameworthy. If a man will not even consider the question of stealing, he is not only less likely to steal but less likely also to do what comes next in badness to stealing. For, if he had considered the question of stealing seriously, these acts would appear less bad by comparison with the still worse act of definitely stealing, and to commit them would tend to seem not a yielding to temptation but an overcoming of it, since they are at any rate not so bad as what he was tempted to do, namely, steal outright. " Sharp practices " that come " near the borderline " would tend to seem an excusable compromise compared to actual stealing.[1] But, where stealing is ruled out as an impossibility, the " sharp practices " a man may be tempted to indulge in are contrasted not with the still worse act of stealing, but with the better course of true, and not only legal, probity.

Of course, this must not be understood as suggesting that the majority of people would steal if there were no punishment for it—I certainly do not think they would—but it does seem to me that a great many more people would be tempted to steal than is the case now, and that among them would be many who do not now want to steal, not because of fear of punishment, but because they think it wrong. The decrease in cases of crime due to punishment does not comprise only those who are deterred by fear, but those who would not have realised the wrongness of the crime if it had not been thus definitely branded as wrong.

There must be added a very important reservation, namely, that a system of punishments will only produce the required effect if it is not sharply opposed to existing ideas on morality. If the State makes punishable a kind of act which the popular conscience approves, it will not have the effect of making the

[1] This is only an illustration ; I am not committing myself to the assumption that all " sharp practices " that come within the law are morally less bad than all cases of stealing.

latter disapprove the acts in question, at least not for a generation or two. It will rather tend to set people against the law and to make them regard with admiration and sympathy those who defy it in this matter. It is only if the law is fairly in accord with, or goes only slightly beyond, popular feeling or ideas that it will tend to strengthen hostility to the acts condemned by it. Unless the badness of the act is already felt the infliction of the punishment will not call attention to its badness, which is not admitted, but rather to the sufferings of the man who is punished, which are obvious and cannot be denied, and it will simply be a ground of complaint against the authorities, except in the case of those submissive people who tend to think of the ordinances of the latter as though they were infallible. People may be deterred by punishment from committing acts which they do not think wrong, but that is not to persuade them that the acts are really wrong. Punishments inflicted for acts which a man thinks good or indifferent take on for him the character of brute force, and the occurrence of many such punishments in the penal code would tend to make him more or less despise laws in general. Nor can the State trick us by punishments into regarding as very bad acts which are not so, unless there is already in our own minds a strong tendency towards that error. It cannot even instil into us a consciousness of shame as regards many acts which are harmful or dangerous but do not imply much moral badness, e.g., riding a bicycle without a light after dark.

It may be objected that, if penal laws only make people think an act wrong when they are already prepared to do so of their own accord, they can be of no use as a moral education at all. Either, it may be said, an act is thought bad already, in which case there is no need for a law to lead us to think it bad ; or it is not thought bad, in which case a law forbidding it will not make us think it bad. This is, however, a misapprehension of the position. The contention is not that the law teaches men what is wrong, but that it tends to bring them into a habit of mind in which they realise its wrongness more strongly and fully. The distinction is between, on the one hand, admitting if challenged that an act is wrong and yet doing it, and, on the other, realising that it is so bad that it " simply must not be done," between a theoretical belief that it is wrong and a practical habit of looking at it as something definitely inexcusable. A new law is not likely to make a man think an act wrong if he would not have been prepared to admit so much without the law, but it may make him feel its wrongness more vividly, and, if he is tempted to do it, there is all the difference in the world between knowing that it is bad and realising its badness in a way that will really check him in face of the temptation.    The chief purpose of punishment as educative is not to create a consciousness that an act is bad, but to strengthen and bring to the front a consciousness of its badness which is already there.    For men commit crimes as a rule not because they do not know that they are wrong, but because the consciousness of their wrongness is lacking in the power to influence action.    The extent to which *new laws* can improve men morally in this respect, however salutary the new law may be in general, is small ; but the case is different with acts prohibited by the laws under which a man has been " brought up " and which strike him as part of the established order and not as a novelty.    For new laws to have their full moral effect in this way we must wait at least a generation ; it would be quite chimerical to envisage the swift achievement of a moral reform in this fashion by additional legislation.

The power of the State in this respect is therefore very limited, but it is none the less real ; one of the strongest convictions of recent philosophy and psychology has been that the importance of the influence of society on the individual is almost overwhelming, and if there is any truth in this view at all the fact that certain actions are so definitely branded " criminal " as they are must have a considerable influence on moral development.

This function of punishment explains certain points which non-retributive theories often leave unjustified and unexplained.    In fact, it paves the way for a view which, while without the *prima facie* irrationality of the retributive doctrine, at least as often interpreted, has much in common with the latter.    In the first place it explains the importance of the reference to the past in punishment and supplies a new interpretation of the conception of " annulment."    The act to be punished is harmful and so its bad effects need to be counteracted, though the act itself with its intrinsic evil is over and cannot be undone.    This counteraction must have reference primarily to the past act, not because we are under an incomprehensible obligation to atone for it irrespective of whether this atonement does good in the present and future or not, but because the only way of restoring a right situation in the present is by counteracting the evil effects of the past act.

Other effects may to a certain extent be counteracted by compensation to the victim, but the moral evil which it produces cannot be removed in this way. We must distinguish here between the moral evil of the act in itself and the morally harmful effects of the act. The former cannot be annulled because we cannot undo the past, but the latter may be to some extent. One of the chief effects of the act is that it tends to make other acts of the same kind in the future more likely both on the part of the agent himself and on the part of others. The act has set a precedent, and, unless something is done to counteract it, a precedent tends to be followed. An unpunished crime encourages other crimes, and failure to punish tends to throw the law and its administrators into contempt.

How is this to be stopped? For the State habitually to do nothing would be tacitly to consent to the breach of its own law. Hence the need of " annulling " the precedent. We cannot annul the past act *per se*, but we can annul its bad moral effects. In so far as these effects are due to the crime as an example, they must be annulled by an opposite example; in so far as they depend on or consist in a setting aside and weakening of the law, that law must be re-asserted, and re-asserted emphatically. The way of doing this is by moral condemnation, and those inclined to commit crimes or hovering on the borderline of the criminal class would hardly take the moral condemnation as serious unless it was rendered more emphatic by having subjoined to it a penalty. With all who have a sense of shame this moral condemnation is certainly an integral and important part of the punishment, while the suffering " brands in " the condemnation in a way in which mere words would not do. This aspect of punishment is well brought out in Bosanquet's essay on the subject. " A bad act has come into being. It has so far established a vicious rule, a precedent hostile to the body or soul of the community. If the rule is not to stand, is not, that is, to become, with a greater or less degree of consciousness, a persistent factor and make-weight on the communal mind ; that is, in every individual mind so far as it is influenced by social contagion, or, more properly, so far as it shares the general mind ; if the evil rule is not in this sense to stand and persist, then the act or fact must be cancelled, annulled or undone. This, I take it, and not the infliction of pain is the essence of punishment. It is the formal verdict or censure of the social authority, marked by some overt act such as the

dullest capacity cannot misread. . . . Now you cannot
formally and publicly undo, or set a brand on, the voluntary
action of a moral agent without checking, cutting back and
repressing his self and his personality."[1]    I am not quite sure
either how far this is believed by the author to be an interpretation of the Hegelian doctrine, or how far it would be a
right interpretation, but at any rate something of this kind
must have been in Hegel's mind and must have made it easier
for him to sympathise with the retributive theory.

But it may be asked—What is the good of all this ?    What
advantageous effects does it produce ?    Who benefits by it ?
Is not " annulling a crime " analogous to locking the stable-
door after the horse has been stolen ?    But, if punishment
serves in this way as a kind of moral education to the community, then it is far from purposeless.    The moral education
of the community is a very important object indeed, and if·it
is desirable for the attainment of this object that crimes should
be " annulled " by punishment, then surely we have found a
fresh purpose to justify the latter.    We must not suppose
that, because we cannot say definitely which persons are
better for these moral effects of punishment, therefore it is
as though no persons were the better ; all its moral effects
are effects on persons.    Because punishment is directed
towards the past, it does not follow that this is its ultimate
end ; on the contrary we have only justified the reference to
the past by showing that without it we shall not obtain the
future effects that are desired by us.    " Annulling " is a
somewhat dangerous term to use, and we are using it here
chiefly because of the weighty authority behind it, but whatever it means it is certainly not supposed to mean literally
" undoing the past " by anybody except some primitive
savages.    We cannot annul the past, but we can to a certain
extent annul the evil effects of the past, and this is what we
are trying to do in punishment.    This is analogous not to
locking the stable-door after the horse is stolen but to trying
to recover the stolen horse.

Besides recognising the essential connection between
punishment and crime, this view also recognises the essential
connection between punishment and the moral improvement
that it is its special function to produce.    Some good effects
of punishment do not follow at all from its intrinsic nature.
A punishment consisting in imprisonment prevents the

---

[1] *Some Suggestions in Ethics*, pp. 190–1.

criminal from committing further crimes while he is in prison and may enable the prison chaplain to help him to reform, but to the achievement of these effects, however valuable they are and however much they ought to be considered in any penal system, the essential nature of punishment is incidental and irrelevant.   A man who is prevented from committing crimes only by the fact that he is in prison would be equally prevented if imprisonment were pleasant to him and were regarded as a reward ; a man who is reformed by the ministrations of the prison chaplain is reformed not by the punishment itself but by something that is no more a punishment than is a lesson at school or a sermon.   The case is somewhat different with the deterrent effect ; this is not merely incidental to but follows from a punishment *qua* punishment. An exclusively deterrent theory, however, goes wrong in treating mere pain as the essence of punishment.   The penalty must not be viewed as mere pain but as pain inflicted for wrongdoing by a recognised authority, and it is as such that it produces its educative effects both on the offending individual and on the community as a whole.   Other good effects are not due to it *qua punishment,* and are, therefore, not in the same degree important for the theory of punishment.

This is not inconsistent with their being of even more importance in practice.   For, while in the theory of punishment we are specially concerned with the effects of punishment as such, in practice we are concerned with the effects of concrete punishments, which are never merely " punishments as such " but include many characteristics not common to all punishment.   The legislator and the administrator of the penal system have to think of these characteristics also, and they may outweigh the effects of it *qua* punishment. It would clearly be wrong to conclude that, because a certain effect was produced by virtue of the essential nature of punishment, it was therefore of more importance than any other effect in practice.   This would be like saying that, because sugar *qua* sugar is sweet, it is good to eat it and enjoy the sweetness even if it be poisoned.   Similarly, whatever the tendency of punishment in general may be, a particular punishment ought not to be inflicted where it is known that it is likely to prove a moral poison.

This view makes disapproval a prior condition and its expression the essential part of punishment, which is of importance in answering the question why only the guilty should be punished. The moral object of a punishment as such is to make people think of a certain kind of act as very bad, but, if it were inflicted otherwise than for a bad act, it would either produce no effect of this sort at all or cause people to think an act bad which was not really bad, and this is why we must first of all ask—Is a punishment just ? Is it inflicted for a wrong act ? If punishment expresses condemnation of acts and persons that ought not to be condemned, it will clearly not be fulfilling its function of expressing moral disapproval in the right way.

What wrong acts it is desirable to punish legally is another question that cannot be settled by these means. It is equally obvious that all cannot be and that some must be, but we should remember that acts generally regarded as wrong, though not legally penalised, tend to be punished by social disapproval or by a semi-conscious withholding of approval that may make life materially less pleasant for the offender. That this often does not come about and, where it does come about, is often insufficient to outweigh the pleasure gained or the pain escaped by the offence, is unfortunate in some respects, but at any rate it carries with it the great advantage of leaving adequate room for " disinterestedness."

We are now in a position also to give a satisfactory reason why a graver offence should be punished more than a lighter one. It is easy to see that, in so far as the moral code of the common man is affected by the penal system, it will be affected adversely if a lesser crime is punished more severely than a greater, for that would imply that the State thought the lesser crime worse than the greater, or at least suggest to men's minds the idea that the lesser crime was worse than the greater. One of the requirements of a good moral code is that there should be a right proportion between values, and, in so far as the penal code affects popular morality, it ought to help and not hinder right judgment in this matter. To take an instance, it is often said that in this country offences against property are generally punished with a disproportionate severity as compared to other offences. If this charge is true, our penal law will have the effect of encouraging the dangerous tendency to attach excessive importance to material wealth, and will in so far do harm to the moral standard of the community. Again, religious persecutions are likely to intensify the bigotry from which they arise.

But is not this to fall back on the old retributive conception that a certain amount of pain intrinsically fits a certain degree of moral badness? No, for all my view presupposes is that in a given society a certain amount of pain is a suitable way of expressing a certain degree of disapproval, just as one tone of voice may be a more suitable way of expressing it than another. To suppose a quantitative correspondence between two things so little susceptible of mathematical treatment as pain and moral guilt strikes many thinking men as extremely difficult and without parallel in the rest of our thought, but everybody must admit that one sign may be better suited to convey a given meaning than another is.[1] Not that the punishment suited to express a given degree of disapproval will be eternally the same ; what punishment is suited to convey disapproval depends not on the badness of the act to be punished alone, but also on the way in which the society in question is likely to interpret a given degree of punishment. The infliction of pain is intrinsically suited to be a sign of disapproval where something so emphatic is needed, but the degree and kind of pain required will vary according to the susceptibilities of those to whom the sign is addressed. The same principles again constitute one of the reasons why the State should make allowance for " extenuating circumstances." Not to do so is to treat a lesser as though it were a greater offence.

There is another bad effect of disproportionate punishments in so far as they involve excessive severity. It is this : if a man is very severely punished for a comparatively slight offence, people will be liable to forget about his crime and think only of his sufferings, so that he appears a victim of cruel laws, and the whole process, instead of reaffirming the law and intensifying men's consciousness that the kind of act punished is wrong, will have the opposite effect of casting discredit on the law and making the action of the lawbreaker excusable or even heroic. Severe punishments are especially liable to produce an effect of this sort on their victim. He will be likely to think the penalty excessive in any case, and the great danger is that this will lead to self-pity and despair, or anger and bitterness, and that he will then simply remain in that frame of mind, thus gaining no moral advantage from his punishment but the reverse. But, if he has really good

---

[1] It may be said that we are still bound to admit a correspondence between *disapproval* and guilt, but this can only mean that we ought to make our judgments about bad acts correspond to the degree of their badness, *i.e.*, merely that the judgments ought to be true, ascribing to them a right degree not a wrong degree of badness.

grounds for complaint, this danger will be doubled. The primary object of punishment is to make both the offender and others realise the badness of the act punished, but, if great severity is shown, they are much more likely to realise instead the cruelty of the punishment. This must be added to the arguments against a very severe system of punishments.

It must not be supposed, however, that it is possible to fix on exact proportion between punishment and guilt. This would involve us in the difficulties which proved fatal to the practical application of the retributive theory. But, it may be argued, by saying that the punishment must not be disproportionate in severity to the crime, you have already entangled yourself in these difficulties. Now in replying to this accusation we must at once give up the idea that the measurement of moral guilt can go very far, but it remains possible to compare the degrees of badness presupposed on the average by different offences, and, having done that, we can lay down the principle that a lesser offence should not be punished so severely as a greater one, e.g., that theft should not be punished so heavily as murder. For, as a general rule, the act of stealing is less bad than the act of murdering, though this may be reversed in individual cases, i.e., *some* thefts are no doubt worse acts than *some* murders. We cannot say exactly how much disapproval a murder deserves, but we can say that it generally deserves more than a theft, and so on. From the retributive point of view it would be necessary that each punishment should be in proportion to the moral badness of each particular crime, but from the point of view of moral education it is only necessary that it should be in proportion to the badness of *that kind of* crime, a very much easier matter to determine. It is not necessary for the formation of correct moral ideas that the goodness or badness of each individual man and act should be assessed, but only that right views should be held as to the importance of observing certain rules and the relative importance of protecting different kinds of values, and this, in so far as affected by the penal law, will depend not on the assessment of the guilt of individuals but on the general rules observed in punishment. Similarly for the individual punished the important point is not to form a right estimate of the exact degree of his own moral guilt, but to realise that he did a very bad act, and this is hardly beyond the capacity of the humblest intelligence. We know perfectly well that certain kinds of acts are very bad and that some of these are generally worse than others, and this is all that is really necessary for our purpose. We can also see that in some cases a punishment is far too small or far too great properly to express our moral sentiment as regards the crime, so great as to arouse horror or so slight as to excite ridicule, and so can avoid penalties of this excessive or inadequate kind. It is not, however, the pain but rather the degree of moral condemnation implied that should be in proportion to the crime. Thus in a more enlightened and milder society the same degree of condemnation may be implied by a punishment that is far smaller. It is certainly not necessarily a mark of great moral sensibility to insist on severe punishments.

We have seen that this view of punishment, which I am calling the " educative " view, justifies certain principles for which hitherto only the retributive theory had found a place. In particular it makes clear how " justice " as the right relation to guilt is a presupposition of punishment doing its work effectively. It does not content itself with maintaining that justice is an end to be pursued for its own sake, but shows its value as a means. This, however, still leaves open the possibility that just punishment may be an end-in-itself as well as a means to other goods, that it may have intrinsic and not only instrumental value. Is this so ? It is very difficult to think of the pain of the punishment *qua* pain as an end-in-itself, but this is not the case with the moral disapproval expressed thereby. For we can hardly deny that a right mental attitude to good acts is of value intrinsically, not only as a means ; but, if so, the same must surely apply to what can hardly be separated from it, a right mental attitude to evil. This would only show moral disapproval, not its expression, to be intrinsically good ; but it seems quite reasonable to hold that the expression shares in the intrinsic value, especially if it is viewed as a solemn moral judgment on behalf of the community. Now this is just what punishment should be. So there seems to be good reason after all for treating it as an end-in-itself. This is on the whole gratifying, because it accords with our intuitive moral judgments and yet does not make pain an end to be pursued for its own sake. It perhaps would not be right to speak of the infliction of pain on the guilty as having value merely as a means, for it may have some derivative value in so far as it expresses moral condemnation in the appropriate way, but this only belongs to it as the symbol of something more important not in virtue of itself but in virtue of what it stands for.

Further the way in which disapproval should be shown depends on the stage of development of the people to whom it is addressed. The pain can only have even this value if it is *the appropriate* expression to *their minds* of the degree of moral condemnation required by the wrong act. When those concerned are sufficiently sensitive adequately to appreciate the condemnation without the pain, the latter ceases to be the appropriate expression and so loses its intrinsic value altogether. For, though truth may be absolute, at any rate no expression of a truth is absolutely appropriate, only appropriate as a translation of the truth to the people to whom it is meant to be conveyed.

There is another reason for regarding punishment as an end-in-itself in so far as it not only symbolises the condemnation of evil but is itself a thwarting, a defeat of the evil will and purpose. This explains very well why, quite apart from human agency, we should think a universe better in which happiness and unhappiness were distributed according to merit than one in which they were not, for we cannot separate the happiness of the bad from their triumph or the unhappiness of the good from their, at least partial, defeat. This principle, however, again makes an end-in-itself not of the pain as such, but of that of which the pain is, at least usually, an inseparable concomitant, the defeat of evil. Further evil is only defeated by punishment in so far as punishment is the best way of meeting it, and consequently the punishment loses its intrinsic value where the evil would be met better by censure alone or by forgiveness. Punishment by an external authority can itself at the best only be a very partial victory.

To say that just punishment is an end-in-itself is not to deny that it should be sacrificed to other more important ends. It is difficult, however, to conceive the possibility of the maintenance of the right mental attitude to crime conflicting with the realisation of other goods so as to force us to choose between the two ; it seems to be only the expression of this attitude that may conflict, and we need not disapprove of the crime any the less because outward circumstances make it inadvisable to express our disapproval fully in punishment. If it be said that a mental attitude is nothing apart from the actions which express it, we may reply that expression in this sense does not include only verbal condemnation and punishment. The mental attitude may be expressed in other ways, especially in abstention from acts similar to the crime in question, or simply in the internal action of thinking on the matter. Its non-expression in definite punishment may involve a sacrifice of some intrinsic value which would appertain to the expression, but this value seems to me very slight indeed, incomparably smaller than the other values furthered by punishment, where it is at all successful in its purpose. It is therefore a negligible factor in deciding for or against the infliction of punishment.

But the question whether the punishment is just is still of the greatest importance, both because injustice is intrinsically evil and because a just punishment is most likely to have good consequences on account of the reasons given above. When I look at the two, injustice in punishment seems to me a *very much greater intrinsic* evil than justice is a good, especially if the injustice consists in punishing somebody for an offence of which he is not guilty or in excessive severity. (If it consists in leniency without good grounds, it is not so great an intrinsic evil as this, but still a greater evil than just punishment is a good.) It is also a most important consideration that the conscious infliction of unjust punishments even if apparently expedient must lead to a very bad " moral atmosphere " in a State (or home). They altogether discredit the moral authority of the State and make people regard it " as a mere matter of force."

We can thus agree with the retributive view on most points, provided this view is not pressed to the extreme of making retribution the only or chief point to be considered in inflicting punishments. We can admit that the first question to be asked is whether a punishment is just, that a reference to the past is an essential element in the nature of punishment, that punishment is an end-in-itself and that the penalty and the guilt should be, if possible, in proportion. But our view still differs from the retributive theory, as usually interpreted, for

(1.) It holds the valuable element in punishment to be not the pain inflicted in proportion to desert but rather the moral disapproval implied thereby. Pain is of value in that case only in so far as it is needed to express and " brand in " that attitude, and the infliction of pain beyond what is directly caused by the moral censure as such should be omitted altogether if the beneficial effects of punishment can be secured without it, for that the offender should suffer pain is in itself evil.

(2.) Without denying the intrinsic value of this attitude of disapproval or even of its expression in punishment, it justifies punishment rather as a means to good than as an end-in-itself. Punishment is valuable not chiefly because it expresses a right attitude of moral disapproval but because it has good consequences ; an attitude of disapproval that banished all thoughts of future consequences for the offender and for the community would emphatically not be right.

It may be objected that I am here guilty of a vicious circle, because the good consequences in question consist mainly in a cultivation of the right attitude towards crime, but I do not think this criticism is justified. For to say that punishment is valuable mainly *as a means to establishing* a right attitude towards crime in the offender and in the community in general is quite compatible with denying that it is valuable mainly *as an expression* of a right attitude towards crime in those who inflict it. The important point is not that we should express this attitude in verbal condemnation or punishment, but that we should cultivate it. Punishment is valuable mainly not as an expression of a theoretical estimate of moral evil but as a means towards its destruction.

Even if our view is " retributive " it cannot then be called " mainly retributive," and I should prefer to avoid the term altogether owing to its associations and owing to the fact that it commonly stands for a view which makes the end-in-itself not only or chiefly what the pain expresses but the pain itself. It is, however, desirable to make somewhat clearer my attitude on the question whether just punishment is an end-in-itself or not. I hold that the punishment as a whole is such an end, but that this is not because it involves pain in proportion to desert, it is because it expresses appropriately a just condemnation of evil and is itself a *defeat* of evil. If and where evil could be as effectively defeated and condemned by censure without any other punishment, the latter should be avoided altogether. Nor does just punishment seem at all an important end-in-itself if we abstract from its effects. Its importance lies rather in the fact that justice is a necessary condition if punishment is to produce satisfactory consequences, and also in the fact that injustice is intrinsically very evil (usually very much more so than justice in punishment is good, it seems,[1] though I do not claim to give reasons for

---

[1] Similarly lying is a greater evil than truth-telling is a good, except where the truth is told in face of a very great temptation when it has the value which belongs to all moral acts done under such conditions.

this intuitive conviction). We must not, however, ascribe whatever intrinsic value punishment has to the pain alone, but to the whole fact of punishment. This is to commit an illegitimate abstraction, for it is not pain alone that constitutes a punishment, but moral condemnation expressing itself through pain. But, someone may ask, if the intrinsic value of the punishment is due to its being an expression of condemnation, why do we apply the retributive principle where the pain is due not to human agency but to nature or accident, as we call it ? It is generally held that a world in which the best men were miserable and the worst happy would be inferior to a world in which the same total happiness was distributed more in proportion to merit. This may undoubtedly be explained largely by theistic conceptions ; justice in the distribution of rewards and punishments is an essential part of goodness, therefore a good God must distribute happiness and suffering justly, and the sufferings of the bad can be regarded as an expression of God's condemnation.[1] But I think there is also another reason, namely, that the pain may be taken as symbolical of the actual defeat of evil, not only of its condemnation. Nay more, it is an inseparable element in this defeat, for the latter must involve either the thwarting by external means of evil purposes in men or the repentance and self-condemnation of the sinners, and both must involve their pain. The idea of symbolism explains the special satisfaction which we are apt to feel when a man falls into the trap which he has himself set for another, or suffers through natural processes a punishment analogous to the crime, for such punishments symbolise with special vividness both the condemnation and the defeat of evil. It is still, however, not pain as such but pain as an inseparable element in the defeat or condemnation of evil that is intrinsically of value. If the pain were an end-in-itself it would surely be the part of a good man to gloat over it, to rejoice in its intrinsic value ; but this is not the case. It is the mark of goodness to rejoice over the defeat of evil but not over the sufferings of the evildoer. This is, perhaps, the strongest argument against the retributive theory. For, even if the pain has a slight derivative value in virtue of that which it expresses, this value is quite outweighed by its evil, as pain, and could by itself never serve to justify its infliction.

[1] Not that this conception of punishment is free from great abuses, v. p. 230.

The above considerations suggest the possibility of dispensing with the special infliction of pain[1] and confining ourselves to verbal condemnation. The moral purpose of the pain as regards the man who suffers it is to " brand in," to print indelibly on his consciousness the iniquitous character of certain acts, but this would clearly be unnecessary if of his own accord he sincerely and fully realised what a wrong he had done, and if this realisation were strong enough to afford an adequate safeguard against a future relapse. In such a case, if we could only be certain of its genuineness, pardon after censure would be more suitable than further punishment, and we can easily imagine a golden age in which all offences would be treated in this way. Indeed censure, or even tacit condemnation, without deliberate infliction of pain, already can and does exercise a considerable moral influence on men. It is fear of social disapproval and not fear of other punishment that is the main external sanction against a breach of those unwritten laws which are regarded as socially, though not legally, obligatory. It is certainly an effective sanction, very often far too effective for moral progress. Similarly the part which should be played by verbal admonition in the education of children is obviously very large. The pain in punishment is only needed for the education of the offender because of his insensibility to moral considerations, which makes it necessary that they should be forced on his attention in a way more obvious and more calculated to leave a lasting impression.

So much for its effect on the offender, but what about its effect on others ? Here again the only need for the addition of the obvious pain of punishment to the censure of a crime springs from a certain insensibility to anything less emphatic. Men will know that, if an act is censured by the State, that act is deemed wrong, but the wrongness tends to be less strongly realised when it is not associated with the more tangible stigma of a definite punishment. Unless it punishes as well as censures, the State, at the present stage of development, does not seem to be " taking it seriously," and therefore will not give the requisite impression. But we are very much nearer to a community in which censure or admonition could generally take the place of punishment than we are to a community in which no important offences would be committed. The situation is complicated by the fact that social disapproval generally has as its natural consequence certain other drawbacks which may be regarded as punishments, but

---

[1] *i.e.*, over and above that which follows naturally from the realisation of the wrong done, a pain which, if the censure is to do its work, must be regarded as inevitable, *v.* pp. 116–7.

it is quite clear that the mere consciousness that other people disapprove of an act, apart from any other harm or loss apprehended through their disapproval, is a very important factor in determining conduct.

We must remember also that the moral effectiveness of pain in punishment, at least as regards those other than the offender who suffers it, does not depend in any important degree on its actual amount[1], but rather on its amount relatively to that inflicted for other offences. Thus, in a community where punishments generally are light, a much smaller punishment for a given offence may do the moral work that a larger would under other conditions. If so, this is a gain, not a loss. We must not say—the more we condemn moral evil the better, therefore the severer the punishments we inflict the better, but rather—the more sensitive the community is to the badness of moral evil, the less need is there to use pain to brand in a consciousness of this.[2] The better a community the less severe need be the punishments. The external infliction of pain is not the inevitable or sole expression of moral condemnation ; it is only a last desperate remedy, necessary because and when milder ways of expressing the same condemnation will, owing to lack of moral sensibility, fail to produce the lasting impression that is needed. Its value disappears the moment the requisite degree of disapproval can be adequately conveyed without it.

In any community save a perfect one some offences will be committed, but it is not absurd to suppose a community which, while still far from perfection, was governed as effectively by censure as ours is by censure plus further punishment. Needless to say, this does not mean that the abolition of punishments other than censure is a practical proposition for us. It would need a bold man to maintain that the general moral development of the community was far enough advanced for that. Would an ordinary thief be influenced very much by the censures of the judge apart from other punishment ? But all the same we must not overlook the fact that the fear of social disapproval is generally a sufficient sanction for the so-called " respectable " classes. It only

---

[1] Provided the punishment is not so small as to appear ridiculous, in which case it would certainly be preferable to have censure without punishment.

[2] Again we must remember that the more prosperous a community is the more acutely sensitive are its members to misfortune, and so the same external treatment is a much severer punishment than it would be under rougher and more primitive conditions.

operates effectively against certain kinds, not all kinds, of wrong acts, but the same applies, much more strongly still, to ordinary legal punishment.

The practical harm of paying too much attention to the pain, whether as an end-in-itself, or as a deterrent, or as an educative remedy, lies both in the fact that it encourages excessive severity, and in the danger that it may by associating duty with brute force and unnatural constraint make it appear distasteful to a free man. In so far as the punishment consisted only or mainly of moral condemnation, the feeling of constraint and the idea that it was merely a case of *force majeure* would be much less prominent. Punishment is liable to involve such great pain both for the victim and others and such danger of moral evil that it is of the utmost importance that it should be replaced by censure or condemnation alone, where possible without grave damage to the interests of society.

These remarks are specially applicable to the education of the young. We may concede to the opponents of punishment in education that the deliberate infliction of pain or even the deprivation of pleasure as a special penalty should be usually replaced by admonition[1] in some form or other ; but it must be clearly realised that, if you do away with punishment, you must find something else to do its work. The work of punishment is to make one realise the importance of not doing wrong, and the fulfilment of this function is obviously essential for the good life. It is necessary that a child should be brought to realise this, if possible, by verbal advice and encouragement, or, after the act, by blame, but it is very difficult to believe that these will always impress sufficiently without something further of the nature of punishment. The function of punishment is to make the culprit take the matter seriously, to make him remember that " he must not act like that." If this can be done without punishment, all the better. Punishment is a crude means, only good because of a strong strain of crudity in the nature of the person who suffers it, and it involves the risks of a confusion between " punishable " and " wrong," with the ethical dangers of an egoistic utilitarianism, but it may still often be necessary. Further, if it is omitted, it is important that the same lesson should be taught by other means, and all such means have as their

[1] I do not limit it to verbal admonition. To show the child the harm he or she has done may often be more effective than any words could be.

object bringing the child to see that the act he has done is wrong, that is, they include the condemnation which we saw to be the essence of punishment. This sounds perhaps rather grandiloquent language to use about the little "naughtinesses" of a child, but, if it is worth while preventing the child repeating them, it is worth while making him realise that it is wrong to act like this, and to take action to make him realise this is essentially the same as to condemn him. The principle is the same as with grave crimes ; it is the degree that is different.

It is in the treatment of children that punishment may best do the work of reforming the offender ; in the penal system of society it is more likely to be effective as a moral education for others than it is for those who are themselves suffering it. The reform of the latter is much more likely to be brought about by auxiliary educative influences associated with the punishment than by the punishment *per se*. On the other hand the penal code will have an important effect on the general morals of society, and this effect will be due to the inherent nature of punishment as such, not to any auxiliary additions.

Our view certainly leaves ample room for the duty of forgiveness, and there is no difficulty in reconciling this with a rightful disapproval of the act forgiven, in fact forgiveness would have no meaning if the wrongness of the act were not recognised by the person who forgave it, though it does not follow that he need always overtly express this. As we have seen earlier,[1] forgiveness does not involve remission of the penalty if one is desirable in the interests of society. It should be added, however, that in personal offences forgiveness may often be a far more effective means of morally benefiting the offender than any punishment could be.[2] But to achieve this purpose it must lead to the man being ashamed of his act, condemning himself, and this is what punishment by another road essays to do. Forgiveness is a better way in personal relations, but it must not be construed as weakness and it hardly applies to the law-courts. A judge cannot show the virtue of forgiveness except towards any private enemies of his own, for this quality consists in putting aside rancour at personal grievances, and is only likely to produce a good moral effect on the offender because and where it is the person wronged who, in spite of what he has suffered,

[1] pp. 30–32.
[2] *v.* p. 30 for reason of this.

forgives him. On the retributive view there would be something lost when a man is reformed by forgiveness instead of punishment, namely the intrinsic value of the just suffering. On our view it is a clear gain, for punishment is only intrinsically valuable in so far as it is the appropriate expression of disapproval, and if the man can be cured through forgiveness without punishment, the latter is not the appropriate expression, because it is not needed to bring home to him his wrongdoing.[1]

We must admit that punishment, even if it only consisted of censure, must always involve pain, since it is unpleasant to be disgraced and to realise that one has done wrong, and this is no doubt true. This kind of pain is an essential part of educative punishment, though it may vary greatly in degree. The infliction of pain by external means may be avoided, but not this psychological consequence of justifiable censure, at least if the censure is to do good to the offender. Further, a man who has done wrong and really repents must suffer in a further way, if under " suffering " be included partial loss of happiness as well as actual pain. If he really repents, he will wish and try to do better, but this will be harder just because he has done wrong. Because he has done wrong in the past, he will be partially thwarted in his efforts to do his duty, and, if he really wishes to achieve success in this, he is bound in consequence to be somewhat less happy than he would have been if he had not made his character worse by previous wrongdoing. Each offence tends to make the process of recovery from the fault a less smooth and pleasant one. For this effect to be realised it is not necessary that the man who is being reformed should reflect self-consciously on the amount of progress he has made and regret that it is not more ; the mere fact that it is harder and begins at a lower level will tend to make the process less satisfactory, even though he is as little introspective as anybody. The less he is what he should be, the more on the whole will the good activities in which his reformed (or, rather, reforming) character is expressed be thwarted through faults in his nature, and so he will be less happy in so far as his happiness depends on unimpeded activity, for, even if we do not go as far as Aristotle, we must admit that it depends on this to some extent. Nor is the pain of a conflict between his moral

---

[1] Except in so far as punishment is needed (whether as deterrent or educative) for the sake of the community in contrast to the individual offender.

aspirations and desires, which have been first strengthened by a life of sin and then repressed by his new and better will, a negligible penalty. This is quite apart from any specific pain of remorse or qualms of conscience such as moralists are so fond of speaking about, and no doubt these may be a source of suffering too. Enough has been said to show that the retributionist was right in holding that any real reform of criminals does presuppose something of the nature of suffering. But this may be necessitated mainly by internal and not by external causes, and, if it is, all the better.

It must be added that, even if we confine ourselves to the milder method of censure and avoid other punishment, many of the dangers of the latter present themselves in a somewhat milder degree. In particular the offender must not be disgraced so much that he feels himself permanently put in a class of " specially bad people," and the degree of disgrace that it is wise to inflict depends on individual temperament and cannot be fixed merely by reference to " deserts."

But some may still feel that we have not said enough. Suppose a man to have sinned, been condemned, and then realised the extent of his sin enough to set him on the path of reform. It is often felt that this is not sufficient, that, quite apart from any utility which pain may have as a means, he ought to " expiate " his sin by suffering, simply because he has sinned and not because the suffering is likely to improve his character or deter others. This view can only be based on " intuition," but the case for it is the stronger because men very often feel not only about others but even about themselves that they ought to endure suffering not as a medicine but as an atonement, not because it will make them better, but simply because they have done wrong. But we may point out :

(1.) That the condemnation which helps a man to realise his sin necessarily involves something of the nature of suffering, even if it is only the condemnation of his own conscience, not of an outside authority.

(2.) That pain is, so to speak, the material expression of condemnation. The attitude of a penitent man who is genuinely convinced, not merely through habit or authority, that he ought to expiate his sin by suffering, may be due to his being so ashamed of himself that he wishes to express his hostility to his old self in some definite way, and the most obvious way is by the infliction of pain. It also symbolises the defeat of the evil in him.

(3.) Even if a man fully realises the wrong he has done, the suffering may be psychologically useful as branding this in further, expressing in definite form and thus strengthening his detestation of it. It may relieve his feelings of remorse, and, once it is over, may give him the sense of a fresh start. Further, the consciousness that he had needed all this suffering to atone for the crime would tend to prevent him from repeating it.[1] On the other hand, most men of the present day cannot help feeling that there is a certain element of morbidity in the attitude in question.

(4.) The belief that the pain is an end-in-itself may be due to a confusion between the symbol and what is symbolised, the means of expression and that which is expressed. An aversion to committing wrong acts is very important and very valuable both intrinsically and in its consequences, and this aversion may be strikingly expressed by willingness to suffer pain for past wrongdoing. Hence it is easy to see how the symbol may come to be regarded as having intrinsic value even when divorced from what it symbolises.

(5.) But we may go a long way to meet the advocate of retributive punishment. I have already admitted that the expression of aversion to evil may have some of the intrinsic value belonging to that which is expressed, and so the pain itself may derivatively have some intrinsic value as long as it is the expression of genuine horror at wrong. Only this value will not belong to the pain as pain, but to the pain as expressing and in so far as it is needed to express the valuable moral attitude in question. Whether this value can outweigh the intrinsic evil of the pain as pain is another question, which I should answer in the negative in general ; but the moral attitude of the man who takes his punishment gladly as expiating his crime, or even meets it voluntarily for that reason, is something which, whatever we think about its expression or the theoretical basis of it, we cannot but admire. The pain may not be of value in itself, yet the act of accepting it may be of the greatest value intrinsically and not only instrumentally. But the man who accepts the pain gladly as part of his moral education, or as a necessary consequence

---

[1] In so far as expression strengthens the disposition expressed, he will also tend to abhor the act more on account of his suffering, but there is the opposite danger, too, that the suffering may be treated as a substitute for amendment, that his ardour may cool when he has suffered, and that he may just think—" Now I have paid for my crime, so I may have a good time and not bother."

of offences against the social order, is equally deserving of admiration.

It is, however, only fair to look at the question from another angle, from the point of view of the spectator, not of the suffering individual. If we do this, it becomes difficult to hold that we ought to welcome additional suffering not needed either for moral education or for social purposes. If the additional pain is not on the whole evil in itself but good, why should not we rejoice to see a man undergo it ? A good man should enjoy what is good, but we can only enjoy another's pain if we are animated by revengeful motives, *i.e.*, not in so far as we are good but in so far as we are bad.

I think I have now said enough to reconcile my position with the data of the relatively[1] immediate and unreflective moral consciousness on punishment. I have not indeed accepted these data in quite all respects as they stand, but I think I can say that, if my view be true, this intuitive consciousness has come as near the truth as could reasonably be expected of it. For, in order to come nearer, it would have to make finer distinctions than it is capable of doing. We cannot expect " intuition," unsupported by conscious detailed analysis, to distinguish between the view that pain is to be inflicted on evil-doers for its own sake and the view that it is to be inflicted as a symbol and inseparable concomitant of something valued for its own sake, and therefore the intuitive conviction that the pain of the guilty is an end-in-itself does not, I think, prove the former view to be true.[2] If, however, anybody thinks this intuition must be accepted at its face value, he can without contradicting the rest of my theory still admit the presence of an intrinsic value in the pain over and above what can be explained by anything said here. I cannot prove such an admission to be false ; all I can say is that it cannot be proved, and that I do not myself see it to be justified by " intuition." What is justified is the view

[1] Only " relatively," for no " intuition " stands by itself quite alone. It is probably always inference plus intuition, only sometimes the former predominates and sometimes the latter.

[2] We should note that the " intuition " which seems to support the retributive view is not an " intuition " as to what to do in a particular case or cases, but an " intuition " as to general principles, implying a very considerable degree of abstraction. This greatly lessens its authority and value, since it may so easily be an " intuition " of something else rather like but not the same as the principle asserted on the strength of it, and this is in fact what I hold it to be. (The practice which we feel we ought to adopt in regard to punishments can be easily explained on a non-retributive view.)

that punishment as a whole is an end-in-itself, and this I hold to be true.

The "educative" function of punishment must not be treated as the only one, but requires to be supplemented by the ordinary reformatory and deterrent views. If it is important to reform a man by punishment *qua* punishment, it is equally important to reform him by other means such as training in prison, and, since these latter means are more likely to prove successful, they are more important in practice as regards the offender himself, though not as regards the moral education of the community. Also, since it is at least as certain that punishment will deter to some extent as that it will reform some offenders and do its " educative " work for the community, this end must be considered also and may sometimes justify more severity in punishment than would otherwise be admissible. Deterrence must not be regarded as merely a means to lower goods of no ethical significance, for, after all, if it is needed for the attainment of security and the protection of rights, it is needed for something which is a most important condition of the higher life. On the other hand, since the " educative " effects are real and important, we must hold that they ought to be considered in practice as well as in theory.

Further the deterrent effect itself is greatly increased by the knowledge that the punishment is a merited disgrace, *i.e.*, a condemnation of wrongdoing. To do even its deterrent work most effectively it needs to be more than merely deterrent, it needs to be " educative."

In two directions the " educative " function seems to be of very special importance :—

(1.) In the effects of the penal law on the moral standards of the citizens generally and the habitual attitude to crime of those who have not themselves been punished for it. As regards its practical effects this is mainly an argument against sacrificing justice too lightly to expediency, since the primary condition of the fulfilment by punishment of its educative function is that it should be just. It shows the importance of not being led by the deterrent purpose to try excessive severity and of maintaining a fair scale of penalties. It is not so much a new criterion for detailed modifications as the main reason for justice and against either capricious leniency or excessive severity. It is also an effect that ought to be considered carefully in determining the manner of pronouncing sentence and the manner in which the penalty is carried out. It is important, if possible, to make the offender as well as others see that the punishment fits the crime and that it is the product of reason, not of the blind impulse to retaliate or of brute force. Variations here are easily possible without appreciably altering the degree of severity.

(2.) In the education of the young, especially if we include under punishment admonition and regard further penalties as only a means of bringing this home. It may be said that, when punishment is justified in this sphere, its main function must be the educative one, provided we use this term to cover effects of the kind described in this chapter on the person punished or threatened with punishment, and do not confine it to others than those concerned immediately, as we sometimes did in speaking of State punishment. That is very important because after all this is a part of life with which far more are primarily concerned than with the administration of the criminal law ; it is here, if anywhere, that most people will have a chance of putting into practice any theories that they hold about punishment. And here, more than anywhere, it is of the greatest practical importance to remember that the essential feature of punishment is the expression of disapproval and not the infliction of pain. It follows, first, that wherever a child is punished it should be made clear that it is because he has done wrong, and secondly that no further penalty of any kind beyond verbal blame is desirable except where the blame is not likely adequately to impress on the offender the wrongness of his action.

I fear that I may seem to have given far too laudatory an account of punishment since I have dwelt mainly on its good effects, as was indeed inevitable in a special philosophical study of its function, for the function of anything consists in doing the good of which it is capable, not the bad ; but I hope the reader will not think that I am either ignoring the fact that, although it plays a part in moral education, this part is only very small, or passing over the grave dangers and evils which may accompany its use and sometimes go far to outweigh the advantages of which I have spoken. In order to counteract this impression, it seems only fair to conclude by a list of the chief moral drawbacks which attend its use by the State :—

1. It tends to arouse resentment and bitterness, especially as a man is always apt to think his own punishment excessively severe.

2. The disgrace involved makes it harder in many respects to gain a fresh start and may lead to despair. It also may suggest — Act up to or " down to " your bad reputation.

3. From the nature of the case it is depressing and hence may weaken energy.

4. It involves the risk of substituting for repentance the opposite impulses which are liable to be excited by any application of force.

5. It may tend in the direction of making a man dislike duty and consider it an interference with freedom.

6. It may help in leading men of crude minds to regard external respectability as all that matters and to confuse the moral law with brute force or think of it as a mere means to personal safety.

These are dangers, not certain harm, but we must admit that they are serious dangers enough. We must never forget that the moral evil and pain involved constitute a very grave factor on the debit side of punishments and a very strong argument for lightening them and restricting their scope in a degree which would not be desirable if we considered only the deterrent and educative effects on the rest of society. It is necessary in some degree to sacrifice the criminal to society— otherwise we find ourselves sacrificing society to the criminal —but humanity has at last realised that this must not be carried too far. The situation would be different if there were sufficient likelihood of the punishments inflicted by the State being reformatory to make it worth while imposing them for the criminal's own sake; but this hardly seems to be the case. It is doubtful whether imprisonment is more likely to reform than the reverse, and, therefore, it must be justified in the main not by its effects on the man punished but by its effects on the rest of the community.

It is not indeed beyond the scope of human ingenuity to devise means of punishment which are less open to objection than the present system ; but these would still have to face all the six difficulties mentioned above, if they were punishments at all. Many evils are due to points in the penal system which can be remedied ; but any conceivable penal system must, for the reasons above given, produce or at the very least incur a grave risk of producing some bad ethical effect on the offender. It may also produce good ethical effects on him, but it would always be difficult or impossible to feel confident that the good for the man punished himself outweighed the evil, although we might be sure that the good for society as a whole including the man often does so.

But this is not an argument against making punishment reformatory. The fact that it involves all these dangers is in itself rather a special argument for trying to secure that it shall work some counterbalancing moral good, and it seems about as practicable to estimate whether particular modifications for reformatory purposes are likely to do good in this direction as it is to estimate whether they are likely to make punishment considerably less effective as a deterrent or not. It would be an argument against inflicting on purely reformatory[1] grounds a punishment that was not required by the deterrent or any other social purpose, except where those who inflict it have special knowledge of the individual character and needs of the offender, as in the education of the young. But then, as we have seen, there are various other grounds for the infliction of punishment by the State, and, granted that punishment ought in any case to be inflicted, the fact that it involves certain moral dangers cannot possibly be an argument against trying to make it as morally beneficial and as little harmful as possible, though it would be a valid argument against incurring those moral dangers for the sake of a problematical moral good to the offender alone. We must also again remember that if the criminal were not punished but left to himself without interference of any sort, there would still not be a very good chance of reform.[2]

It is only in education that the reformatory purpose can become the sole object of punishment, and there it is possible to have more knowledge of individual character than we can have in the case of State punishment. But the evil effects just catalogued are only too likely to occur in the education of children also, though in a rather mitigated form because any particular punishment will be a great deal milder and less important in the life of its victim than is the case with the criminal law.

Further, five, at any rate, of the drawbacks I have men-

---

[1] *i.e.*, for the moral good of the offender alone as opposed to the rest of the community. These dangers, excepting (6), concern mainly the morality of the man punished, not the effects of the punishment on the community in general.

[2] Nothing that I have said must be taken as debarring recognition of the fact that many "criminals" are cases for medical and not for punitive treatment. The discussion only applies to those who have a real measure of responsibility for their criminal acts.

tioned, *i.e.*, all except (2), do not apply in such a marked degree to censure in some form without other punishment, and this constitutes a very strong argument in favour of that milder method, which is certainly to be preferred where at all practicable. It is obviously not practicable with hardened criminals ; but it may often be so with first offenders against the criminal law, and in the education of the young. But even that method obviously has grave dangers ; it may rouse only antagonism and bitterness, or again it may dispirit. Whether it does this or not depends largely on the way in which it is administered, but there is no royal road to success. Further it must be admitted that there are some temperaments which may be influenced for the better by a moral conviction of their own, but never by censure or punishment.

Further, as has often been pointed out, we must remember that convicted " criminals " are not necessarily always much worse than the average man. They have committed certain specially grave offences of a kind that can profitably be prohibited by law and they are responsible for their acts, but it is impossible to assess the strength of their temptations and so estimate the *degree* of that responsibility. We cannot say confidently what sort of lives we ourselves should have lived under their circumstances, nor how many of them are really more to blame for their grave offences than are people of better natural disposition and opportunities for comparatively quite minor acts of selfishness. This does not obviate the necessity of punishment. They are to blame and they perform bad acts, therefore their acts need condemnation and they need reform ; their acts are socially dangerous, so society should be warned of the fact and, if possible, others should be cured of or deterred from the tendency to follow their example, although it remains the case that there may be many other acts equally bad which it is not practicable or desirable for the State to punish. But, while these considerations do not excuse those who have fallen, they should certainly debar us from over-emphasizing the retributive element in State punishment ; and, whatever our theory of punishment may be, they certainly add emphasis to our obligation to treat the offenders as human beings and to strive for their improvement even to the extent of incurring a slight degree of risk, either in lessening the deterrent effect of the punishment or in giving the offender work after his emergence from prison with the chance of a

" fresh start." *How much* risk we should incur in that fashion cannot be decided by general rules ; we must beware not only of a hard self-righteous contempt for criminals as merely criminals and nothing more but also of the humanitarian sentiment unguided by reason which leads us to incur *unwarranted* risks for their benefit, a course of action which is not only foolish but morally wrong, sacrificing the interest not only of the man who takes the risk himself but of society.

Finally it must be remembered throughout that my defence of punishment is not a defence of the existing penal system, but only an assertion of the need for some kind of penalties.

# CHAPTER V

## Reward

How far can those principles which have guided us in dealing with punishment be applied to reward? The latter is a subject which now calls for consideration on our part, both for its own sake and because of the light it may incidentally throw on punishment. There is another reason also, namely, that since Bentham reward has hardly been discussed systematically at all in any book on moral philosophy. This is indeed somewhat surprising, for although special direct and deliberate rewards given by the State have a much smaller part to play than the corresponding punishments, yet, if we include under the heading salaries, rewards given to children in education and " the rewards of a good reputation," most of our life seems to be covered by it. The way in which I shall deal with the subject is by taking each of the different aspects or functions of punishment that I have discussed and touching upon the corresponding aspect of reward.

The first is the retributive. " Retributive " is not a term usually applied to reward, but there is unfortunately no other adjective in use that will serve to take its place and describe that aspect or theory which corresponds to the retributive aspect or retributive theory of punishment. We might call it the " merit " aspect. For, just as there are theories of punishment which maintain it to be an end-in-itself that the wicked should suffer pain simply because they have done wrong and in proportion to their wrongdoing, so it may be held that it is an end-in-itself also to reward the virtuous and not merely a means to other advantages. That seems to be in fact the view of " common sense," in so far as it can be said to have a view. Its prevalence is shown most strikingly by the very widespread, if not almost universal, belief that the just reward of the righteous is essential if God is to be regarded as good, and by the intuitive conviction that, if a good man suffers misery or fails to gain happiness, it is a blot on the universe in a way in which a bad man's sufferings never are.[1] The good are clearly regarded as having a special claim to happiness just because they are good, not because their happiness will make them still better or be itself a greater happiness than that of the bad, nor even because it will enable them to do good to others more effectively, but simply as an end-in-itself which requires no further justification. When we say that a man " deserves " good fortune, we do not mean that it will be advantageous to society for him to have it ; if we did we could not make the judgment without first considering the consequences his good fortune would have for society. On the contrary our judgment follows without further mediation from our estimate of the merits he possesses. This does not indeed prove that reward is an end-in-itself, but the marked intuitive conviction deserves at least respectful and sympathetic consideration.

We may, however, derive the intrinsic value of reward from grounds similar to those which led us to accept the intrinsic value of just punishment. In dealing with the retributive theory of punishment I argued that, although the pain as such was not an end-in-itself, it symbolised and expressed something that was, namely, a just condemnation of evil. Can we apply this argument to reward ? We need not deny that pleasure enjoyed through the reward is like all pleasure intrinsically good, but we may say that the reward, where just, is also the expression of something else intrinsically valuable, namely, a right approval of the good on the part of those who bestow it.[2] The intrinsic value possessed by this may vary greatly, but surely any right approval of the good must have some. This may be illustrated by the fact that we rate the enjoyment of what is really beautiful, or the admiration of what is really noble, very much higher than we do an even greater enjoyment of or admiration for what is mistakenly thought beautiful or noble but is really not so.

---

[1] This must, of course, be taken as meaning merely that happiness should be in proportion to goodness, not that all mankind could be divided into two sharply defined classes, the good and the bad.

[2] It may also be urged that the value of happiness cannot be separated from the value of the activities and states of mind which it accompanies, and that these will be on the whole better the better the man. But this is not mainly because the happiness is deserved, but because of the specific nature of the activities in question. It is intrinsically better that A should enjoy Shakespeare than that B should enjoy his dinner (in an equal degree), because an æsthetic experience of that kind is of greater value intrinsically than the experience of eating a good dinner, even where the pleasure in the two cases is equal, but this would be so even if A was in general a worse man than B.

It is not merely that we think the good ought to be happy but that we think they ought to be recognised or manifested as good, and the most impressive form of recognition is by bestowal of the means to happiness. For the same reason we are inclined to think it incumbent on divine justice to secure the happiness of the good, because without that we cannot picture the good as really triumphing. Even if the happiness flows necessarily from their inherent nature and is not bestowed from without, that only makes it a more signal manifestation of their superiority and their victory. Just as from the moral standpoint it is held that we ought to recognise, honour and reward the really deserving, and not the undeserving, so from the religious standpoint it is held that the cosmos itself or its guiding principle must give final recognition to the superiority of the good because they are good, and the superiority and triumph of the good are inseparable from their ultimate happiness. But it is intrinsically good not only that moral virtue as such should be recognised, but that other kinds of value should be, which explains our attitude to rewards for æsthetic and intellectual achievements or feats of skill generally. In any sphere it is good that the best should be recognised as such and not ousted from the position of honour by the inferior. We are not here talking of a mathematical or quasi-mathematical proportion between happiness and goodness, but of a right valuation of the good and an expression of this valuation in an appropriate manner. Thus rewards have a further intrinsic value, over and above the pleasure they give, for a reason strictly parallel to that which gives intrinsic value to punishment.

Where rewards are an expression of gratitude, this inherent value is enhanced. Both gratitude and its expression are generally recognised as inherently valuable ; and I see no reason to reject this view. How far the bestowal of public rewards provides a fit sphere for the exercise of this virtue and how far its expression in individual relations can be brought under the heading of " Reward," it is more difficult to decide. The gratitude of a nation as such certainly does seem to add something to the rewards conferred on a man for a really great public service ; but on the other hand gratitude can only attain its full value as an element in friendship, which is essentially a relation between individuals, and should be too free and too little mercenary to be much concerned with definite rewards. Spontaneity, however, *per se* naturally adds to the value of a reward.

Now, just as some hold that punishment ought to be entirely determined by the retributive principle without regard to consequences, so it might be held that the corresponding " merit " aspect ought to be paramount with reward. It might be maintained that a right proportion between virtue and happiness was the only or the chief end to be pursued in assigning rewards. But this view is liable to the same objections as the corresponding theory about punishment.[1] It may be a good that happiness should be in proportion to virtue, but it is certainly not the only or the chief good to be considered. Further a general establishment of this proportion is an end that it would be totally impossible for the State to achieve and most harmful for it to seek. The State cannot give rewards for merit in general, but only for specific meritorious achievements.

So much for ideas of reward based mainly on the duty of justice as an end-in-itself. What is there that corresponds to the other, non-retributive functions of punishment ? Deterrence is the inducing of people to abstain from wrongdoing for fear of subsequent penalties, so the corresponding function of reward would be to encourage people to do good for the sake of a prize they had not yet received but hoped subsequently to gain by their efforts. One might call this the " encouragement " function ; it is what would generally be considered the chief purpose of reward.

Now it must not be supposed that the desire for reward is on a higher moral level than the fear of punishment ; both may be described as non-moral. It is no more creditable to do good simply because you are bribed by a promised reward than to abstain from evil simply because you fear punishment. But we cannot conclude from this that no use ought to be made of rewards. If the principle of reward for services could be altogether swept away at one stroke, there would be no incentives left to work except the love of it and the desire to do good or act rightly ; and it would certainly be Utopian to suppose that at the present stage of moral development these motives are sufficient to secure the doing of all the necessary work without help from motives that would generally be described as more "material" or more "selfish." Even Socialist schemes would either give extra pay for work or inflict punishments for idleness. Those who cry out against the use of rewards in education forget that our

[1] v. above, pp. 17–19.

whole social system is built up on a scheme of rewards in the shape of salaries and wages.[1] If material rewards are needed, as almost anyone would admit, in order to get the work of the world done, it would be unreasonable to expect children altogether to dispense with such a stimulus, and so in this respect be more moral than adults.

The first reason for rewards, as for punishments, is that there are certain acts which society must see performed irrespective of motive. If they are done from a higher motive so much the better ; but it is very much better that they should be done from a " low " motive than that they should not be done at all. It is very much better that men should produce food from purely selfish motives than that they should for want of these selfish motives leave everybody else except themselves to starve, just as it is very much better that a man should escape being murdered simply because the would-be murderer fears the penalty of the crime than that he should perish because that fear is absent.

Secondly, to deny that an appeal to " lower " motives can ever be of any ethical value is to be the victim of a crude psychology which forgets that what is not in itself moral may yet serve as a means to morality. The stimulus of a hoped-for reward, in fact, may be and very often is only needed in order to overcome the inertia which prevents a man from starting a habit or course of action that, once begun, he will carry on not for the reward but for its own sake or even for moral motives of service, which may not be sufficiently strong to give him the start and yet strong enough to carry him on once he has started for other reasons.

But I need not repeat here what I have already said about punishments.[2] The arguments in defence of the possibility of punishments producing good moral effects apply, *mutatis mutandis*, to reward also. Further the desire for reward, though itself no more moral than the fear of pain, seems capable of closer association with desires of a higher order. It is not as though there were only two alternative states,

---

[1] Wages and salaries differ from special rewards in (1) being dependent on contract, (2) being given normally not for special but for average achievement. If, however, reward is defined as the bestowal of some good for a service rendered, they clearly come under this heading. Also their main purpose is the same as that of reward, namely, to induce people to render services, and they imply at any rate a modicum of approval. At least we can speak of the general system of wages and salaries as having the effect of a system of rewards.

[2] p. 80*ff*.

one in which a man was moved by merely selfish desires, and another in which his motives were purely unselfish and moral. A man who is stimulated to activity by the desire for a reward may seek the latter not only for the pleasure or monetary gain it brings, but also partly for the sake of his family, or because of the sense of worth associated with its attainment. We must not speak of these motives as merely " selfish," unless we are prepared to adopt the standpoint of egoistic hedonism in regard to desire. The desire for a happy life for oneself, the desire to keep one's family " well," the desire to be a useful and worthy member of society, the desire for a good reputation and the love of one's work may be intermingled in such a way that it is quite impossible to say of a man's professional activity by which of these motives he is actuated ; and the first, though it can in a sense be called the lowest motive, may strengthen and support all the rest because the man has come to view the satisfaction of the other four as indispensable conditions of his own happiness, as even in a sense identical therewith. The " higher " motives may thus be strengthened and not weakened by a system of rewards which makes them more likely to run with and not against the so-called lower motives. If these different desires were in continual conflict, it would be impossible for the man to give his best, since he would either sacrifice the more important ends to the less important, or, if he resisted the temptation to do this, his attention and energy would still be distracted by the struggle against desires which he could not cease to feel, however much he might strive to prevent them from influencing his overt actions.

The prospect of reward may serve the purpose of carrying men steadily through periods of depression and slothfulness, of keeping their mind fixed on the object when otherwise they would " let things slide." Few people need the thought of reward all the time, but everybody needs it some of the time. It is sometimes objected against the use of rewards that, when we are at our best, we feel above them and should be annoyed at being offered them in a way which implied that they were the object of our work, but this is no valid argument. For they are needed not for our best moments, but for our worse. To say that, because we do not need them in our best moments, we do not need them at all, is like saying that, because the best men do not need to be sent to prison, nobody ought to be. Nor are they useful merely as leading men to do what they otherwise would not ; they are still more useful as making them do steadily, perseveringly and effectively what they would otherwise have done spasmodically and without constancy or much real exertion.

But all the same we must not overlook the grave danger involved in a system of rewards, namely, the danger of impairing that " disinterestedness " which alone makes the higher virtues possible. This is one of the chief reasons why the State can do so little in the way of rewarding virtue as such. The danger is worse than it is with punishment, because, while punishment has to do specially with the worst, rewards for virtue would have to do specially with the best. For a man formerly given to crime to abstain, even from merely prudential motives, is a step upwards, but for a man who previously did good actions irrespective of reward to come to do them for the sake of reward is decidedly a step downwards. Those who most deserve punishment have no " disinterestedness " to spoil ; those who would best deserve rewards for virtue must have sufficient " disinterestedness " not to be benefited by them morally. Rewards for virtue as such could only rightly be given to people who were not virtuous for the sake of the reward and did not need the reward to make them so.

Also, it is easier for a man to be deluded into thinking laudable an act which he does merely for the sake of reward than into thinking his action in abstaining from an offence laudable when his motive is merely to avoid punishment. The former will be liable to appear as definitely meritorious, the latter as merely " decent." For the mere passive avoidance of crime is in any case not something on which he is likely to pride himself specially. Also the fact that the desire for reward is more capable of association with higher desires than the fear of punishment makes it easier for a man who is really acting mainly for the sake of reward to be deceived into the belief that he is acting from the best motives.

Rewards are, however, usually bestowed not for virtue in general but for the production of certain tangible results, that is, ultimately, for industry plus ability.[1] Hence the danger of sapping disinterestedness does not arise to the same extent as it would if the rewarding of virtue in general by the State were a practical possibility. But it must be remem-

---

[1] The same applies to wages and salaries.

bered that there are also rewards in the shape of respect and honour, and that, so far from it being impossible to give these rewards for qualities like unselfishness and purity of motive, it is inevitable that they should be given in a community which appreciates the value of these virtues—not indeed bestowed formally by order of the government but growing quietly out of daily intercourse. If one values unselfishness, one must think better of a man for displaying it, and this higher opinion will favourably affect his relations to other people.

Such rewards, dependent on what may be called the specifically social sanction, are almost all-pervasive and therefore far more potent for good and evil than any practicable government system could be. The same indeed applies to punishment, if we include under the latter heading the loss of popularity and respect consequent on wrongdoing (or what is considered to be wrongdoing). Besides the direct though indefinite gain in honour as a reward, there is the indirect influence that the good opinion of others will have on a man's chances of gaining advantage or satisfaction, which must naturally be added to the reward in question, and the same applies to punishment, *mutatis mutandis*. Rewards in this wider sense can incite to a steady and prolonged course of action that may occupy most of a man's life. Indeed one can go further still and say that it is difficult to find any action in any part of life on which they cannot (and do not usually) have any influence. Again the same applies to fear of punishment (in the wider sense), but here it is very difficult to say where absence of reward stops and punishment begins. What precise amount of respect and favourable consideration ought to be regarded as the minimum to fall below which is punishment and to rise above which is reward ? Clearly this point is not capable of exact determination and varies very much for different social classes and different individuals. Or are we to say that any diminution in respect, etc., from what we previously enjoyed is punishment and any rise reward ? If we did, that would lead to some curious results. We do not usually think of a man as enjoying a " reward " for virtue if he comes to be regarded only as a thief instead of as a murderer, and of an athlete as being punished by society for lack of skill if he comes to be regarded as the second-best in the country after being the first. A more satisfactory way of distinguishing the two would be to regard punishment as always inflicted for what is considered a definitely bad act and reward as bestowed for what is considered a definitely good or in some way meritorious act, but then the absence of reward often is by this definition a punishment, because to omit a good act which we can perform without violating a more paramount obligation is itself wrong. In practice, however, we may usually distinguish with ease an attitude conveying or suggesting blame (punishment) from a mere absence of special praise or approval (failure to obtain reward).

Rewards in the shape of honour, whether deliberate and government-bestowed or the natural result of spontaneous admiration expressed in normal social intercourse, seem somewhat less unfavourable to " disinterestedness," as being more closely associated with the genuinely moral motive. Consequently they may be and are used, even by the State, to a certain extent where pecuniary rewards would seem obviously unsuitable.

Reward may also improve certain ethical virtues (if I may be permitted to employ this old-fashioned but useful term), directly as follows. Moral virtue in general depends on rightness of motive, but there are also a number of particular " virtues," which, in so far as each can be separated from the others, depend not on rightness of motive in general but on rightness in regard to one particular kind of motive.[1] Thus courage consists in not being influenced by the motive of fear beyond what is desirable, temperance in not being unduly influenced by the desire for certain physical pleasures, perseverance in not abandoning one's efforts too soon on account of rebuffs or natural weakness and slothfulness. Now, whatever views we may hold about the unity of the self, it is an empirical fact that a man may possess some of these virtues without possessing others, and it is therefore necessary to take special measures in order to cultivate those which are lacking. Perhaps a man could not have any one virtue in perfection without having all the rest, but at any rate he may possess a very high degree of it and yet be most faulty in other respects. Now a particular vice consists in yielding to a particular kind of temptation, and therefore good work in curing it may be done by a reward which appeals to desires of a kind *different* from those which lead to the vice in question. Courage does not presuppose the highest motives but only the overcoming, where desirable, of one particular kind of motive, namely, fear (in its usual sense,

---

[1] I do not say that this is necessarily the correct way of defining all the virtues.

fear of pain or danger), and therefore it may be attained by following any motive except this kind of fear ; perseverance may be developed by following any motive except love of ease or whatever is regarded as the desire antagonistic to this virtue ; temperance by following any motive except love of the pleasures in question. Presumably this is why it is possible for a man to display these virtues in deliberately doing what he knows to be evil. We need not consider a man less brave, persevering and temperate if we find that he practises these virtues simply for the love of gain, though we may have a much lower opinion of his general character in consequence of this discovery. For the vices to which these virtues are opposed consist in yielding to other temptations, not to the temptations provided by the love of gain. Courage, for example, does not depend on rightness of motive except as regards the one passion of fear, and therefore we need not think that, because a reward does not appeal to the highest motive, it will not help to make a man brave, provided only it does not appeal to that fear. It may be said—for the same considerations apply to punishment—that, though a man may be stimulated to fight by fear of being put to death or flogged if he runs away, he could not be stimulated thereby to show real courage, only to give way to the greater fear. On the other hand, in so far as the punishment for cowardice consisted in disgrace or even in a pecuniary fine, that would constitute a stimulus to show real courage in the battle, since courage of this sort does not consist in overcoming the fear of disgrace (or financial loss) but in overcoming the fear of pain or death. But, suppose that what is sometimes called " moral courage," or the courage to do what one thinks right in face of adverse opinion or apparent disgrace, could be rewarded by a system of honours, this would hardly be likely to further the virtue in question, since it would not help a man to overcome the fear of disgrace.

It may be argued, therefore, that rewards cannot be of any help in cultivating a virtue when they appeal to motives the same in kind as those which they are meant to overcome, but only when they appeal to motives different in nature. Certainly the virtue of temperance could hardly be stimulated effectively by offering free drinks as its reward,[1] or the virtue

---

[1] Similarly we should not regard it as an instance of temperance in food if a man abstained now so that he might indulge more at the next meal, but we should if he abstained to save money or avoid the pains of indigestion.

of modesty by publicly presenting modest men with laurel wreaths.    Rewards the same in kind as the temptations which it is desired to conquer may be effective in " getting the external acts done," but they will not be effective as a moral education.    It may be said that an act done in order to obtain the reward will not in such a case be an instance of the virtue which the reward aims at developing, since the virtue is shown in overcoming a particular kind of desire and so cannot be exemplified by an act done because of that desire.

This is true in the main, but it is going a little too far. For the attainment of the reward presupposes at least the ability to postpone the satisfaction of the desire, and this, though not very much, is better than nothing.    It, moreover, *may* be the first step towards a real overcoming of the desire. To postpone a present pleasure for the sake of a greater one in the future presupposes at least a power of temporary abstinence ; to fight for fear of being afterwards shot if you run away involves at least the ability to overcome the fear of the more present danger in order to avoid another that, if greater, is also more remote ; to work hard now in order to idle later shows at least the ability to conquer sloth for a time, if not permanently.    Such achievements may not be very meritorious, but even so much as this would be impossible if a man were completely mastered by the desire in question.    In some cases this power of postponement is all that can be expected in the first instance of children or people morally undeveloped, and then it may serve as a necessary preliminary to further advance.    The reward may still be morally useful for the same reasons that hold with deterrent punishments, though on the other hand it could never by itself establish anything like real virtue or even *a particular* real virtue.

To sum up, rewards can directly stimulate qualities[1] valuable as a means in carrying out any ends, meaning by this that they can be an immediate cause of acts exemplifying the good qualities in question ; but a " virtue " which consists in seeking the right ends they can only stimulate indirectly, if at all.    They can directly stimulate qualities like industry, courage, temperance, because these virtues do not consist in possessing the right motive, but only in not being unduly influenced by certain particular motives, and therefore may be exemplified in acts done for the sake of

[1] Including under this head both ability of all kinds (v. p. 137) and certain ethical virtues.

reward provided the reward does not appeal to those particular motives. They may sometimes stimulate the qualities in question indirectly even if they appeal to the same motive as that which the particular virtue aims at overcoming, provided they involve a postponement of its satisfaction, *i.e.*, they will not in that case by themselves lead to really brave or temperate acts, but they may possibly set up a habit which later develops into real courage or temperance. Similarly they *may* stimulate indirectly even that virtue which consists in seeking the right ends by encouraging a habit which makes its subsequent development easier, but there are so many moral dangers in this use of rewards that it is not *usually* desirable to employ them for this purpose. They are often more likely to corrupt this " disinterestedness " than to further it.

These remarks call attention to the function of rewards as cultivating ability rather than goodness. Moralists are too apt to talk as though rewards were usually intended to be primarily for " virtue " ; but, though they may be given for virtue and should always be given for merit of some kind, they are in general more effective in cultivating those qualities which constitute ability than those which are commonly dignified by the name of virtues. Ability, although it does not possess the kind of value which moral virtue does, is valuable both to a certain extent as an end-in-itself and as a means to the attainment of other ends. We must not underestimate the enormous importance of intellectual ability in producing good consequences for society, and the difficulties as to motive which limit the effectiveness of reward in the cultivation of virtue do not so seriously lessen its beneficial effects in the direction of stimulating ability. It would be better to cultivate the ability mainly from motives other than those supplied by any rewards which an external source can offer, but these considerations do not alter the fact that the quality of the skill, once cultivated, is independent of the motives which led the man to cultivate it. If A and B have otherwise equal skill, the knowledge that A only cultivated his skill from bad motives does not make us regard him as the less skilful. While it must be admitted that skill or ability used for a bad end is liable to do more harm than good, it cannot be denied that the cultivation of skill or ability is one of the chief objects of education. Without this a man is even " with the best of intentions " liable to fail both in seeing and in doing what is right.

Reward possesses a great advantage over punishment in the fact that it and the hope of it are stimulating, while punishment and the fear of punishment are depressing. This must tell both on those who gain and on those who merely strive for rewards. While pain and fear involve checks of some sort in development, joy and hope are associated with continued advance. The importance of this advantage possessed by reward is well stated, though with some exaggeration, by Bentham : " Reward not only calls forth into exercise talents already existing, but even creates them where they did not exist. It is the property of hope, one of the modifications of joy, to put a man, as the phrase is, into spirits ; *i.e.*, to increase the rapidity with which the ideas he is conversant about succeed each other, and thus to strengthen his powers of combination and invention, by presenting to him a greater variety of objects. The stronger the hope, so that it have not the effect of drawing the thought out of the proper channel, the more rapid the succession of ideas ; the more extensive and varied the trains formed by the principles of association, the better fed, as it were, and more vigorous will be the powers of invention. In this state the attention is more steady, the imagination more alert, and the individual, elevated by his success, beholds the career of invention displayed before him and discovers within himself resources of which he had hitherto been ignorant. On the one hand let fear be the only motive that prompts a man to exert himself, he will exert himself just so much as he thinks necessary to exempt him from that fear and no more, but let hope be the motive he will exert himself to the utmost, especially if he have reason to think that the magnitude of the reward (or, what comes to the same thing, the probability of attaining it) will seem in proportion to the success of his exertions."[1] It is important to note that here we have an exceedingly strong argument for the use, where practicable, of reward in preference to punishment.

I shall now pass on to the equivalent in reward of reformatory punishment. The deterrent end in punishment is distinguished from the reformatory end because the latter is thought as affecting only the offender punished himself, the former as affecting others. Similarly we may distinguish the effects of a reward as :

[1] *Rationale of Reward*, book I, Ch. 7.

1. Encouraging men who have not yet attained it to make efforts for its sake. This affects all the candidates for it, the unsuccessful as much as the successful, at least in so far as they have equal or almost equal hopes of success, and even where the hope is very slight this effect is considerable.

2. But we may think also of the subsequent effects of the reward on the character and work of the man who receives it. This corresponds to the reformatory effect in punishment ; we might call it the " ameliorative " function, since " reformatory " is not a suitable term here.

The first would be generally held to be much more important than the second ; indeed it may be doubted whether the latter set of effects are usually beneficial rather than the reverse. It is practically certain that a reward will stimulate some people to make greater efforts ; but whether its subsequent effects on the character of the man who receives it will be good seems too doubtful in most cases for this " ameliorative " purpose, if taken apart from its other effects, to serve as a sufficient justification for giving it.

Now in my account of reformatory punishment I laid great stress on the function of punishment as an expression of social disapproval and as consequently forcing on the offender's mind the realisation of the fact that he has done wrong. Rewards as an expression of social approval and praise necessarily have the contrary tendency of impressing upon a man that he has done well, but unfortunately, while it is generally admitted that a vivid consciousness of the wrongness of the acts punished is needed for true reformation, it is much more doubtful whether a vivid consciousness of the good one has done will have a salutary effect on character.

Still in some cases where it is important either to restore a shattered self-respect, or to remedy an unjustified congenital lack of self-confidence, this function of reward may be of great utility. A public authority cannot ordinarily adjust its rewards to the character of particular individuals ; but in education, especially within the family, this is possible, and there one ought to consider the question whether a particular child needs to be made more self-confident by reward, including praise, when he acts well, or whether he is self-confident enough already and it would tend to make him undesirably conceited. Also, curiously enough, rewards have a similar function of considerable importance in the treatment of criminals, for it is generally admitted that the giving of rewards to well-behaved and hard-working prisoners may often be of value in helping to restore self-respect and counter-balance the evil effects of overwhelming disgrace. For the disgrace of being definitely put in a special " criminal class " subject to extraordinary penal treatment is bound to be in some ways harmful to character ; and this special danger ought to be counteracted as far as possible by providing a chance of rewards. The fact that rewards heighten a man's opinion of himself, though it usually carries with it certain moral dangers, is an additional argument for the reward where the dangers lie rather in an opposite direction.

But perhaps the way in which reward is most likely to be beneficial to the character of the man who has received it is by making him " want to live up to it." " To disgrace an honorary reward is to be a traitor to oneself ; he that has once been pronounced brave, should perpetually merit that com-mendation."[1] The standard according to which the man who is rewarded values himself is likely to be raised. He may no longer be content to be mediocre, and he may be more vexed by any fall from his comparatively high position than he would have been by the consciousness of real and definite inefficiency before he received the reward. He may acquire the habit of expecting more of himself. However much we may deprecate the evils of conceit and insist on the fact that, if we are too well satisfied with what we already are, we are less likely to try hard to improve, still it must be remembered that there is an important connection between self-respect and both virtue and ability. But the man who receives a reward will only " feel bound to live up to it " if he regards it as an honour rather than as mere profit in business (though he might even in the latter case think it desirable to " live up to it " for pecuniary or hedonistic con-siderations, which is quite a different matter). For a reward to do any moral good to its recipient it must be a mark of approval for merit. This characteristic of reward can be shown to be a presupposition of the fulfilment of all its most important purposes.

But both with the reformatory effects of punishment and with the corresponding effects of reward, we have to oppose to the credit balance a somewhat formidable array of possible or likely evils. In the case of punishment they are the evils of resentment, bitterness, discouragement and despair ; in the case of reward they are the evils associated with the undue stimulation of conceit and the ordinary temptations of

[1] Bentham, *Rationale of Reward*, Bk. I, Ch. 11.

prosperity. Common to both are the dangers of spoiling what is usually called " disinterestedness " and of confusing the right with the externally satisfactory or, still worse, with what is profitable to oneself. With either it is doubtful whether it can be justified by the subsequent moral effects on the person who has received it alone, if these are abstracted from their effects on the rest of society. In fact it seems that as regards the ethical character of the individual on whom they are bestowed the rewards of life, including in these even rewards of honour, are, once given, less likely to make a difference for the better than for the worse. It is proverbial that " success corrupts," though it is impossible for all that to eliminate " success." The benefits of reward, other than hedonistic, lie rather in stimulating efforts to gain them than in their effects after they have been gained. We need not necessarily apply this conclusion to education, where much allowance is possible for the individual, though it is a truism that the use of punishment and reward is accompanied by great dangers even there.

To pass on, the function of punishment as a means to " vindictive satisfaction " may be paralleled by the function of rewards as expressing and satisfying the sentiment of gratitude on the part of those who bestow them. But there is a great difference between the two cases. Whereas the pleasure of vindictive satisfaction is, at least when felt in any at all intense degree, an undesirable one that ought not to be encouraged, the pleasure[1] of expressing and satisfying grati-tude is perfectly justifiable and very laudable. The result is that, while the first (vindictive satisfaction) cannot rightly be regarded as an end which punishment should aim at producing, the second is certainly something that deserves our approval and is quite a legitimate object to pursue. The expression (or feeling) of gratitude is, however, more (though perhaps not only) an end-in-itself in the case of an individual who bestows gifts or renders services (not, strictly speaking, rewards),[2] than it can be in the case of a State or other organiz-ation which gives rewards.

[1] Though I have used the term, pleasure, I certainly do not imply that the value of gratitude is merely hedonistic. I regard gratitude as having an intrinsic value over and above the pleasure it gives and its other good consequences.

[2] Because they are not conferred *expressly* for a previous service or as a mark of special virtue or ability, but as the result of a general senti-ment partially created by previous services.

Next, as the equivalent of the preventive function of punishment, comes what I might call the "*enabling*" function of reward. Punishment may be beneficial through "preventing" a man from doing further evil, reward through "enabling" a man to do further good. For it may provide him with means of service or self-development[1] that would otherwise not have been at his disposal. There are many rewards of which this is the chief purpose, *e.g.*, scholarships, and most have the effect in some degree.

This should be distinguished from the function of a reward as "*compensating*" the winner for any expense or trouble in which he may have been involved. Like punishment reward should aim, if possible, at compensating. Only the person who should be compensated is different. In the case of punishment it is not the doer of the act but the person to whom it was done; with reward the opposite holds good. It must be added, however, that mere compensation is not a reward. It would seem to follow from this that a reward, to be a reward, ought always to exceed in amount what is required for compensation, and, if it is wholly and merely pecuniary, no doubt it must. But the argument does not necessarily apply if the reward is not pecuniary, or if, though pecuniary, it is regarded as also an "honour" and not merely a "payment" of money. For a reward, in itself insufficient to compensate, may be sufficient to outweigh the loss involved in seeking it, just because it is an honour and distinction, or when combined with other, natural or adventitious, advantages liable to be brought by the action rewarded it may do so, though alone it would be insufficient. A reward that appeals to the desire for honour appeals to certain motives which cannot be assessed on the strictly pecuniary basis usually implied when we speak of compensation. The Victoria Cross cannot be said to be sufficient to "compensate" a man for risking his life or losing a limb, but it may still be effective as a reward. There are many actions which would never be done for the sake of the reward if there were no motive for them besides desire of the reward, and yet where the reward is useful as strengthening these other motives in face of obstacles and dangers, and so perhaps turning the scale where a small additional incentive may make all the difference between action and inaction, or at any rate encouraging the man to act more steadily, vigorously and efficiently

---

[1] The latter is directly for the good of the man rewarded himself, but indirectly for the good of the community.

than he would otherwise have done. Or a reward may out-weigh the cost of the action rewarded not by virtue of what it is in itself but by virtue of the motive of " self-assertion " or also more " moral motives," which are aroused to a high pitch by the desire to be worthy of the honour conferred by the reward. For an honour alone apart from the sense that we had done something to deserve it would lose most of its appeal. No high-minded man would care very much for an honour that he was certain had been unfairly bestowed and did not imply that the giver of the reward thought he deserved it on his merits, even though nobody else knew of the unfairness but himself. In fact he would feel ashamed at rather than honoured by such a reward, even though he were not to blame for the unfairness in question. But, while we must not slip back into the idea of a natural equality to be established by reward between service and return, we obviously ought to consider the compensatory function in determining the amount of a reward.

Reward also has hedonistic advantages not possessed by punishment. Punishment gives pain, not pleasure, to him who suffers it, and even restraint by fear of punishment is painful rather than pleasant ;[1] but reward on the other hand gives both pleasure to him who has gained it[2] and the pleasure of hope to all who seek it. Whether this pleasure of hope is greater than the pain of disappointment depends too much on individual psychology for it to be safe to generalise, but at any rate it is usually felt for a much longer period. In the case of punishment there is no doubt pleasure felt by those who fear to suffer it and then escape it, but where this pleasure occurs it is generally (or always) a sign that punishment has failed of its purpose in some degree, because the end of punishment is defeated either if the guilty escape or the innocent fear it. We must add that the joy of receiving a special reward (as opposed to ordinary wages) is likely to be very much greater than the joy at the acquisition of its

---

[1] Except that there are cases where a man may be glad to have a strong motive for doing his duty.

[2] The cost of the reward to the giver of it may balance this, but that still leaves reward with an advantage over punishment here, because the pain of the man who suffers punishment is not balanced by the pleasure of those who inflict it, so that punishment is in so far a loss, while in reward the receiver gains what the giver loses. Besides the pleasure of receiving is apt not only to balance but to exceed the loss of pleasure due to expenditure on it, since what is given in the way of reward has an especial value just because it is a reward.

monetary equivalent by normal means. This naturally increases considerably both the hedonistic value and the stimulating power of reward. These are obvious and simple ends which I mention for the sake of completeness and because account ought clearly to be taken of them in giving rewards.

Another function of reward is the "*testing*" function. Rewards may be useful because they select the best and so provide knowledge that may be of value for future use. Punishment has perhaps a similar function in supplying information as to what men are dangerous or not to be trusted, but it may be questioned whether in any case this information depends on the punishment and not on the detection and conviction which precedes the punishment. It is rather different with reward, for in many cases the competition which reveals the good work of certain candidates would never have taken place but for the offer of a reward, while it is difficult to think of instances in which a penalty is deliberately fixed in order that people may reveal their bad character by committing offences on account of the penalty ! One of the chief objects of many rewards is to *discover* and not only to encourage ability ; they serve as a criterion of talent and not only as an incentive to effort.

The fundamental reason for reward on which depends this diversity of functions is the importance of bringing about good and beneficial actions or developing the capacity to perform such actions, just as the fundamental reason for punishment is the importance of discouraging and condemning bad actions. From a certain point of view reward may be regarded as merely a mercenary means of making it worth while for people to do good. This is analogous to a merely utilitarian conception of punishment as deterrent and externally reformatory, and like the corresponding view of punishment it may be admitted to be " true as far as it goes." This is part of the function of reward and not an unimportant part. We must beware of sacrificing solid, if uninspiring, advantages of this sort for the sake of mere theories as to possible moral gains from reward, especially where the actions rewarded are of a kind which it is better to get done from whatever motive than it is to see that they are done from a motive of an exalted kind. But we must not say that reward is merely a bribe to do good any more than we ought to say that punishment is merely a matter of brute force. Even if we could draw such a sharp, clear-cut line between mercenary and disinterested desires as that would imply, we could not rightly neglect the moral importance of the " honour " generally involved in reward. Just as it is of the essence of a punishment to be a disgrace, so it is of the essence of a reward to be an honour.

Now we have already seen that the effective fulfilment of its other functions presupposes that reward is an honour, or at least that a reward will necessarily fulfil its function much better if this is so. It will encourage effort more if it is valued as an honour and not only for what it is in itself ; it is most likely to be good for the man who gains it if he regards it as an honour which he ought to " live up to " ; its value as a sign of distinction or worth will compensate for much trouble in attaining it and greatly add to the pleasure of success ; finally its intrinsic value (" merit " aspect) and its power to satisfy and express the sentiment of gratitude both depend on it being assigned for a real service or real worth. This brings us to the one function of punishment for which I have not yet pointed out a parallel in reward. That is what I called the " educative " function in relation to the community as a whole.

Rewards, like punishments, clearly express the opinion of the body that gives them as to the value of certain services, or the merits of certain pieces of work or certain actions. The possible moral effects of this expression of opinion on the man rewarded have already been discussed, but we must suppose that it is liable also to have moral effects on the other members of the community and on the social standard in general. Just as I said earlier that it was obviously desirable that the members of the community should have a right attitude towards evil and that one of the good effects of punishment was the help it gave in establishing and maintaining such an attitude, so I must now insist that it is desirable that they should also have a right attitude in the appreciation of good and that rewards may be of value in furthering that attitude, not only in those individuals who gain or seek to gain them but also in the community as a whole. For they help to a certain extent in fixing the national standards of merit and particularly in impressing on men the high value of certain achievements or acts. Rewards by the State play less part in this than do punishments, because they are a much less common institution, but where given they must have some effect of that kind. State rewards[1] to a great artist or scientist may

---

[1] Including especially honours.

help, though to a limited extent, in impressing upon people the value of art or science.   That will not indeed help them to appreciate art and science in detail, and therefore the effect is apt to be of little value, but it must be mentioned all the same.   It is desirable that those who have little capacity for appreciation in such matters should still realise that they are important, so that they may try to develop what capacity they have and so that popular opinion may not hamper real scientists and artists.

Rewards tend to impress on men the value of certain actions just as punishments intensify their consciousness of the bad- ness of certain offences.   They do not usually impress directly on men the value of moral virtue as such ;  but they do tend to enhance their consciousness of the nobility and desirability of doing good work and of rendering public services.   Their function is, however, only fulfilled to any large extent in education and through the informal rewards which come naturally in social and economic life but are not officially bestowed by the government, or any other organisation or authority.   The importance of rewards in this respect, for good or for bad, is shown by the extent to which people tend to correlate wealth with real worth, wealth being regarded as a reward for ability or services.

But here we find an effect of rewards that we cannot but deplore.   It is not good that material wealth and real worth should be correlated in people's minds ;  it greatly increases the desire for the former and consequently promotes the evils which moralists are so fond of describing as characteristic of " this money-loving age."   It is important to note that, in so far as the wealth acquired by a man in the ordinary pro- cesses of business is regarded as a reward, it tends to confuse real public service with the acquisition of money for oneself. From the mere fact that a man makes a profit of ten thousand pounds a year we cannot tell how much of that sum comes from really serving the public and how much from outdoing rivals in a way which does not serve the public at all.   In so far as the profit is made by a supply of better goods a public service is being rewarded, though probably to excess ;  in so far as it is made by a more ingenious use of advertisements than his rivals are capable of, something is being rewarded which is hardly public service at all ;  in so far as it is made by cornering a commodity, using sweated labour, or by tricking rivals and customers, a reward is being conferred for what is the reverse of a service.   Yet others, having no chance of distinguishing how much of the profit is due to each of these factors, only know that the man has had the ability to make a profit of ten thousand pounds and will tend to estimate him in proportion to his wealth, not in proportion to his real public service, since they have no means of judging that except from his wealth. Unless he passes beyond certain very wide limits in the means he uses, a man attains as much honour through making a fortune in ways that are of very little benefit (or none at all) to the public as he does through making it only by the supply of a real need at a fair price. This is no doubt one of the reasons for the strength of the tendency to treat money-making in business as the end rather than public service. Money becomes the aim rather than service partly because it is treated as the measure of service without really being so. It is a more disputable question whether these or equally bad drawbacks depend on our particular economic system or, human nature being what it is, are inevitable under any system. Any all-pervasive system of pecuniary rewards must tend in the direction of identifying the acquisition of money with the rendering of service in the public estimation and by making the former an honour increase man's natural love of material wealth ; and also it will tend to produce a wrong relative estimate of service *in so far as* it fails to distribute wealth in proportion to real service, for it can hardly avoid some failure there.

But rewards in the shape of honour, or comparatively occasional pecuniary rewards which derive their value rather from being an honour than from their amount, are not liable to these objections in anything like the same degree. There is still the drawback that good acts tend to be identified with acts that are rewarded, but this is only a serious objection against a system that seeks to reward most actions, not a system which rewards a comparatively few exceptional ones, for the acts that are rewarded, being exceptional, could not be supposed to be the only good acts.

It does not seem right to look on reward as morally on an inferior level to punishment. Punishment may be viewed and treated as a mere deterrent, reward may be viewed and treated as a mere bribe ; but such a way of thinking is inadequate to express the full nature and real function of either, it is a partial truth that becomes untrue when made absolute. It is not right to say that reward makes people do good *merely* by bribing them any more than it is right to say that the function of punishment is limited by its deterrent power.

Just as the good effects of punishment are due partly to its being a disgrace and an expression of condemnation, so the good effects of reward are due partly to it being an honour and an expression of approval or praise.    Where a man is stimulated to action by reward, this is partly because the prospect of it appeals to him as an honour and not merely as a profit, an appeal which would not affect the man who was merely " economic " or merely hedonistic.    Now it is through being not merely hedonistic or pecuniary but an expression also of approval and praise that reward must affect the standards of the community.    How it does so we can see from the analogy of punishment.    Again much that I have said of the " educative " function of punishment may easily and with equal justice be applied to reward.    Reward is an impressive declaration that the rewarding body values certain things highly, and as such it is apt to set the standard, so to speak, and to exercise a powerful unconscious influence on the valuation of merit.

Bentham, utilitarian though he was, laid great stress on what I have called the " educative " function in the case of reward in so far as the latter is used to arouse and direct public esteem.    In fact his account of its benefits in this respect errs in the direction of exaggeration.[1]    " An inquiry into the causes of the high respect in which, under certain governments particular virtues were held—why the virtues of a Curtius, of a Fabricius, of a Scipio, were nourished and developed at Rome—why other countries and other times have produced only courtiers, parasites, fine gentlemen and wits, men without energy and without patriotism—would require a moral and historical analysis only to be completed by means of a profound study of the political constitutions and particular circumstances of each people.    The result would, however, prove that the qualities most successfully cultivated, were those held in most general esteem.

" But public esteem, it may be said, is free, essentially free, independent of the authority of governments.    This copious fund of rewards is therefore withdrawn from the hands of the supreme authority !    This, however, is not the case : governments may easily obtain the disposal of this treasure. Public esteem cannot be compelled, but it may be conducted. It requires but little skill on the part of a sovereign to enable him to apply the high reward of public esteem to any service which his occasions may require.

[1] *Rationale of Reward*, Book I, Chap. 16.

" There already exists a degree of respect for riches, honour and power if the dispenser of these gifts bestow them only upon useful qualities—if he unites what is already esteemed to what ought to be estimable, his success is certain. Reward would serve as a proclamation of his opinion, and would mark out a particular line of conduct as meritorious in his eyes. Its first effect would be that of a lesson in morality."

Rewards rightly administered should help to train the public standard by pointing out and so turning attention to both the merits of individuals and the value of certain kinds of action. For it is important that both should be rightly appraised. It is desirable that the best should be known both because it is intrinsically good to know it and in order that it may be treated as best. This applies alike to the relative estimate of different *kinds* of actions and to taste in judging of the merits of individual men, though the function of reward is no doubt of more importance in the former direction. If a certain kind of action is rewarded it will, *pari passu*, tend to be more valued. On the other hand, Bentham overlooks the fact that a system of rewards cannot be very much, though it may be a little, in advance of public opinion if it is to have any such effects. The promotion of good qualities by government action is not nearly as simple a matter as he seems to have imagined.

An illustration of the effects of the informal natural rewards of social life is seen in class distinctions and in the different valuations men attach to different occupations as being more or less " respectable." This is probably a bad effect on the whole, and certainly the esteem expressed on such grounds does not usually correspond to real merit ; but the powerful influence which these distinctions have on our valuations, even against reason, shows the importance for our value ideas of the way in which other members of society and the community in general express theirs. Surely at least as much could be done by rewards when they conform to reason as is done when they conflict with it. But in any case the conclusion as to the importance of this kind of reward follows from the platitude that the social esteem and disapproval of others is a factor of the greatest importance in fixing our own ideas of value. It is in fact the chief ethical education provided by society. It may be a bad education because the ideas impressed on us are crude and ill-proportioned, but whether used wisely or foolishly, for good or for evil, it remains the principal or only means of communicating ideas on value and morality. For to communicate them we must express them, and expression of ethical opinion when directed towards acts actually done must take the form of approval or disapproval.

But in this we have transgressed rather beyond the proper limits fixed by the ordinary meaning of rewards. Definite rewards by a recognised authority have no such wide scope. But the " educative " influence even of these may be more far-reaching than we usually think, if the influence of rewards in the wider sense is so great and paramount. What is praised and greeted by obvious and impressive signs of the praise will tend to be valued highly by those who see it rewarded or hear it praised.

Of special rewards, as of special punishments, it seems true to say that they cannot discharge their " educative " function if there is a sharp conflict with popular ideas on the subject of the goodness of the actions rewarded. If a government rewards acts generally considered bad, it will not make people think these acts good but rather still worse than they did when they were unrewarded (e.g., spying not held to be justified by military necessity, enrolment in the garrison of a tyrant). This even applies to acts that are obviously serviceable to the community but unpleasant to those immediately affected by them, e.g., tax-collecting. Such acts have by many nations been regarded as bad when done for reward, because to earn payment in that way was to make money out of the troubles of one's fellow-citizens. That may be foolish, but the point it shows is that to offer rewards for unpopular acts does not cause these acts to be in any way esteemed but rather to be condemned more violently than before. If the rewards are material, they are in that case likely to appear simple bribes ; if they take the shape of special honours, ridiculous flattery. Rewards can only develop the moral standard and outlook of the community effectively by encouraging further a certain tendency already present (though perhaps not avowed in words or even recognised by self-consciousness), or by establishing through association and usage a conventional view which in the absence of a definite opposing opinion tends to become fixed and genuine. The same limitations hold good here as in the case of punishment.[1]

Special rewards by the government or by organisations within the State play a much smaller part in developing the

---

[1] v. above, pp. 98–100.

moral standard of the community and impressing more firmly on men half-realised moral ideas than do State punishments.  For (1) they are less commonly used ; (2) there is little divergence of opinion on the merit of the kinds of act that deserve reward, however much divergence there may be on the comparative merits of individuals ; (3) rewards are generally not so much for moral qualities as for ability.

In the education of children, however, special definite rewards certainly can play a very large part in fixing standards by association and through the fact that for the child's parents to reward an act is to stamp it with the mark of their approval and authority.  A very serious difficulty is left in the way of the use of honours as rewards, namely, they are apt to lose their attractiveness to many and their real utility to others[1] by offending modesty.  This can only be avoided, if at all, by a very circumspect application of the principle.

But, if we include under " rewards " the increased respect naturally paid to a man whose worth is well-known and any such informal acknowledgment of merit, and the advantages, hedonistic, material and social that result from it, we must regard reward as one of the most potent factors in moral development.  The kind of reward of which we are now speaking is just the natural expression of the opinion of " people in general," or people in a particular circle of society, as to the goodness of certain acts, and it surely cannot be denied that this expression of opinion reacts very powerfully on the standard of any one individual.  It is much easier to realise the obligatoriness of a certain act, if it is expected from us by " society " than if it is not.  Needless to say, I am not maintaining that this influence is wholly good, only that it is very important and so has enormous power both for evil and for good.  Without it—if we can imagine a world from which it was wholly eliminated—there would be very much more frequent conflicts between apparent interest and duty and, what is more, the chief instrument of moral education by society would disappear altogether.

What is the relation between external rewards and the fact or supposed fact that " virtue is its own reward ? "  This dictum may mean simply that the practice of virtue makes a man more virtuous, or it may mean that virtue brings pleasure in its train.  In the first case it is not an adequate argument

---

[1] i.e., those who are attracted by them may become over-conceited as a result of their bestowal.

against the addition of external rewards. For, although virtue is the greatest of goods, it is not always appreciated as such. Virtue is valued ; pleasure is liked and enjoyed. Virtue unfortunately appeals much less than many other ends to the natural man, and therefore needs to be supplemented by other attractions, where it is socially important that a certain kind of action should be performed. We cannot argue that, because, if humanity were better, we should be above external rewards, we therefore do not need them now. People do, in fact, often appreciate external rewards very much more than virtue, so the rewards are needed to supply a stronger motive, even if their real value is very much smaller.[1] So it does not seem to me legitimate to use against reward the argument that real good does not consist in rewards capable of being bestowed from without,[2] as long as goods capable of such external treatment appeal somewhat in fact to all men and more than virtue to the great majority. I do not say the great majority make a practice of sacrificing virtue to them in case of conflict, for a sense of duty very frequently prevents that ; but I do say that the great majority would be more *pleased* by an acquisition of external goods than by an acquisition of virtue. Men regard virtue as better than these things and to a certain extent *act* accordingly ; but, if we consider only their desires or likings, surely there are very few who would not dislike, *e.g.*, severe toothache more than they dislike the consciousness of having committed a minor act of selfishness or lost their temper. Nor ought circumstances that contribute to happiness and are necessary for the satisfactory exercise of much intrinsically valuable intellectual and æsthetic activity to be ignored as of no value, even from the ideal standpoint.

The doctrine that virtue is its own reward has, however, often been understood and maintained in the sense that virtue by a natural process inevitably brings with it the happiness which it deserves. The eighteenth-century British moralists, in particular, seem to have thought the establishment of a doctrine of this sort to be one of the chief objects of moral philosophy. No doubt a firm belief in this would carry with

---

[1] We must not, however, go too far in underestimating the value of external rewards. The exercise of the virtue (or proficiency) rewarded may be very much facilitated by the additional happiness, or again by the addition of other external advantages like opportunities of intellectual intercourse, a good social standing or increased material wealth.

[2] As, *e.g.*, Princ. Moberly does, *Proceedings of Aristotelian Society*, June, 1925.

it the advantages belonging to an absolutely all-pervasive system of rewards, but it would carry with it at least some of the disadvantages. But we are not discussing here the practical effects of believing this doctrine ; suffice it to say that, while it is quite possible to show that virtuous conduct on the whole tends towards happiness, at least when not very far in advance of the practice and ideas of contemporary society, it seems quite impossible to establish the *universal* agreement of virtue and happiness on empirical grounds, nor do I see that this is a necessary postulate of either morality or religion. Granted that a fair proportion between virtue and happiness is a good, it may have to be sacrificed to other goods such as the moral regeneration of humanity, which is clearly much more important, or even to the greater happiness of the greater number. We must not, therefore, say that, unless happiness is proportioned to desert, the universe cannot be ordered for the best or God cannot be righteous. For we have no guarantee that a distribution of happiness in proportion to virtue is necessarily always conducive either to the greatest happiness or the greatest virtue, and it is such an unimportant good compared to these that, if they conflicted, it would in a universe ordered for the best clearly have to be sacrificed to them. It is not the prosperity of the wicked and the misfortunes of the good that constitute the real " problem of evil," but the presence anywhere of pain and of wickedness.

It is right for the good man to desire that he should be happy ; but it would be selfish for him to desire that none who are quite as good as he should be quite so happy, and that every sacrifice which he makes should be balanced mathematically by a grant of future happiness. It does seem to be a fact that virtue *per se* in general makes for one's own as well as others' happiness ; but this is not to say that the gain is never outweighed (hedonistically) by unfortunate external circumstances or that every increase in the degree of one's virtue makes one happier. A particular advance may often have the reverse effect if it is sufficient to make a man dissatisfied with what he has been doing and yet insufficient to make him abandon it wholeheartedly, so that he is continually conscious of a painful conflict which he is yet not good enough to resolve, or if it brings him into conflict with the moral standards or selfish interests of his associates. It is easy to show that a very good man will be happier than a very bad man, but not that one man is always happier than another who is slightly worse.    We can say to a man—if you try to improve your character you will probably be in general considerably happier than if you do not, whether in this life or in any future life that it may be considered necessary to postulate for religious reasons—but we cannot say more, we cannot say that he will gain in happiness proportionately as a reward for every part of his advance.    And it is perhaps well that we cannot,—for this is sufficient in some degree to touch self-interest, and yet insufficient to reduce virtue to a kind of commercial bargain with the universe or God.    Virtue does bring its own specific happiness, but this happiness must flow from its inherent nature and not from external circumstances artificially combined with it, and may be sometimes outbalanced by the latter.    To say that, where this occurs, there is " no point in being virtuous," would be to deny morality outright and to assert that we need think of nothing but our own selfish interest.    Duty is duty whether we gain by it or not, either in this life or another.

If it is not a necessary and universal law but only a general tendency (limited by many exceptions) that virtue carries with it corresponding happiness, then the fact cannot possibly be made the basis of an argument against external rewards, for they may be needed to supplement and strengthen the general tendency and to make it more obvious to the eyes of the multitude that virtue brings advantages to its possessor.

The majority of rewards, however, are in practice given for ability rather than for virtue, and nobody would maintain that it is a necessary postulate of morality or an immutable law of retributive justice that happiness should be in proportion to ability (though it would generally be admitted, and rightly so, that in fact increase of ability mostly carries with it increase of happiness).    Rewards for this are in the main utilitarian in purpose and character.    They do not convey special moral approval, and still less can they be said to aim at establishing a right retributive proportion between goodness and happiness.    Physical skill or intellectual ability as such are not usually considered moral virtues.

On the other hand ability is undoubtedly valued both in itself and in its results, so the reward of it may be said to involve an approval of value, but not value of the specifically moral kind.    This being the case, we have still quite as much right to say that the approval of non-moral values[1] is likely

---

[1] *i.e.*, things good-in-themselves other than morality, not of course anti-moral or in conflict with morality.

to affect popular standards as that the approval of moral values will do so. In fact æsthetic and intellectual standards may certainly be affected very much by the wisdom (or folly) shown in selecting what work should be adjudged worthy of reward. Thus, for example, an educational institution in which rewards were given mainly for memory of facts, or again for merely verbal brilliance, would encourage these qualities to an undesirable extent at the expense of others. Again we must regard a right estimate of intellectual and æsthetic work as not only instrumentally but intrinsically valuable. A theory which founds the intrinsic value of reward on the fact that it is an appreciation of what is good[1] and not on the desirability of establishing a fitting proportion between virtue and happiness has no special difficulty in recognising that it may be an end-in-itself to reward ability as well as virtue.

To sum up, reward is our way of expressing appreciation of good and as such participates in the intrinsic value which must belong to a right attitude towards good. As such also it impresses on the community the value of the act or acts in question in a way which may be of much importance as affecting standards of valuation. Its more utilitarian function as encouraging desirable actions is probably still the most important, but at any rate this emphasis on values must not be neglected in an account of reward. It is for this reason that reward is considered an honour, and this makes it far more effective in stimulating even outward acts and special skill than it would be if it were considered only a " gain." Against these advantages we must set the obvious moral danger of destroying " disinterestedness " and the fact that rewards are often morally harmful rather than beneficial to the persons who gain them. But to try to do without any form of reward seems to me quite chimerical ; and we must ascribe much value, even moral value, to the effects on character and capacity of the effort called forth by the desire to gain reward. (The beneficial results of a reward are chiefly produced prior to gaining it and not afterwards.) We must remember, however, that rewards are not and cannot be awarded for moral virtue as such but for proficiency in outward acts, i.e., chiefly, though not entirely, for ability. Even ability, however, has some intrinsic as well as instrumental value, so that throughout reward retains its character of approval of values.

# CHAPTER VI

## The Bearing of our Moral Theory on Practice
### (or How we are to decide what is right)

THERE is one criticism that will certainly be brought against this book by " the practical man." It will be said that I have, after all, not told the legislator or judge what penalty he ought to impose for particular crimes, nor the educator what punishments and rewards are most likely to be good for a particular child, or even a particular kind of child. I might well retort that this is not really a charge against me but against all moral philosophers, or that the business of the philosopher[1] must always be primarily theory not practice, to understand the nature of the good and right whilst leaving to others the task of practical application. But I cannot agree with the cavalier way in which most modern philosophers dismiss the question how we are to decide what is right in particular cases. It is all very well to say in a lordly fashion that it is not the business of Ethics to decide particular cases —and in a sense I quite agree with this statement ; but if so, how are they to be decided at all ? We decide them in practice and rely on our decisions as to a large extent justified. We even sometimes give seemingly good reasons for them. How is this possible ? If our reasons are ultimately based on general ethical principles, surely they ought to fall within the scope of Ethics as a department of organised knowledge ? If they are not based on them, surely they cannot possibly provide an adequate reason for considering any action right ? Must there not be some way of justifying our conclusions ? Has Ethics nothing to say in the matter ? ·Can no account be given of our practical decisions at all ? It is no use to say that this is not the business of Ethics but of " casuistry " ; the objection seems to me purely verbal. If I am allowed to talk about this topic at all, I do not mind what name is applied to it, provided only the disreputable associations of the word, " casuistry," due to certain abuses on the part of the Jesuits, are not allowed by the reader to prejudice him against what

---

[1] *i.e.*, *qua* philosopher. *Qua* man he is, of course, concerned with ethical practice.

I have to say. Also, secondly, if ethical principles do not apply to particular right acts they can hardly be true even for the philosopher ; and if they apply at all, their application cannot be without interest for Ethics. Even if it were treated as a separate science, Casuistry[1] would have to be a deduction from Ethics. To reason about what we ought to do can hardly be useless, unless it is bad reasoning (*i.e.*, fallacious).

The only way of avoiding the responsibility of helping in decisions as to what we ought to do is for the philosopher to say frankly, as Prof. Prichard[2] does, that there are no general ethical principles, but we know immediately what is right in each particular case, and leave it at that. This view involves the frank abandonment of all attempts to systematise, even partially, our knowledge of what is right ; but we cannot at the present stage of our argument exclude the possibility that we may eventually be driven to this. But, before we abandon the attempt, we must at any rate make it. The problem is an urgent one for every branch of Ethics. How can we decide what is right in particular cases ? Can we deduce it at all, or must our decision be " intuitive " ? If " intuition " and inference both play a part in it, what are their respective functions ? What is the relation of theoretical Ethics to practical life ? I have in the previous chapters given an account of the good and evil done by punishment and reward ; but my task would not be completed if I did not say something about the bearing of that on particular decisions as to what punishment (or reward) was right in a given case. I cannot indeed attempt to make any definite suggestions for reform because that would require a knowledge of other subjects than Ethics ; but if I fail to do this I am all the more bound to say something about the general relation of ethical theories to practice, though the problem seems to have been shirked by most recent philosophers. It is not, however, a matter that can be discussed in relation to punishment (and reward) by themselves, but only as a general question common to all branches of ethical theory, and it is as such that I must deal with it. Those who do not wish for a general disquisition on Ethics as a branch of knowedge may omit this chapter, as the views maintained here are not presupposed in my treatment of punishment (and reward) elsewhere. But I cannot

[1] In so far as deducible at all.
[2] *v. Mind*, 1912. Even if its conclusion may seem exaggerated, Prof. Prichard's very valuable article there raises many important points, some of which I discuss later.

possibly do justice to my own topic without going back to more general principles at this point.    The present chapter is therefore intended as a contribution to general moral philosophy, an attempt to work out my own theory of it as regards certain of its chief problems ; and, incomplete as it necessarily is, I should be very glad if it received attention as a modest attempt towards developing such an outline theory of Ethics as will meet some of its most pressing difficulties.

As we turn to our problem, we see at once that there is one simple solution which must have occurred to almost everybody who has ever studied Ethics.    Why should not Ethics provide a set of general principles by a direct application of which we can decide what is right in all particular cases ? Why should not all our particular duties be strictly deducible from Ethics as a science giving us general principles ?

There are two methods by which it has been held possible to effect such a deduction.    The first is by appealing to universal laws.    According to this view, of which Kant is the most celebrated exponent, an act is right not because of its consequences, or because it does good, but because it is a particular instance of a universal law known *a priori* to be obligatory in all cases, *e.g.*, a particular lie is wrong, not because it produces bad consequences for anybody, but because there is a categorical imperative—Thou shalt not lie, and it is part of the nature of any categorical imperative (*i.e.*, moral law) to admit of no exceptions whatever.    The chief defects of a view like this, when universalised and applied to all questions of conduct, are (1) that it breaks down where two different laws conflict, *i.e.*, an exception must then be admitted to one at least of the two laws ; (2) that, since it would clearly be wrong, other things being equal, to produce evil consequences by an action of ours if we could help it, we are driven after all to consider the consequences, and these will be different in each individual case ; (3) that there are very few, if any, universal laws which can be, even plausibly, held to be capable of being known and formulated without introducing a reference to the consequences they will produce in different instances.[1]    For example it was very easy

[1] The laws—thou shalt not lie, thou shalt not break promises, thou shalt not commit suicide—and a few other negative principles like this, which seem, at first sight at least, capable of formulation without reference to consequences, clearly are insufficient to tell us what is right in all cases.    Even if it is always wrong to break these laws, there are also many wrong actions that do not break them or any law to which we can give a universal formulation of this kind.

for Kant to lay down the general rule that we ought to develop our talents, but he could on his principles hardly answer the question—what talents ?  We ought not and are not able to develop them all equally, so—which is to be preferred to which ? and—how much time and what method ought we to devote to each ?  The answer to these questions will be different for each individual case, and it would be totally impossible to deduce the answers simply from universal laws without including in the laws a reference to the varying capacities of different individuals and to the effects of education on these, *i.e.*, the reference to empirical circumstances and consequences which Kant was so studious to avoid. Otherwise we should have no guide as to which faculties ought to be developed and in what degree.  As a result of considerations like these there are now hardly any philosophers left who would hold that we can deduce from universal laws what it is right to do in all particular cases.[1]  On this point it would be almost unanimously held, even by Kant's greatest admirers, that his system breaks down ; it may be of the highest value as an account of the general nature of moral law and duty, but it cannot be used to deduce our *particular duties*.

But there is another principle of deduction which has greater plausibility and is still popular among ethical theorists. The view to which I am referring is as follows.  It is held that the right action under any given circumstances is always the action in the agent's power which is likely to produce the greatest good and that this is the only and sufficient reason why it is right (though not necessarily the definition of rightness).  After all, it is said, what can make an act right but the good it does ?  It can surely never be right to perform any action except the one which will, as far as we can see, be likely to produce the greatest good possible under the circumstances for all concerned ?  In particular cases, therefore, we have to decide what is right by determining how much good is likely to be produced by each of the alternative acts between which we are choosing.  Now there are various kinds of things[2] which are good in themselves and not merely

---

[1] Though it may easily be possible in *some* cases.
[2] I have been obliged throughout to use " things " in the widest possible sense of the term so as to include not only or specially physical things but experiences, activities, and even different elements in one experience that are distinguishable though really inseparable from each other.

as means to something else, for nothing would be good even as a means unless it produced something that was good-in-itself, *i.e.*, good otherwise than as a mere means.  The justification of an act always lies ultimately in the production of these goods or the removal of corresponding evils.  But, since the good (and bad) effects of an act are generally manifold, we can only determine the total good likely to be produced if we sum the good of these varied effects.[1]  (Here and throughout this chapter " good " is used not in the narrower, though very important, sense of goodness of moral character alone, but as including all kinds of real value other than value merely as a means.  Thus moral character, knowledge, experience of beauty and pleasurable sensations would be all goods of different kinds and degrees.)  The method will therefore consist, first, in seeing how much good *of each kind* is likely to be produced by each alternative act, secondly, in putting these quantities together so as to deduce from them the *total* amount of good likely to be produced by each act, and, thirdly, in comparing these totals so as to see which act will produce the greatest.  Thus of two alternative courses one may yield more pleasure, but the other be more conducive to intellectual development, or of two rival systems of training one may be better æsthetically, but the other supply more knowledge and stimulate thought more effectively, so we should have to decide between them by determining the amount of æsthetic, intellectual and hedonistic (pleasure) value of various kinds that each would give, adding these amounts so as to determine the total value of all kinds likely to be produced in each case and then choosing the act which produced the greatest.  In making our calculation it would be necessary also to subtract any incidental evil, *e.g.*, the unpleasantness of any boredom which may be involved in the process of learning or any of those risks which affect in varying degrees all human activities.

It must be admitted indeed that we may be practically certain that an act is right or our duty without having first summed up the good which it is likely to do and proved this to be greater than the good likely to be done by alternative courses of action, but it is possible to admit this and yet hold the only ultimate reason why it is our duty, the only real justification for it to be that indicated in the above description of the method.  If it is the right action it must be because its rightness is deducible by this method, though we

---

[1] For reply to objection that number of effects is infinite *v.* pp. 169–70.

in fact may not have deduced it. The function of Ethics is, then, first to determine what is " intrinsically good " or " good-in-itself " (a knowledge which, as would usually be admitted by the supporters of the view, cannot be reached by strict logical proof but only with the help of something of the nature of what is commonly called " intuition "), and afterwards to apply this knowledge to particular cases in the way just indicated. This is the view both of " Utilitarians," in the ordinary sense of the term, and of writers like Dr. Rashdall.[1] It may be held equally by someone who regards pleasure as the only good and by someone who believes in a number of goods of quite different kinds, including but not confined to pleasure.

This doctrine has been expounded at some length here because it is the only theory according to which it can reasonably or plausibly be maintained that all particular duties are completely deducible from more general principles of Ethics, i.e., according to this view, principles as to what is good-in-itself. The method of Kant, even if applicable to some duties, is clearly not applicable to all, and there are few indeed who would now put it forward as a universal method of determining what is right. But the only alternative method suggested is a deduction of the right from the good produced in the way given above, and it is therefore our first task to consider whether it can achieve all that is claimed for it. If it cannot, we shall have obtained a negative answer to the question whether Ethics can deduce completely what is right in particular cases. This we may be able to use later in building up a positive solution of the difficulty.

Now the doctrine under discussion depends on two assumptions; (a) that the right action is always the action likely to produce the greatest good,[2] (b) that the total good[3] likely[4] to be produced by an action can be inferred from our knowledge of the different elements of value in this total taken separately—let us call them the " constituent goods " —by some process analogous to numerical addition. (The same would naturally apply to evil except that we should have to subtract it from the total instead of adding it. The

[1] The fullest account of this view is given in Rashdall's *Theory of Good and Evil*.

[2] And/or the least evil.

[3] In this good may be included the intrinsic value of the act itself over and above the value of its consequences. For a defence of this against objections v. p. 170–1.

[4] Not necessarily " actually produced," v. p. 188–9.

diminution or averting of evil would have the same relevance for determining the rightness of an act as the production of a corresponding good.)    Here we shall confine ourselves to the second assumption.    The answer may throw some light on the first also.

The theory with which we are now dealing starts from a knowledge of what is *good* in itself, not from a knowledge of universal laws dictating what we *ought* or ought not to do. According to it laws as to what we *ought* to do are only valid because and in so far as their observance furthers the greatest *good* ;[1] they must be justified by the good they produce and broken in any case where they cease to be for the greatest good.    This enables us to avoid the objections brought against the ethics of Kant and yet to claim knowledge that is in the true sense universal.    We seem forced to admit that the laws as to what we ought to do are not truly universal because they are not valid in *all* particular cases, but we may still be able to say that a particular kind of effect is good in *all* cases without exception.    This does not mean that we ought always to produce it, for it may have to be sacrificed to a greater good, but it is still good even if it is our duty not to produce it.    If a particular kind of act, A, is right once, it does not follow that it will be right under different circumstances, but if A is once good in itself it seems to follow that it will always be good in itself whatever the circumstances. It is true that other considerations may make it wrong to produce A, but this does not alter A's goodness.    Similarly, if in any single case it be right to lie, there can be no *universal* law that lying is *wrong*, but there may still be a universal law that lying is *evil*.    Though it is conceivable that it might in some exceptional cases be our duty to choose it as the lesser of two evils, it will still remain an evil even in those cases. So here is a field in which universal laws seem really to apply. It seems quite obvious that the pain incurred, *e.g.*, in an operation, is always an evil, though it is sometimes right to inflict it in order to avert an evil which would be still greater.    And it is still more obvious that something good may have to be sacrificed to a greater good and yet remain itself also a good ; the fact that I ought to interrupt my study of philosophy to save a drowning man does not imply that the study of philosophy as such is not good, though in this particular case

---

[1] This is, I think, quite compatible with admitting that one of the factors in deciding may be the intrinsic value of the act itself, and not merely its consequences (*v.* p. 170–1).

it had to be sacrificed to a more important good. (Perhaps the reader should be again reminded that " good " is used throughout to cover all kinds of value except value merely as a means, both in my statement of others' theories and the elaboration of my own. " Good " is inclusive of but not synonymous with " moral good " in the ordinary sense of this term.)

Before we go any further, there are one or two ambiguities in our statement which it is necessary to clear up. I have spoken of deducing what is right, or what we ought[1] to do, but these phrases may either mean (a) the right act under the circumstances, (b) that act which under the circumstances known to us, we should, if we decide rationally, hold to be right. According to the view under discussion, whether an act is right in sense (a) will depend entirely on the good it actually does ; whether it is right in sense (b) on the good which we should, if we estimate probabilities rationally, expect it to do. In practice we have to be content with determining what act is right in sense (b) in the hope that it will at least approximate to the act which is right in sense (a). We know that it will be not indeed certain but at least far more likely to do so than if we had left the decision to chance or mere guesswork, and in many cases this likelihood would approach certainty even if we based our conclusion on consequences alone.

Again the problem before us is not the determination of the moral worth of acts already done but the decision as to what act it is right to do. I do not deny that, *granted* we think a given course of action our duty, it is right in a sense for us to do it, but before we have reached this stage we must settle the question whether we ought to think it our duty or not. If I hold the opinion that A is right I ought to do A, but how am I rationally to form that opinion ? It is my duty to *do* what I think right, but it is also my duty to do my utmost to *think* correctly in this important matter and form rational opinions before I act. The question of this chapter is how I am to fulfil this prior duty.

Thirdly it should be noted that the same problem arises both in questions of duty and questions of " prudence," if we distinguish the two kinds of questions. In both we have to decide which of a number of alternative acts is preferable, and the answer I shall eventually give, as well as my criticisms of other views, must be taken as covering both kinds of action.

[1] *v.* p. 3 for relation between " right," " ought " and " duty."

For it is not in logic or method of decision that they differ essentially but in motive and moral worth.

But, to return, are we to accept the doctrine that Dr. Rashdall calls " Ideal Utilitarianism," the doctrine that the right is to be inferred by summing the " constituent goods " which it is likely to produce ? We must now proceed to examine the criticisms that have been brought against this view. The first is directed against the notion of " good-in-itself." It is pointed out that it is quite impossible to draw a sharp line between good as an end and good as a means. Most good things are good both as end and as means, their goodness depends on their context, and we cannot hold that in a different context they would necessarily be good at all or at least that the degree of their goodness would remain the same. Nothing is good in itself, because nothing exists by itself apart from other things. We cannot say that it would continue to be of equal value any more than that it would remain the same in other respects if surrounding circumstances were changed ; its value is relative to its function in the whole, and this must clearly depend not only on itself but also on the rest of the whole.

These objections seem valid if by " good-in-itself "[1] is meant something that would necessarily still be equally good even if everything else were different, because the differences in other things would, or at least might, alter its nature and therefore its value. A pleasant sensation, for instance, could not be good in itself in this sense since, if there were no conscious beings or if conscious beings were differently constituted, the sensation would not occur at all and would therefore not be good except in the sense in which a thing that is not real at all may be said to be good. But this is surely not what anybody who uses the term, " good-in-itself," can have meant by it ; they cannot have meant to deny that the things to which they applied this attribute were causally affected by circumstances other than themselves. But a distinction is possible here : we could easily admit that something would or might be made different by differences in other things, and yet assert that it was good in itself in the sense that its value would always be the same *as long as it remained unchanged in other respects*. This certainly would not be true of what was good merely as a means, since such a thing would cease to be good if its end could not be

---

[1] I am referring not to " good-in-itself " as a universal but to any particular things which are good-in-themselves.

achieved,[1] but it might conceivably be true of anything in so far as it was good in itself. This much seems to be a necessary presupposition of the theory which we are discussing if the latter is to be maintained in its full rigidity. For, unless we hold this to be true, we shall not be in a position to give any universal laws about what is good, since we could no longer say that, if a thing is good-in-itself in one case, it will always be so.

But, thirdly, if we consider the way in which the term, " good-in-itself," originated, we shall find that it was primarily used in distinction from " good as a means." So, when I have used the expression, it has always been intended to signify *good otherwise than merely as a means to or condition of something else which is good.* This, if not the whole, is at any rate the most important part of what is usually meant by the assertion that something is good-in-itself, and it does not necessarily imply that the particular thing in question would always be good, only that it is good *in this case.* For it might have real value otherwise than as a means to or condition of something else, and yet this value might be affected by other things, just as a penny may be round although it would cease to be round if reduced to a molten state or sufficiently battered by a hammer. In this sense I have asserted certain effects of punishment and reward to be good-in-themselves, and this is all that is meant by the assertion. It may indeed be objected that in this sense of the term everything which is good at all is good-in-itself, because " good only as a means to or condition of something else " really signifies " not good at all but a cause or condition of something else which is good," and that therefore the addition of the words " in itself " is unnecessary. This criticism would be quite sound if it were not that " good " has been habitually, though perhaps confusedly, used to signify both " good as a means " and " good as an end," and that therefore for the sake of clearness some further distinction is required.

But I do not see that the admission that some particular thing is " good-in-itself " in this sense necessarily implies that it is always good in any sense of the term, still less that it is always equally good, any more than the fact that a piece of coal is of such and such a size and density now implies that it will always be of that size and density, or would have

---

[1] *e.g.*, a sharp knife, though it remained unaltered itself, would lose its value if there were nobody who wished to buy it and nothing that it was desirable to cut.

been of the same size if the circumstances had been different. It may be true that the value of a thing could only be different as a result of the thing being different in properties other than value, but I do not see that we have any right to assume this ; and, unless we do assume it, the theory we are discussing is at the best logically incomplete, since in that case it is no longer possible to lay down strictly universal laws about the good-in-itself any more than about the right action. It does follow indeed from the conception of goodness or value that the value of something cannot be different except as the result of some other difference, but this difference need not necessarily lie in the thing itself, it may lie in something else.[1]

We cannot therefore say that the intrinsic value of any quality will always be the same under all circumstances. We may know indeed sometimes that its presence will always be a good or an evil, but not that it will always be so in the same degree.[2] It may be said, however, that, though we cannot lay down absolutely universal laws about what is " good-in-itself,"[3] we can lay down laws which are approximately universal. Approximate, not absolute, universality is all that even physical science claims, so perhaps the theory is little impaired by this criticism.

We must further note that it is quite possible for some particular thing to be good both as an end and as a means, and yet for us to be able to distinguish in it between its two kinds of goodness. We can easily enough distinguish between the intrinsic value of an unselfish act and the pleasure it brings to persons other than the agent and can evaluate them separately. We can say that the act was a noble one

---

[1] It is true that, if we adopt the " internal " theory of relations, a difference in something else will mean a difference in the thing itself, call it X ; but (a) the internal view of relations is itself fatal to the doctrine that strictly universal laws can be laid down as to what is good in itself any more than as to what is right ; (b) where the whole makes a difference to the value of its parts, the difference of value in X does not seem to result directly from any difference in X's other properties, even if there is such a difference, but from something other than X ; (c) the difference in the properties of X, if it exists at all, is often so small as to be practically negligible.

[2] e.g., the pain of an operation is as such always an evil, but how much of an evil it is will depend on the way the patient bears it and not only on the degree of the pain itself.

[3] " Intrinsically good " is a term frequently used as equivalent to " good-in-itself." When I use it, it is in the last of the three senses indicated. I have, however, except where I made a definite statement to the contrary, always used the terms " good " and " value " to signify " intrinsic good," never to signify " good as a means."

but foolish or not really worth the price, or that of two valuable experiences one was worth more in itself but that the other was better for the man " in the long run," *i.e.*, more conducive to mental or moral development.

It is also said that the view in question does not make duty unconditional, because according to it duty still depends on an end beyond itself.  But the unconditionalness of duty does not mean that no conditions affect the question what our duty is, but only that once granting a certain act to be our duty for whatever reasons, it is unconditionally obligatory on us.  What our duty is in a particular case must be decided, at least partly, by reference to particular conditions ; but once it is decided nothing can excuse us from doing it.  The duty to take certain measures in order to save life is none the less unconditional because it has an object, the saving of the life, and may possibly not be universal.  It is unconditional in so far as, wherever it is a duty at all, we are bound to do it whatever our desires may be and whatever the circumstances. This is not altered by the fact that we have to consider particular circumstances[1] (including in some duties, as in the choice of a profession, even our own desires) in order to decide whether it is a duty.  Nor would it be altered if we found it not to be a duty in all cases, because it would still apply with undiminished force in those cases where it was a duty.  It is indeed of the utmost importance to realise the special feature of duty as not only having value but carrying with it an " ought " ; but we are not discussing here the special features of all duties, we are discussing how we can decide which acts are duties.

Another objection to the theory is that it presupposes the possibility of comparing and measuring against each other quite different kinds of good.  It may be asked how we can possibly say what amount of pleasure in conversing with friends is equivalent to what amount of æsthetic value in reading Shakespeare, what amount of increased security = what amount of personal liberty sacrificed, how much improvement in capacity for scientific research = how much practical ability, and so on.  Yet it would seem that, if we are to determine in particular cases what is the line of action which will secure the greatest good, we must be able to do this at least approximately.

It is partly to avoid these difficulties that utilitarianism of

[1] Otherwise we shall not know what are the best means of saving the life that is in danger.

Bentham's type is adopted. It seemed to simplify the problem very much if there was held to be only one kind of good, pleasure. But, apart from the other objections to the view that pleasure is the only good, it does not really remove the present difficulty. For, in the first place, we should find it almost or quite as hard to compare two experiences of very different kinds in respect of pleasure as in respect of goodness or value.[1] Further—and this second point has been surprisingly neglected—it should be noted that there are cases of comparison between different kinds of values which even a thoroughgoing utilitarian can hardly reduce to a comparison of pleasures. Take the case of marking examination papers. Here we are often quite certain that one candidate is in general much better than another, though in some respects he may be much worse, e.g., he may be less accurate about details, but show more grasp of the subject as a whole, or he may show less originality but more common-sense. In these cases we do balance different values against each other, yet we succeed in reaching a conclusion that we are bound in very many instances to accept as true. Such a comparison certainly cannot be reduced to a comparison of pleasures, even if that were possible with more specifically ethical reasoning, as the utilitarian would maintain. It is certainly not a question of judging how much pleasure these different characteristics of the candidate's work give. Even if the value of the characteristics displayed in the examination were ultimately dependent only on their pleasure-giving capacity, we are certainly able to compare them without any reference to this ; and, though there are many doubtful cases where we are very uncertain about relative merit, it remains pretty certain, e.g., that, where the examiners are competent, all the candidates placed in the third class have done worse papers than any placed in the first class, though it may be very doubtful whether a given candidate ought to be placed in the first or the second class.[2] The same necessity of balancing different values against each other and deciding that

---

[1] Utilitarians would have not only to do this but to say how much pain it would be worth incurring for a given pleasure, or how much pleasure it would be worth losing in order to escape so much pain, i.e., besides comparing pleasures quite different in kind they would have to compare pleasures to pains. So they are as much hampered by the difficulty in question as the advocates of the other view.

[2] This does not eliminate the possibility of a candidate having not done his real merits justice in the paper through illness or bad luck with the questions, but then the examiners are not judging of this.

a deficiency in some is outweighed by a superiority in others occurs in comparing the qualities of different articles offered for sale, choosing lodgings, estimating the merits of a book, selecting from candidates for a post, deciding whether it is worth while incurring a particular expense, etc.

It is therefore futile to say that the comparison of different values cannot be made, because we in fact do make it. It is obviously impossible in many cases to make it with certainty ; but it would be quite absurd to say that such comparisons have no validity and that we can never rely on their results. We are at any rate sufficiently certain of this power of comparison to stake on it the whole of men's careers, for there is no other means whatever of judging their relative fitness. We must take this power as a fact, though that does not excuse us from the obligation to give the best account we can of it. If in our practical activities we are to consider consequences at all, we must admit the possibility of rationally preferring one set of consequences to another as better, although the advantages which each of these alternative sets of consequences possesses, the " goods " which they involve, may be quite different in nature.

Another objection is that the inference suggested by the theory in question can never be carried out because the consequences of any act are infinite, since its immediate effects will influence the events which come next, these the events afterwards and so on *ad infinitum*. I can never tell that events in the year 1,000,000 A.D. might not be different in some material respect as the result of any action performed to-day, for on them it must certainly exercise an indirect causal influence through the long chain of intervening events. If we can never know all the consequences, can we possibly know which act will produce the best ?

This criticism clearly debars the inference from being *certain*, but in any case it could not be more than probable because it depends on causal laws discovered not *a priori* but by induction from experience. But this applies also to all the conclusions of natural science, and we need not surely be sceptical about ethics merely because it does not possess a greater certainty than the best-established conclusions of the physical sciences. In making all its predictions science also has to ignore the influence of unknown causes, yet this does not prevent it from forecasting so accurately that it can anticipate correctly the day and precise hour of an eclipse. Can Ethics expect more certainty than this ? As a matter of fact, however, its position is a good deal less favourable than that of astronomy, because, while we can be pretty sure that there are no causes at work which will considerably alter the time of the eclipse from what we had predicted, we seem bound to admit that in very many cases acts will produce effects which will considerably increase or decrease the total good produced and yet cannot be predicted.    But, since there is no reason to expect that these unknown effects will favour any one alternative rather than any other, it is rational and justifiable simply to ignore them in our choice.    By the rule of probabilities they must not influence our choice, because the uncertainty affects *all* alternatives *equally*.

Their presence, however, should remind us that we can never be certain what the right act is, since what we think the right[1] act may always be really wrong because of unknown consequences.    This uncertainty is due not to any defect in our power of moral insight (though I certainly do not say that this is infallible), but to our defective knowledge of facts and the rules which govern facts.    Further it suggests that it may often be a better method just to do what we think expresses the best general principle, trusting that such acts are always most likely, though not certain, to produce the greatest good, than to rely exclusively on the calculation of consequences.[2]

We must add, however, that the importance of remote consequences is greatly diminished by the fact that an act can never be more than part-cause of these, and will as such grow progressively less important in proportion to their remoteness.    For the further removed they are the greater will be the number of other causes which contribute to them, and so the smaller the share of our act in their production.

A further objection is that an act itself often has intrinsic value as well as its consequences, and that likewise in many cases the reason why we ought not to commit an act lies rather in the nature of the act itself than in the nature of its consequences.    This can be met by saying that any intrinsic good or evil belonging to the act itself should be counted in determining the total good produced, and may therefore play a part in deciding what we ought to do.    The fact that an action possesses intrinsic value might then be an additional reason for its being right and might even outweigh other reasons against it.    But in that case we have to face the

---

[1] In the first of the two senses of " right " which I distinguished on p. 163.

[2] *v.* below, pp. 199 *ff.*

charge of a vicious circle. It is contended[1] that the fact that a certain action possesses intrinsic value cannot be given as one of the reasons why it is right, because that intrinsic value itself depends on and presupposes the rightness of the act. Only right acts are intrinsically valuable, and they can only be so because they are right. But it is possible to overcome this objection by the use of a distinction which seems to me very important for Ethics.

(1) All acts that are right possess intrinsic value just because they are right, at least where there is any difficulty about doing right or any temptation to do wrong; but this value, unlike the good produced in its consequences, cannot be a reason why the act is right. To make it a reason would be to say that the act was right because it was right and so to fall under the objection.

But (2) certain kinds of act may have an intrinsic value of their own over and above the value involved in being right. Now this value may be one of the reasons that makes a course of action right, e.g., one of the reasons for studying philosophy may be that there is an intrinsic value in the studying of it even apart from its effects, and apart from any value accruing to it in given circumstances *because* it is right. Yet, since this value is only *one* of the goods which an act is capable of producing, it does not always make the act which possesses it right. For this good may in some cases be outweighed by other goods which would be produced by an alternative action in greater degree. This will not take away the intrinsic value of, e.g., studying philosophy as such, but it will make it wrong to do so in the given circumstances where more good could be produced by not doing it. Similarly there is a special evil about lies over and above that which belongs merely to wrong acts as such, and this evil may well be part of the reason why lies are wrong since it does not itself result from the lie being a wrong act but simply from it being a lie, just as the specific value of an æsthetic experience is not due to its being right to undergo the experience, but simply to the character of the experience as æsthetic. There is no vicious circle here.

Worse difficulties are raised when it is maintained not only that we can compare different goods, but that we can and ought to find the total good which an action is likely to produce by " summing " these different goods. At first sight it seems quite absurd to talk of summing goods, just as it would

---

[1] *v.* Prof. Prichard's article in *Mind*, 1912.

be considered absurd to suppose that we could add up the yellowness of a flower, the greenness of the adjacent leaves, and the brownness of the flower-pot in which they are placed, thus arriving at a sum-total of the quantity of colour. Further any summing of goods seems to imply that we can say not only that one is better than another but that it is, *e.g.*, $2\frac{3}{4}$ or $1\frac{1}{5}$ times better than another. Are not quantitative, mathematical conceptions totally inapplicable here? It would seem quite impracticable to use them, and most philosophers would think the very idea of it absurd.

But there is a consideration that makes me pause in my sweeping condemnation. It is well known to all who have had to do with examination papers in whatever capacity that it is quite possible to represent qualitative differences numerically by giving marks, and though this is admittedly in some degree inadequate it serves its purpose fairly well. It should, therefore, be possible to universalise this method, and determine what course is right in all cases by giving so many marks for each of the goods realised (*e.g.*, 5 for immediate pleasure to agent, 16 for pleasure to others, 10 for increase in knowledge, 14 for improvement in intelligence, etc.), and then adding up the total. In this way we could arrive at our conclusion by genuine mathematical inference, though we should be summing not indeed the goods but numbers substituted for them. This is not a method we usually adopt in making decisions about what is right, but it might be said that in our ordinary life we proceed by some more inexact *quantitative* reasoning analogous to this. The possibility of giving marks proves that we can not only compare different kinds of value but fix a quantitative equivalent for each, thus bringing them under a common numerical standard, and then arrive by a process of inference at the total value which they make up ; and it might be said that, although it is not practicable to follow this method of marking always, we can and commonly do proceed by a looser kind of quantitative comparison and summing. Examinations at least disprove the view that the method of summing is always an impossible one. But this is not to say that the claims of the view before us to have provided a *universal* method for deducing what is right are in the least justified. For it is the limitations of this view that we must now consider.

In the first place, as Dr. Rashdall allows, it presupposes that we know immediately (*i.e.*, not by inference), (*a*) what things are good-in-themselves, (*b*) what is their relative degree of goodness.[1] It therefore falls far short of being a *complete deduction* by inference of what is right in each particular case. This the adherents of the view would usually admit. Even the hedonist must presuppose an immediate perception that pleasure is good and that one pleasure is worth so much more than another.

Secondly it is an indubitable psychological fact that this is not the way in which we always infer what is right, and while it may be held that it is the best way it must certainly be admitted that in many cases we discover what is right without using it. What the nature of our ethical reasoning is I shall try to say later ;[2] but it is certainly not always in fact reducible to any kind of " summing." It may be said that, wherever we form a true judgment as to what is right, it *could* be justified by summing the good produced ; but the mere fact that we have been able to reach it at all without " summing " shows that this is not the only way of attaining ethical knowledge.

These objections would still seem to leave the suggested method in the position of the best, though not the only or the all-sufficient one ; but, thirdly, it has the further practical and logical defect that its premises are apt to be more uncertain than its conclusions. It is generally easier to estimate the value of a total concrete good than it is to estimate the value of its constituent elements, because it is so difficult to abstract the latter from each other. We, therefore, have a better chance of knowing the conclusion without the premises than we have of inferring it from the premises, which makes the inference useless except possibly as a slight additional confirmation where such is needed. We can as a matter of fact compare the complex but concrete goods of life with a fair chance of being right ; but when we try to abstract the different distinguishable elements in these concrete goods and estimate their value separately we find ourselves in hopeless difficulties. This is shown by the fact that, while different philosophers are fairly in agreement about most ordinary ethical questions involving the comparison of concrete goods, they are in grave disagreement as to the relative value of the different constituent elements in these goods. Utilitarians and non-utilitarians make similar decisions in moral matters,

---

[1] I had better remind readers again that " goodness " is throughout used in a very wide sense to cover not only " moral goodness " as such, but all kinds of intrinsic value without exception.

[2] *v.* below, pp. 128 *ff.*

yet the utilitarians deny the value of all the elements in a
set of consequences that the latter hold to be good except
the particular feelings of pleasure.  Few philosophers even
agree as to which of these constituent elements are good in
themselves, let alone as to their relative value.  Yet, while
there is so much dispute about the supposed premises, we can
often be fairly certain of the conclusion, for we may very often
be pretty sure that an act is right or that one concrete good is
better than another.  Therefore the conclusion cannot be
merely an inference from the premises.

We must admit in any case that we can perceive certain
things to be good without inference, but if so why should it
only be the parts, or constituent elements, that we perceive
to be good, not the whole?  Why can we not perceive it of
the whole straightway without summing up the value of the
parts at all?  In any case it must be admitted that we
perceive it of some wholes analysable into further constituent
elements, since we never carry the analysis to its furthest conceivable point.  Then why not of the larger whole?  Surely
it is easier to see that one whole complex experience is superior
in value to another than it is to estimate separately and then
sum the æsthetic, moral, intellectual and hedonistic values of
each of three or four successive stages into which we may
divide the experiences?  Can we possibly, even in the most
approximate way, decide how much of the value of a state of
unselfish love is due to the pleasure felt, how much to the
intrinsic value of love as an emotion, how much to the moral
value involved in unselfishness, and then add the three
together?  We cannot abstract these three elements sufficiently to estimate them separately.  Yet it remains true
that we must take them all into account in estimating the
value of the whole.  How these two statements may be
reconciled I shall try to show later.

Fourthly, it is at least very doubtful whether we can assign
marks to different qualities except by considering what share
they each have in the total value of some larger whole.
Certainly, once the maximum for each quality was fixed we
could give marks for each without further reference to the
whole, but we could not fix the maxima fairly except by
asking what part of the total value is due to each quality,
and this itself seems to involve a reference to the whole.  We
seem to have been entrapped in a vicious circle, for while we
sought to derive the value of a whole entirely from the value
of its parts we now find that the value of the parts cannot

be determined except by reference to the value of the whole.

If the summing theory were an adequate account of the matter, it would be inexplicable that we can be as nearly certain about many ethical decisions as we are. It can serve neither as a sufficient account of the way in which we actually form our judgments, nor as a sufficient reason for their validity. The quasi-mathematical guise which the method assumes is feigned, not genuine, for quantitative determination here can never be exact and the thought-process involved is not adequately described by the metaphor of " summing."

A further objection is that, if we are to deduce the value of a whole from the value of its parts, A, B, and C, we must assume that the value of the whole is equal to the value of A plus the value of B plus the value of C. This assumption we have no right to make unless we have first disproved what Dr. G. E. Moore calls the principle of " organic unities." To quote his words,[1] in some cases, " *the value of a whole*[2] *bears no regular proportion to the sum of the values of its parts.* It is certain that a good thing may exist in such a relation to another good thing that the value of the whole thus formed is immensely greater than the sum of the values of the two good things. It is certain that a whole formed of a good thing and an indifferent thing may have immensely greater value than that good thing itself possesses. It is certain that two bad things or a bad and an indifferent thing may form a whole much worse than the sum of the badness of its parts. . . . However we may decide particular questions, the principle is clear. *The value of a whole must not be assumed to be the same as the sum of the values of its parts.*" For instance, the experience of a beautiful object can be analysed into the consciousness of the object plus a certain pleasure, but its value is very much greater than the value of the consciousness itself plus the value of an equal pleasure derived from something else. Again, a true belief that some beloved person has certain good qualities adds greatly to the value of the love though by itself the belief would be almost without

---

[1] *Principia Ethica*, pp. 27–8. I do not mean that Dr. Moore would necessarily agree with all the instances I give of the principle or the conclusions I draw from it.

[2] As Dr. Moore distinguishes between the value " on the whole " and " as a whole," I had better say that what I am referring to is the former, *i.e.*, not only the extra value accruing from the combination of the parts but this together with the value of the parts.

intrinsic value (as opposed to value as a means). In some cases the value of a whole is increased by or even totally dependent on the presence of some element which, taken by itself, is an evil. For instance, the intrinsic value of a morally noble state of mind may be actually increased by the pain of sympathy with the sufferings of others. (A feeling of love for them without this pain might be very much less valuable than a feeling of love with it.) Similarly the æsthetic value of witnessing a tragedy depends on a certain pain of sympathy with the hero. Yet pain taken by itself is always an evil. Again the evil of certain bad states of mind, *e.g.*, cruelty, actually increases, and does not decrease, in proportion to the pleasure the man takes in them. The state of mind of a cruel man is the worse the more he revels in his cruelty, though pleasure as such is always a good and not an evil. To take another instance, the æsthetic value of a picture is certainly not equal to the sum of the values of its parts ; and the same must surely hold of good states of mind and good acts as of physical beauty. It would be generally agreed that right acts of self-sacrifice have a high intrinsic value, but this value must depend largely on the presence of an element of pain, which is evil in itself, since otherwise it would not be a case of self-sacrifice.[1]

Consideration of points like these forces me to accept the principle of " organic unities," at any rate on its negative side as a denial that the good of a whole is necessarily equal or reducible to the sum of the good of its constituent parts. The only doubt is whether the values of the parts can in all cases be separated from each other and summed[2] so as even to allow us to say that they are greater or less than the value of the whole ; but if they cannot this is *a fortiori* a refutation of the theory which makes that summing the one method of Ethics. Now the principle of organic unities is in flat

[1] I do not deny that the pain may be so great as to make the sacrifice an evil except as a means to another good, but the evil is always at least mitigated by a certain value involved in the moral nobility of the act, and this is inseparably bound up with the sacrifice and pain.

[2] It is very doubtful, *e.g.*, whether there is any sense in separating the value of the activity of loving and the value of the pleasure it gives, reckoning the two values apart and then adding them together. But whether this is possible or not, one thing seems clear, namely, that the value of the whole experience is *not* reducible to a sum of these values, and that is all we want to prove. The reason may be either that the sum is different, as Dr. Moore thinks, or as most other philosophers hold, that they cannot be summed at all.

contradiction with the theory that the total good of a whole can be determined by summing the values of its parts. If any comparison can be effected at all the good may be more (and possibly in some cases less) than would be expected from the value of its parts. But if so, how can we reach it by summing its parts ? Dr. Rashdall refers to Dr. Moore's view approvingly in a footnote,[1] but does not seem to realise its total incompatibility with his own position. He admits that the different elements of the good modify each other when brought together and that the whole is, often at least, more than the sum of its parts, but it remains true, he says, that " we could give no intelligible account of the good except by regarding it as a combination of goods,"[2] because in all thought some abstraction is necessary. But it is not a question merely of abstracting. Dr. Rashdall maintains that we must determine the value of a whole by summing the constituent goods which are parts of it ; the principle of " organic unities " lays it down in so many words that the value of a whole need bear " no regular proportion to the sum of the values of its parts." Both views cannot be true. We may abstract the parts, but we could only deduce the value of the whole from their value if we were justified in assuming that the abstraction had made no appreciable difference ; but the instances given seem to show that it cannot be effected without making not only a difference but a very appreciable one.

It would seem to follow that we cannot, in all cases[3] at any rate, infer the good of a whole by summing its constituent goods, and therefore that this is not a possible way either of universally determining what is right. Further it would equally prove that we cannot infer in all cases the value of a whole from the value of its constituent parts in any way other than summing. This is of some importance, because otherwise it might be said that the objections commonly brought against the view are only due to the use of an inadequate mathematical analogy and that the good of the whole might still be inferred from the good of the parts, though this inference cannot adequately be described as summing. But,

---

[1] *Theory of Good and Evil*, Vol. II, p. 40 n.
[2] *Id*. Vol. I, p. 220.
[3] I do not deny that we can do so in some. Some wholes are, if organic unities, at any rate not sufficiently close ones to vitiate the method. It is only because he (1) makes the method universal, (2) views it in too mathematical a fashion, that I am criticising Dr. Rashdall.

whether it is summing or any other mode of inference, the method when universalised is still in any case open to our objections that, first, it proceeds from premises which are less certain than the conclusions based on them, and, secondly, it contradicts the principle of organic unities which we are bound to accept in the realm of value, for this principle says that the value of a whole cannot be reduced to or inferred from the values of its parts, since it does not vary in proportion to the values of the parts.

But let us quote Dr. Rashdall's main argument.[1] " How we can arrive at an estimate of the amount of a whole without putting together a number of parts is to me unintelligible. . . The idea of a quantity—a quantity occupying time—which does not consist of parts, and is not made up of the addition of parts, will remain to most minds an unintelligible paradox. If it consists of parts, the parts must surely all be looked at before we can pronounce upon the pleasurableness of the whole. . . . If such a process of estimating a total quantity after estimating the constituent quantities, is not to be called addition and subtraction, I should be grateful to any logician who will tell me more precisely what mental operation it is." The passage refers only to the summing of pleasures, not to the summing of good in general, but he applies his principle also to other kinds of good, and the argument would justify this equally, if valid. Now it is undoubtedly right to say that in order to estimate the value of a whole we should *take account* of its constituent parts. But is this the same as saying that the value of a whole is always *the sum of* or *inferable from* the values of its parts? I think not. In order to appreciate fully the beauty of a picture we should see all its component parts, but it does not follow that our cognition of its beauty is an inference from the beauty of its separate parts. And neither is it so in the case of the good, if my reasoning has been right. In order to discern the value of a whole we must take into account all the constituent " goods," or elements of good (and evil), which it contains, as far as humanly possible, but it does not follow that its value is a deduction from the value of these. We do not *infer* the value of the whole from that of the parts ; but a knowledge of the value of the parts puts us in a better position to perceive the value of the whole without further inference. Once we know the whole properly we see its value ; but to know the whole properly we must know the parts. We know the total good of a concrete

[1] Vol. II, pp. 29–30.

set of results by a cognition which is not itself a mediate inference ; but this " intuition," if it is an " intuition," pre-supposes a careful analysis and survey of the parts. Nor need we deny that we can sometimes infer what is right in a par-ticular case without the " intuition," for *in some cases* the good may not be an organic unity, and *in some cases* again general principles may be applied with safety.[1] But we must deny that it is possible to do so in most or all instances, and we cannot lay down beforehand which the exceptions are.

The above seems to apply to our knowledge both of what is good and of what is right. If we cannot arrive at the total good likely to be produced by an act through a mere inference from the constituent elements of that good, neither can we infer the rightness of an act in that way. With this vanishes our only hope of ever being able completely to deduce from the science of Ethics what acts are right. Only two ways of doing this have been put forward ; the first is by appealing to universal laws as to what we ought to do, formulated irres-pective of particular circumstances and consequences, but it is generally agreed now that it is not possible to deduce what is right in all cases by this method even if it is possible to do so in some.[2] The second is the method we have been discuss-ing ; and we have come to the conclusion that it likewise must abandon its full claims. Even if the rightness of an action depends on its being likely to produce the greatest good, neither the greatest good nor the right action can always be deter-mined by inference from any more general ethical principles. They must sometimes at least be cognised immediately in the particular instance ; but I have not excluded the possibility that this immediate cognition may be helped by previous inferential thinking. It is on these lines, I think, that we must reconcile the " rationalist " and the " anti-rationalist." But more of this later.

While I am dealing with the method described as the summing of goods, it is desirable to point out that it has a certain considerable value for ethics provided we do not forget its limitations. It is only in the case of goods realised simultaneously in a single complex experience that the objections to the inference of the value of the whole from the values of the parts seem altogether fatal. They are by no means always so serious where we are concerned with the goods of different persons or the goods realised by the same

[1] *v.* p. 199 *ff.*
[2] For a summary of objections to the method, *v.* above, p. 158–9.

person in successive times, for these goods are less likely to constitute an " organic unity " of the close kind that involves a considerable difference between the value of the whole and the value of its component parts. For I have not said that all wholes are organic unities in respect of value, only that some are. Nor is it true even in the case of all organic unities that there is a *considerable* difference between the value of the whole and the value of the parts, only that it is so in many instances, like those I cited. There are a great number of practical cases in which even arithmetical summing is a suitable method for deciding what is right, *e.g.*, where food has to be distributed in order to relieve a famine it is rational to decide between alternative schemes by adding up the number of lives likely to be saved by each. Again it is practicable enough to decide a candidate's merit by giving a mark for each separate question and then adding the marks.[1] In other cases it may be rational to have recourse to " summing " of a loose kind. If I am choosing between entertainments A and B either for myself or for somebody else, it may be rational for me to decide in favour of A on the ground that the time spent on it will be on the average about as enjoyable as that spent on B, and that for the same money I can enjoy two evenings of it instead of one, provided I am satisfied that my friend or I will not be tired of it by the second evening so as to counterbalance this advantage.

We must not, however, assume that successive times and different persons cannot constitute an organic unity in respect of value. We must not say that the intrinsic value of reading a great poem is necessarily reducible to the sum of the values of the experiences of the successive lines which make it up, nor that the intrinsic value of a community as a whole is necessarily equal to the sum of the values of the individuals who compose it (though I admit that the community is not a mind over and above the minds of its members).[2] Further,

---

[1] This is the usual method adopted. It would be possible to use the method of giving separate marks not only for different questions but for different qualities shown in the answer to one and the same question, so many for memory, so many for originality, so many for understanding of general principles, etc. This would correspond to the method of summing as applied to goods realised simultaneously in the same complex experience, and would not, I think, be generally considered at all a good system of marking.

[2] The principle of justice provides special difficulties for the view which determines the right action by reference to the greatest good, for " justice " seems to say—prefer a fair to an unfair distribution for its

in practice it is generally easier to see the value of the results of an action as a whole than first to see separately the value of the constituent elements of these and afterwards infer from them the value of the whole, even where it is not impossible to do so with fair accuracy.

We must also remember that, even where something like numerical summing is practicable, it is not, strictly speaking, the values that are summed.   In a few cases we may add up marks which are taken as equivalent to the values but are not themselves the values ;  in others we effect the summation by assuming that one portion of the time taken by a given experience or the enjoyment by one individual of a given external good is *on the average* equal in value to another equal portion of time taken by the same experience or the enjoyment by another individual of the same quantity and kind of external good, and then concluding that a greater number of such units is preferable to a lesser.   Now there is no objection to this procedure in so far as the assumption is justified, and *in practice* it may be.   When there is no reason to suppose a difference we must act as though there were an equality of value ;  and if the calculation covers a large number of units, we are fairly likely to be approximately right, since a surplus of value above the average in some cases will be compensated by a deficiency in others below the average.   And, in so far as this is so, there is room for an arithmetic of ethics, and one that cannot lie open to the caviller.   Since the units in these cases have to be assumed to be homogeneous, this is not to claim that we can fix the mathematical ratio between different kinds of good, or even between two goods of the same kind but of different intensity ;  nor does it even necessarily imply that the life or enjoyment of twenty people is twice as good as that of ten, all that it necessarily implies is that we must, for certain purposes at any rate, treat it as twice as important. We may leave aside the very difficult question whether and in what sense there is a quantitative relation between goods and yet admit that we can in these cases proceed quantitatively.   I can give A 60 marks and B 20 without committing myself to the view that A's work is *three* times as good as B's.

own sake even if the fair distribution does not yield a greater quantity of good.   The most hopeful way of reconciling this with the view that the right action is always the action likely to produce the greatest good would be by appealing to the principle of organic unities and saying that, even if the sum of the goods enjoyed by the different individuals affected is not greater on a fair than on an unfair distribution, the good of the whole may be so.

I can admit that all men's lives are not equally valuable, and yet hold that the only practicable rule in cases of famine is to treat them as if they were. Consideration of the summing theory has suggested to us some very important conclusions. It seems now that it is not possible logically to deduce all particular duties from universal principles by any process of reasoning. Only two methods of doing this have been suggested, the Kantian and the summing method, and both are unable to substantiate their claims.

Nor can we solve the difficulty by falling back on induction from and verification by experience, which is the course adopted by many positivist writers and also in a recent book by Prof. H. L. Roth, *The Science of Morals*. For induction can only tell us what happens, not what is right or good, though when we have seen what it is in fact we *may* afterwards be able to see that it is right or good. The specifically ethical problem is not what the consequences of acts will be, but which set of consequences is preferable ; and this problem still remains when we have determined all the facts. Induction supplies valuable data for decisions, but cannot decide alone.

So I am led to abandon the idea that all particular duties are deducible ; but this does not preclude me from admitting the importance of inference in Ethics *as a help,*[1] as bringing us into a position where we can the better see immediately what is right. The strength of the summing theory lies largely in the truth that the value of the consequences it is likely to produce[2] must be at least a very important factor in determining whether an act is right,[3] and that we are not assessing this factor adequately if we overlook any important elements of value in the consequences (any " constituent goods "). Now, since we obviously ought to consider the important values involved before deciding what to do, and yet cannot deduce from them either the total good produced or the rightness of a particular act, the process, in cases where

---

[1] Or perhaps even as essential (*i.e.*, a necessary condition of any intuition), *v.* below, p. 193-4.

[2] I do not mean that the consequences actually produced alter the morality of an act, *i.e.*, it does not make the act immoral or even mistaken if an unfortunate consequence occurs which the agent could not be expected to foresee.

[3] What our duty is, therefore, depends to a large extent on the likely consequences, but this is quite compatible with the unconditional obligatoriness of a duty, as soon as it is seen, for whatever reason, to be a duty (*v.* p. 167, 216).

we judge only after full consideration of the consequences,[1] should be of the following nature. We forecast the probable consequences of each alternative course of action, and (if we decide with care) take account of all the important advantages or disadvantages (good or evil) involved in these consequences. We then take the effects of the alternative actions as a whole, and now find ourselves in a position to judge which is better by an act of comparison that is not itself an inference. Or rather we compare in this way not the effects alone but *the actions taken in conjunction with their effects.* We do not strictly infer our conclusion from the various goods produced, but must be said to perceive it "immediately"[2] (*i.e.*, by an act of non-inferential cognition,[3] or, as it is popularly called, " intuition "). But, on the other hand, unless we analyse and consider the different advantages and disadvantages involved, our " intuition " is likely to be wrong or only " right " by accident. It must be added that this non-inferential cognition has to supply not only the conclusion but some of the premises. It is required to tell us which of the consequences are good or bad in themselves, and in what degree they possess these qualities. But most people would agree here ; the subject of contention is whether we require non-inferential cognition for the conclusion, *i.e.*, that this act is right, not whether we require it for some of the premises about the goodness of the consequences. I should insist that it is required for both,[4] though it does not follow that it is the only thing needed for either purpose.

Now that we have reached this view, it is easy to explain how people came to hold that the rightness of an act was to

---

[1] This is not, however, by any means the only way of judging whether an act is right, as we shall see later, though it is the most important way and the necessary way for most acts.

[2] The term, "immediate," is, however, misleading, for the acts of non-inferential cognition to which it usually refers are not by any means necessarily immediate in the sense of being attainable without a process of thinking. They are not necessarily " judgments at first sight," and are mediated in the sense of being helped by other items of knowledge. It was for this reason, I suppose, and not because he ignored the importance of the factor to which I am referring, that Hegel denied the possibility of merely immediate knowledge.

[3] I do not mean that this is necessarily always a separate act later in time than the inference involved, for it may be better to regard it as a distinguishable but inseparable part of the same activity. That is a question for general epistemology to settle.

[4] It might be objected that we still *infer* what act is right from the situation taken as a whole, though not from the different elements of which this whole consists ; but such an " immediate " inference could

be inferred by summing the good it does. For, if it is a fact that we can only see B to be true after examining A, it is easy to confuse this with our *inferring* B from A. We usually can only determine whether an act is right after examining the different kinds of good which it produces, and from this it is easy to pass to the erroneous view that both the total good produced and the rightness of the act are inferred from these, but it is nevertheless a mistake. This is quite an adequate explanation why it is that the view I have been discussing seems so plausible.

Further I must repeat that I have not disproved the possibility in *some* cases of being able really to *infer* the right from the different elements of good produced.[1] What I maintain is that we cannot do this in all or most cases.

We must not assume that, because we cannot, as we have seen, make our moral knowledge dependent entirely on inference, therefore there is no scope for inference or reasoning at all in Ethics. It does not follow, because reasoning is not omnipotent, that therefore it is useless. We have to rely on something that may be loosely called "intuition," but to put ourselves in a position to make safe use of it we ought first to reason long and hard. It would be admitted by almost everybody that in order to determine what is right, in many cases at any rate, we have to use reasoning for the purpose of forecasting the probable consequences, this being a question of fact, not of values ; but surely it is proper also to analyse these consequences and determine which elements in them are valuable and which are not. That is where moral theory can help, and where everybody ought to a certain extent to be a moral theorist ; for we must not, as we are apt to do, confine ourselves to one or two superficial aspects, but ought to take

not be divided into any different stages, or reduced to the mere application of any universal rules, and is, therefore, only another name for a non-inferential cognition. For inference always consists of a series of non-inferential cognitions, each of these being the perception that one stage in the inference follows from the preceding stage. Therefore, an inference which cannot be reduced to more than one such stage is the same as a non-inferential cognition. Both terms stand for the simple perception that, *e.g.*, B follows from A, and the need for a distinction only arises when we are obliged to introduce a third term to connect the two.

[1] *i.e.*, in cases where these different goods do not constitute a close organic unity and can easily be evaluated separately and compared, (provided also the act is of such a kind that its rightness or wrongness can be treated as dependent on certain definite predictable consequences, as is not the case with, *e.g.*, acts involving deceit or breach of faith).

into consideration all the important values that an act is liable to produce or impair. We have not always time to do this, but where we have time to decide and are really in doubt, we surely ought to have recourse to such reflections as these. For example, in deciding the punishment of an offender we ought not to rest content with an immediate " intuition " as to his " deserts," not preceded by a consideration of the different ways in which the punishment is likely to do good or harm to him and to society, yet it is to be feared that in history the first method of decision has been even more common than the second, though that would not be true now-adays, it is to be hoped. The " intuition " should come after and not before the survey of the various goods produced, and one of the chief reasons why " intuitionism " in the ordinary sense has been stigmatised as unphilosophical is because it forgets this.

There is a vast difference between saying that we decide by " intuition " and that we decide by arbitrary imagination. A true cognition that is non-inferential is just as little arbi-trary and as much expressive of the real nature of the object cognised as any other cognition. The admission of know-ledge by " intuition " does not lend the slightest countenance to the view that we make an act right by thinking it right. It is important to mention this because there is a real practical danger that people who hold a more or less " intuitionist " view of ethics will be content to accept a passing fancy at the first moment instead of taking pains to make as sure as possible that their supposed intuition is a genuine and true one. They cannot *prove* it to be right ; but if they look at it carefully and honestly they are at least more likely to see if it is wrong, especially if they have availed themselves to an adequate extent of the help given by inferential thinking. We have no golden rule, no infallible criterion to tell us when we are right ; but we must just do our best with the capacities at our command. To try to form a true judgment about what is right is just as much our duty as it is to do what we have already decided to be right.

I know that even so I shall be charged with gross obscur-antism for having fallen back on " intuition."[1]  But, before

---

[1] I have suggested elsewhere (p. 183) that this " intuition " might possibly be described as an " immediate inference " from the whole situation ; but I see no difference between " immediate inference " and " intuition." When I call it non-inferential it is *mediate* inference that I am excluding and inference according to general principles. This terminology seems sufficiently in accord with usage.

my opponents can force me to plead guilty, they must show a way of proving moral judgments by strict reasoning without introducing a single premiss or conclusion that is not itself inferred from something else according to proved universal principles and rules of logic.    If they can I shall readily abandon my " intuition " ;  but if they cannot they have no right to blame me for admitting the fact frankly.    We do make moral judgments, and we must believe that in many cases they have a very good chance of being approximately true at the very least.    Yet they cannot be justified wholly by inference.    Even if some philosopher of the future should discover a method of reasoning by which we could deduce what is right in each particular case, it would remain true that we have in fact acquired some moral knowledge without using that method and that therefore moral knowledge is derivable otherwise than by reasoning, though it might *also* be derivable by reasoning.    Even those who deny " intuition " most strongly are not so hostile to it when it bears the name of " practical judgment " or " good sense."    They generally admit that you must leave the decision of what is right in particular cases to the judgment of the agent at the time and would pour scorn on any attempt to deduce all particular duties in strict logical form.    Yet what is this but a refusal to rely entirely on inference ?    But all I meant in using the term " intuition " was *knowledge otherwise than by mediate inference or by mere observation*.    This word is, I admit, associated with some very unphilosophical modes of thinking, since nothing is easier than to fancy you have true " intuitions " when you really have not ;  and I shall therefore substitute for it the term " non-inferential cognition," if by so doing I may avoid some scandal.

Some non-inferential cognition is absolutely necessary for all reasoning.    In the first place if we are to infer at all we must perceive the connection between one stage in the argument and the next immediately, for otherwise we should have to interpolate a third stage and so on *ad infinitum*.    This perception cannot be itself an inference.    Secondly all inference presupposes the non-inferential cognition that certain particulars are instances of certain universals ;  but if so why should we not be able to cognise that certain actions are instances of the universal, rightness, and certain experiences of the universal, goodness, without having to prove it wholly by inference ?    Even the hedonistic utilitarian has covertly to admit this except that he substitutes for goodness

" pleasure." We need not commit ourselves to the view that the cognition of goodness and rightness is just the same in principle as the cognition of other universals ; but at least the analogy shows that we need not cavil at its possibility. Thirdly all inference not based merely and entirely on sense-data presupposes non-inferential cognition to help in providing its premises, and this seems to be the case with ethics since " good " and " right " are not properties discoverable by sensation. If we are to admit any knowledge at all, we must accept non-inferential cognition as a fact. Nobody can deny that at least the first two reasons given force us to accept it throughout the field of knowledge and not only in Ethics.

What seems strange about the non-inferential cognition that I have discussed in Ethics is, first, that it comes at the end of an inference, not in the middle nor at the beginning ; but even this point of difference seems to vanish, for after all in any inference there must be a non-inferential cognition that the conclusion follows from the premises, otherwise we have an infinite regress since other premises would be required to supply a connection and so on *ad infinitum.*

There remains this point, however, that the conclusion in Ethics cannot be deduced from universal laws, and this might seem to differentiate it altogether from ordinary reasoning. It is the cognition that an individual act in an individual situation is right or an individual complex whole better than another such whole. We see this from the individual nature of our object of thought without being able to justify it entirely by connections of universals. Yet all other cognition, in so far as it is not purely empirical, is held to depend never on the particular *qua* particular, but only on the universal in the particular. This seems to be radically different from the case of Ethics, where we must say *either* that the premises[1] of our reasoning do not imply the conclusion *or* that the only really adequate premiss is the individual situation in all its individuality and not merely *qua* an instance of a universal. The peculiarity of the cognition would therefore be not that it is immediate (non-inferential), but that, although it marks the conclusion of a reasoning process, it does not, like ordinary reasoning, derive its validity merely from a connection of universals. But this peculiarity is less unique than might seem at first sight, for, as I said above, all reasoning pre-supposes the non-inferential cognition not only that certain

---

[1] *i.e.,* the arguments and data that help us in arriving at, but do not, as we have seen, prove the truth of, our intuition.

universal principles hold but that certain particulars are instances of a certain universal. Why should it be considered more extraordinary that we can see an act to be an instance of rightness, than that we can see something to be an instance of the number, four, or of the species, man? In either case, starting from the individual nature of something we bring it under a universal, and in both cases we may need reasoning to determine its nature before we can see that it falls under the universal in question. A complete parallelism between our ethical cognitions and our cognitions of fact is not to be expected; but I think I have said enough to show that they are not totally disparate. This is a satisfactory conclusion, since it gives us a better chance of forming a coherent theory of knowledge than would otherwise be the case, but even if they had been shown to be quite different in kind this would be no argument against Ethics because their subject-matter is different in kind also.

It must not be supposed, however, that we can learn by this non-inferential cognition what is the right act absolutely, *i.e.*, in view of all the circumstances of the case, but only what is the right act in view of the circumstances known to us. What the circumstances are we must ascertain by observation and causal inference, but we can never do so completely since some of the consequences are indefinitely remote and even these might make a difference. I have been discussing only the genuinely ethical part of the problem, and not the way of arriving at the judgments of fact presupposed in all ethical decisions. If we have made a mistake in this point, no non-inferential cognition of the right will save us. We can know hypothetically that if the facts (including consequences) are like this the action will be right; if the facts are not what we think they are the fault lies with our reasoning as to facts, and neither with our non-inferential cognition as to what is right nor with any specifically ethical reasoning. We first ascertain the nature of the proposed action and its likely consequences as matters of fact, and then we perceive that an act of this sort is right or wrong. This perception may give us truth and yet the act not turn out right in the end, because we were not aware of the full nature of its consequences. For what I have been describing is the cognition that such-and-such an act is right, not that a proposed act is really of such-and-such a nature.[1] The discovery of its

---

[1] The nature of the act cannot be ultimately separated from the nature of at least its intended consequences.

nature is a process the same in kind as the discovery of any truth about a particular physical fact based on observation and causal laws, and is therefore no speciality of ethics. Fortunately what we do not know about the circumstances may often be treated as irrelevant, just as science can recognise that everything is affected by everything else and yet in determining the cause of an event cheerfully take as irrelevant the greater part of the universe. Only there are risks that it may after all turn out relevant and so upset our calculations.

A very similar process to the one described by me occurs in examining, estimating the merits of two rival brands of goods when there are several points both for and against each, appraising the works of poets or painters, or choosing lodgings. To take the instance of examining—unless we proceed by the somewhat childish method of merely counting mistakes, which is quite inadequate when applied to any but the simplest work, we find it quite impossible to *prove* that candidate A deserves 6 or candidate B 3 marks, or even that one is better than the other. If anybody disagrees with us, all we can do is to point out in detail, one by one, the relative merits and defects of A and B, hoping that, when he understands these, he will look on it as we do. But this is no " proof " ; there may well be a number of points where B is right and A wrong, and there are no universal laws by which we can determine the relative importance of these. We cannot prove, *e.g.*, that so much understanding of general principles compensates for so many slight inaccuracies in detail. If our critic says—I agree with you that these are real merits and defects respectively, but I cannot see that on the whole B's defects exceed A's—you cannot disprove that statement. You can certainly argue with him by going through the various points where each candidate is wrong, showing just what kind of misconceptions they presuppose and thus bringing out the relative importance of the knowledge they have succeeded in expressing, but in the last resort you can only achieve a conclusion by a process of balancing one against the other which cannot be wholly determined by any logical or quasi-mathematical canons. The only possible course is to try to take account of all relevant points and then after surveying them go by the total impression ; and this is surely what we ought to do, where there is a difficulty , in cases of action. Each of the alternative courses will have some advantages and some drawbacks, and though we may be quite sure that

the one side outweighs the other we could not give a " proof."
Yet for all this there is plenty of scope for reasoning, as in the
case of the examination, even if we are agreed as to what are
likely to be the consequences in fact.    I can point out new
advantages or drawbacks in these consequences that my critic
had overlooked, appeal to the analogy with other cases where
he would have been likely to decide on our side and to general
principles as to relative values, or analyse the character of the
act proposed by him, *e.g.*, show that it involves " letting down "
somebody who had trusted in us.    All this will not strictly
" prove " our case, since the conclusion depends on an estimate of the relative values of two or more courses, both of
which involve some good and some evil, and therefore on a
balancing of these values against each other, a process which
nobody can justify entirely by logical rules showing how it
follows with necessity or reduce to a mathematical calculus.
But it may make him see the situation in a way which will
induce him to yield his assent.

A similar position constantly arises also in cases of argument on matters of fact (and in metaphysical discussions)
where there is room for opposing opinions and the evidence of
experience is not conclusive.    Both contending views have
some points in their favour and some against, and one can
only form a conclusion rationally by estimating the relative
strength of these.    This fact is commonly disguised because
the advocates of one side generally talk as if their view had
all of the advantages[1] and none of the disadvantages, but it is
nevertheless nowadays almost universally recognised in
theory,[2] although most people still neglect to apply it in
particular cases where they hold strong views of their own on
a subject.    Where the evidence is divided and we have to
decide by balancing it, we are carrying out a mental process
which, though it may be greatly helped by inference, cannot
be completely determined thereby.    This does not mean that
our conclusion is necessarily not justified ; it means that it is
not justified by inference.    It does not mean merely that our
conclusion is proved to be more probable but not certain ; it
means that our very estimate of it as the more probable
cannot always be completely justified by any calculation or

[1] I do not here mean necessarily practical advantages but theoretical
advantages in respect of the evidence on which they are founded.

[2] Even the recognition of it as true in general is a very important
step forward, one of the chief intellectual advances made in recent
times.

strict proof, yet may lay claim to rationality. This seems to be commonly involved in the weighing of evidence, and differs radically from cases where the probability is capable of direct proof (*e.g.*, that a die which had 6 on two sides was more likely to fall with the 6 uppermost than a die which had it only on one side). This weighing of evidence, where no strict proof is forthcoming, seems to me, in some respects at least, very similar to the process by which we compare conflicting values.[1]

On one point, however, I agree with the opponents of " intuition." We must not assume straightway that our ethical judgments are necessarily infallible because they are non-inferential. All I mean by " intuition " or non-inferential cognition is a kind of cognition not based wholly on reasoning, and surely the absence of such a basis can be no guarantee of infallibility but rather the reverse. Prejudices and delusions are not based wholly on reasoning, but it is impossible to argue that therefore they are true. I admit indeed that, where our non-inferential cognitions are wrong, the fault lies in our confused minds, but unfortunately we may suffer from a confusion in our thoughts without knowing it. We cannot distinguish which of our opinions are true merely by psychological observation, and it seems in the most flagrant contradiction with experience to maintain, as Butler did, that given goodwill we can almost always know with certainty what we ought to do. But it does not follow because this non-inferential cognition is uncertain and fallible, that therefore it is worthless ; it is at least the best we have to go on and in simple cases it may give us something which approaches practical certainty. After all, when riding or driving in traffic, men are often bound to stake their very lives on a quick " intuitive " judgment of the situation which they certainly have not time to reduce to explicit reasoning (if they waited to do that in emergencies they probably would not live to tell the tale), and nobody would claim that in this matter their intuitive judgments are infallible.

It is arguable that in all cases the error would have been removed by a better analysis and process of inference, and

---

[1] It is sometimes held that, even where strict proof is available, all the proof does is to put us in a position where we can know the conclusion immediately. But, whether this is so or not, it is certainly not all I mean by insisting on non-inferential cognition in ethics. I mean also that in ethical reasoning our premises do *not* necessarily *imply* our conclusion.

that therefore it is always the inference and not the non-inferential cognition which is at fault.   Whether this is so or not cannot be decided without a discussion of the general theory of knowledge for which the present is hardly the place ; but even if the view is true these two facts remain.   Firstly, there are at least many cases in which we could devise no inference adequate to enable us to have a certain and infallible non-inferential cognition, however much we tried.   Secondly, there is no psychological distinction between those non-inferential cognitions which are preceded by an adequate process of inference and those which are not.   Right and wrong " intuitions " (non-inferential cognitions) may be very different *logically* (as true and false judgments are), but they seem the same *qua* events in the mind.   We cannot observe any difference, and therefore it seems to me better to apply the same name to both and to regard the one as successful, the other as unsuccessful cognitions of their object. Where intuitions do differ is in the conviction of certainty or consciousness of uncertainty which accompanies them, but we cannot say that the former is never present when they are false.   If a sharp line is to be drawn between certain and relatively uncertain cognitions we must put at any rate many (I should say most) of our ethical judgments in the latter class, though any uncertainty is due not to its being really doubtful in itself but to a defect in our mind.   As they stand, at any rate most of our non-inferential cognitions are fallible, even if this fallibility is held to be due to the absence of adequate inference.

But to say there is a risk of error is not to say that our judgments are worthless.   We shall be far less likely to fall into error if we use our faculties to the best of our ability than if we do not.   We cannot be certain of *complete* success, but the only course is to do the best we can ; we shall gain some truth about what is right and good, as much indeed as we are capable of, and our capacities themselves will be developed by our efforts so that we come to gain more and more.   In fact experience shows that it is far easier to decide what is right in most cases than we might expect ; the difficulty is more often moral (unwillingness to do what is right) than intellectual (inability to know what is right), though this must not lead us to the extreme view of Butler that there is practically no chance of genuine error in moral matters and that we always (or almost always) can, if we wish, know our duty with certainty.   We must not neglect the duty of taking pains to find out what is right any more than the duty of doing what we have already decided to be right. Ignorance and stupidity that can be avoided deserve moral censure as well as the deliberate doing of what we know to be wrong, and have perhaps been quite as harmful in history. Nor, in view of the great complication of values involved, can we possibly suppose that the decision what our duty is will always be quite simple and obvious. " Goodwill " by itself cannot achieve miracles.

To sum up, " reasoning " (I am not referring to " reason " in the wider sense) cannot by itself *prove* but may *help* us to see whether an act is right or wrong ; and the most important (I do not say the only) factor in the reasoning would generally seem to be a determination of the consequences likely to be produced and an analysis and survey of the elements of good and evil in these consequences, of their advantages and disadvantages. I do not mean merely that the reasoning makes it probable, not certain (as, *e.g.*, consideration of the barometer, etc., may make it probable, though not certain, that it will rain to-day), and that we just accept the probability. It is not uncertain *in that way* except in so far as it depends on causal reasoning about matters of fact. What I mean is that the process by which we come to see the conclusion cannot be wholly reduced to and justified by either probable or certain inference, but must terminate in a non-inferential cognition, meaning by this not one in which the inference is implicit but one that could not be justified *entirely* by any inference at all.

Is inference then only a help or is it always essential ? Can there be non-inferential cognitions in ethics without any inference ? Clearly there may be no explicit inference set out in a series of steps ; but on the other hand it would be a mistake to regard a non-inferential cognition as ever a mere " flash in the pan " unattached to any thought-process at all. So whether we are to say that inference is always essential or no, must depend on our definition of the term. If we mean by it explicit ratiocination the answer is in the negative ; if we mean by it any thought-process that is more than a mere single cognition we must reply yes to the question. It presupposes at least a process of analysis of the situation which must presumably take some time and may be more or less gradual, and it certainly is affected by our previous thought and experience. The important point to realise is that an " intuition " is not just a quasi-miraculous flash of insight standing by itself but part and culmination of a thought-process. Nor is it necessarily a separate act following an inference. Intuition, or non-inferential cognition, and inference are rather distinguishable but inseparable elements in the same activity.[1] In describing the way we know we have to abstract them from each other, but this no more than any other abstraction of thought necessarily implies their real separation.

All ethical judgments seem to presuppose at any rate these three factors : (a) some empirical knowledge of the particular situation or object ; (b) some more or less incomplete analysis of it ; (c) the previous or simultaneous occurrence in the person judging of some desire or emotion relative to something good. The third presupposition has been emphasised very much by the opponents of " rationalism " in ethics, and it is indeed important to realise that in order to have ethical knowledge we must be more than merely cognitive beings. This does not, however, affect the validity of our ethical judgments but only the possibility of our making them. In passing we may note that the emotion or desire need not necessarily be relative to the specific object of the cognition, e.g., it is true that I could not judge a particular lie wrong (except on authority) without having at some time felt an aversion either to a lie as such or to some bad effects of a kind similar to those which I expect to follow from the lie, but I may do so without feeling aversion to the particular lie in question at the time I think about it.

We can now determine the function of Ethics as a science by means of the above considerations. Inferential thinking on ethical matters, under which I include not only Ethics in the narrower sense, but any kind of argument that is used by the plain man to enable him to decide moral questions, does not itself make the decision as to what is right, but prepares the material for that decision. It does not lead to the conclusion directly itself but submits certain considerations which help the mind in reaching the conclusion. We must not think that it is otiose because it cannot claim absolute power, and in fact people are undoubtedly helped in that way. If they were not, there would be no point in using any argument at

---

[1] This does not mean that non-inferential cognition in ethics *always* presupposes one of the modes of reasoning that I give below. But at least one of them is presupposed in most non-inferential ethical cognitions, though perhaps not in the simplest ones and in those cognitions of a particular thing being good in itself which give us our premises.

all about what is right. For instance all " political arguments " which are of any use. at all would fall in this class as helps in deciding, where we have to judge mainly or entirely by the value of likely consequences and where conflicting values are at stake. They cannot, strictly speaking, *prove* but *may* bring us into a position to see that the set of values realised by a measure is likely to be preferable to those which will be realised if it is amended or if it is not passed. Everybody is a moral theorist in so far as he uses reasoning at all in deciding what is right, everybody must and does know something about Ethics, about what is good and bad, right and wrong ; but it is possible to " get on " in practice without having any conscious recourse to the more generalised forms of the theory that we find in Ethics in the philosophic sense. It would, however, be quite against reason to suppose that this has no effect on the more particularised forms and therefore we cannot deny Ethics some practical influence. The chief puzzle is indeed why it does not have more. But the popular argument that Ethics is useless because it does not enable us to decide what is right in all particular cases is absurd. If it could achieve that end, it would be true not only that ethics was useful but that no other branch of knowledge was so. It does not follow that because ethics cannot decide all practical questions it is useless, any more than it follows that shoemaking is useless because people need other articles of apparel which shoemaking does not provide. One of the reasons why Ethics cannot decide all particular cases is because to do so would involve a knowledge of the likely effect of all actions, *i.e.*, a knowledge of all the special sciences ; but another is that as inferential it must be content with the rôle of submitting points to be considered in deciding, it cannot do the work of deciding itself without the aid of this non-inferential cognition.

But, it may be asked, what is the ethical reasoning of which I speak ? Is not all the reasoning possible a mere determination of matters of fact, *i.e.*, prediction of the consequences of suggested acts, a process which is as little a part of Ethics as Medicine is when it tells us the best way of achieving the end of cure from disease. On the ethical side is there anything at all but an immediate apprehension of what is good or what is right, is not the rest simply causal reasoning from an act to its effects ? And, if that is so, is there any such thing as moral reasoning or moral theory at all ?

In a sense I must admit the truth of this objection.

" Ethical reasoning " is in some degree a misnomer, because it is not the reasoning that is ethical but its subject-matter. The subject-matter of Ethics is values ; but the cogency of any steps in argument in Ethics is determined by their logic and not by their ethical value just as much as arguments on non-ethical subjects. The same thing naturally applies to every other study, *e.g.*, the connection between a premiss and a conclusion in chemistry is not itself chemical. It is not incompatible with the fact that a particular subject must use the kinds of argument which are appropriate to it and not inappropriate ones, *e.g.*, mathematics must not have recourse to empirical generalisations, though these are indispensable in biology. In so far as we reason at all in Ethics we must use arguments which, though they may be specifically different from those in other branches of knowledge, would be accepted equally there *if* they were applicable. Ethics can claim no exemption from the laws of logic. Its premises and its conclusions may be ethical, but the connection between them must be that the one implies the other, which is not itself an ethical relation but a logical one,[1] though it may be based on the perception of ethical qualities. This does not diminish the uniqueness of the subject-matter of Ethics.

But the objection further implies that the only reasoning involved in determining the rightness of an act is causal reasoning as to its likely consequences, a matter which falls within the sphere of the theoretical sciences, and that this leaves nothing for the moralist except to apprehend by an indescribable intuition the rightness or wrongness of an act when he has been told about its consequences. This view is taken by Prof. Prichard :[2] he argues that we cannot infer the right from the good produced and that therefore we must simply rely on an immediate knowledge confined to particular cases and not admitting of any help from inferential thought about values or more general principles of ethics. But surely one may admit that inference cannot do everything in ethical knowledge without holding that it can therefore do nothing whatever. Even if we cannot determine the rightness of an act *entirely* by inference from the different elements of value in its likely consequences, it remains true that we have to

---

[1] By this I only mean that the conclusion must follow from the premises *because* they imply it, not *because* it is ethical that it should. I do not mean that anybody could see the implication from logic alone, if he had no capacity for perceiving the good and the right.

[2] " Is Moral Philosophy Founded on a Mistake," *Mind*, 1912.

consider the consequences *to some extent* at any rate, and we cannot do so in a rational way unless we try not only to calculate them correctly as matters of fact but also to envisage what is good and what is evil in them. Now that is a specifically ethical question. In order to decide what is right we need to determine not only what events are in fact likely to happen, but also to estimate the value (or the reverse) of these events. For it is only because these consequences are good or evil and not because they follow in fact that a knowledge of them is needed to decide whether an act is right or wrong. Their value is not a sum of the values of their constituent parts, but we still cannot hope to estimate it successfully without considering the value of these different elements that make it up ; and this requires analysis, not merely unreflective apprehension. Thus the main part of my work in this book has been to analyse the different kinds of good producible by punishment (and reward). This analysis cannot be divorced from a knowledge of facts, but must go hand in hand with it ; yet in very many cases the facts are clear, but certain of the values (or " disvalues ") in them are overlooked or neglected because they are not obvious without careful study. Here Ethics as a science helps us. Even if we cannot decide what is right merely by having recourse to it, this analysis still remains useful for our decisions.

We must not, however, hold that ethical thought is entirely confined to the method of analysing the value of the consequences. We certainly pursue *various* methods in our ordinary thought about moral questions : we appeal sometimes to the consequences, sometimes to the character of the act proposed apart from its consequences, sometimes we argue by analogy with situations where we should be certain what it was right to do, sometimes we ask which of the alternative acts is nearest to a given ideal of conduct, or which is most in accord with the spirit of an ideal man,[1] sometimes we simply have recourse to general laws. These methods are not all equally important or ultimate, but in practical life they are all helpful sometimes ; and it seems important for Ethics at least to consider the ways in which we actually reason in such matters. If these methods do all help us in deciding what is right, some arguments of each kind must have at any rate a

[1] To use this method we must have some prior ethical conceptions, but this does not mean that it involves a vicious circle any more than algebra involves a vicious circle because it presupposes arithmetic. It would if used to deduce *all* ethical judgments, but not otherwise.

certain limited validity and are therefore entitled to consideration by philosophic Ethics. An account of them, besides bringing " Ethics " more into touch with our real ethical thinking, should at any rate remove the fear that there is no such thing as ethical thinking.

Further, if we analyse merely the good and evil in the consequences we are neglecting the fact that an action itself may be intrinsically good or evil, and not only its consequences.[1] When we consider some possible acts we seem at once to see that they are wrong without any calculation of their consequences, perhaps because their intrinsic evil is immediately perceived to be so great as to outweigh any good that they might conceivably do,[2] perhaps because we in these cases perceive the wrongness of the act directly without any reference to the good or bad produced. A man who before deciding to miss any particular opportunity of cheating always calculated carefully whether the harm to his victim would outweigh his own gain, and whether the consequences to everybody would be on the whole good or bad would hardly give the impression of being highly moral, yet if the method of consequences were the only one he would deserve praise and the man who shrinks from the dishonest act without having calculated the particular consequences blame, since he would not in that case have taken the one step necessary if he was to know whether his abstention was justified. *Even if* it be the case that the bad consequences are the only reason why we ought not to cheat, at any rate *we can see* the wrongness of cheating someone in particular instances *without* calculating these consequences. Further, even if the rightness of an act does always depend solely on the good produced—and this has not been proved—in the good produced must surely be included any intrinsic value belonging to the act itself over and above the value of the consequences. Not that the act and its consequences can be separated completely, but they can be separated sufficiently to make the distinction an important relative one. It is the act and its consequences *taken together* that we have to consider, but sometimes we look at it rather from the side of the act itself in its intrinsic character, sometimes rather from the side of the consequences.

---

[1] This is recognised by Dr. Rashdall in his *Theory of Good and Evil,* so the above remark must not be taken as a charge against him.

[2] For my reply to the objection that this involves a vicious circle *v.* p. 171.

Secondly, the prediction, analysis and quantitative estimate of the particular consequences of an act are liable to be very difficult, and therefore in some cases we are more likely to make correct decisions if we have recourse to different methods.   Very often we know that the tendency of a certain kind of act is in general for the bad without being able to specify the particular evil consequences which any specimen of those acts is likely to produce, so that a universal law based on this general tendency may be a better guide than a calculation of the consequences in each particular instance.   This is the case with many lies and acts involving unfairness or deceit which *appear* to be " expedient " but are felt by us at once not to be right.   So *even if* an act is only made right by the good produced and we have to fall back on that as the ultimate justification, there are a number of proximate methods which are in certain cases more helpful.   The fact that we can never know whether very remote effects may not be sufficiently important to make a considerable difference to our reckoning greatly increases the uncertainty of the method of calculating consequences, and is a strong argument in favour of supplementing or replacing it by others.

Of these other methods I shall proceed to mention as many as occur to me.   In some cases we may fall back on a general law established both by a consideration of the consequences *usually* produced by a certain kind of act and a non-inferential cognition that the act taken in itself is bad,[1] *e.g.*, the prohibition to tell lies.   This does not necessarily imply that the general law holds under *all* circumstances, but only that the *present* circumstances are clearly not of such an exceptional nature as to make it worth while discussing whether they justify a breach of the law.   Or we may just hold that, though the case is doubtful, we are less likely to go wrong if we follow the general law.   It is not correct, however, to say that in these cases we ought to take no account of the particular consequences at all.   We could hardly pronounce a lie wrong if it were certain that it was the only possible means of averting the total destruction or permanent moral degradation of a large number of individuals, and that it would really produce no counter-balancing evil consequences ; and we therefore need at any rate the negative knowledge that there is no reason to suppose this to be the case.   Some knowledge of (or opinion about) the consequences of avoiding

---

[1] " Bad " does not necessarily mean *always* wrong, because it might conceivably be right sometimes to choose it as the lesser of two evils.

the lie is always presupposed, we know or assume at any rate that they are not likely to be harmful in such an overwhelming degree.   We do not formulate and are not explicitly conscious of this, but that is only because it is so obvious that the very suggestion of the possibility seems ridiculous, and unless we took it for granted our judgment that the lie is wrong could hardly be maintained.   I may justifiably think a lie wrong though the consequences of avoiding it seem harmful, I may even be right in saying that a situation could never arise in which the consequences of this particular lie or one like it would be so desirable as to justify me in telling it ; but that is because I do not anticipate that a situation ever could in fact arise in which the consequences of truthfulness surpassed a certain degree of evil.   The lie would not be wrong if it really were the only means of averting the total destruction of the human race ; but then I am aware that according to the laws of physical nature and human life such momentous consequences can hardly follow from my action in this matter.

I further know that *in general* the consequences of lies are bad apart from the intrinsic evil of untruthfulness itself, and this is undoubtedly one of the reasons which makes it our duty to tell the truth, though not the only one.

Although we are morally bound to consider consequences, we are not bound to consider them more than is necessary for determining what is right or wrong ;  and the two items of knowledge just mentioned, limited as they are, generally provide all that is needed to help us in our cognition that the act is wrong.   Not that men always explicitly formulate this knowledge in deciding not to lie, but they justifiably take it for granted, just as in deciding what to do when a motor-car approaches we justifiably take for granted without explicit formulation that the impact on us of a heavy body advancing at a great speed is liable to be physiologically injurious and that it is undesirable that our body should be injured.   But, though it needs to be supplemented by at least some negative knowledge or opinion of the consequences, it remains true that by far the most important factor in determining us not to lie ought to be the intrinsic evil of untruthfulness.   We are in danger of forgetting this if we pay too much attention to the consequences.

Even here, however, the method is twofold.   On the one hand the wrongness (or rightness) of a given act may be simply deduced from a general rule.   This is an ordinary process of reasoning and is no more entitled to be called non-inferential than is any syllogism in Barbara. It is also legitimate within certain limits, for sometimes we are justified in taking it for granted that a general rule holds or at any rate that we are more likely to be right if we follow it than if we decide each particular case afresh on its merits. I did not say that all cognition of what was right was non-inferential, only that some was. In these cases, however, the general rule itself must be based on some non-inferential cognition as to the rightness or wrongness of acts, so it is no real exception. But such general laws must not be regarded as premises from which to deduce *all* particular duties, otherwise we are again in the untenable position of Kant. We must not think of them as the primary factor, for in Ethics at any rate we see the particular before the general. They seem to bear the character rather of generalisations from what we already know to be right in particular. But that does not destroy their utility. For in the first place they absolve us from the necessity of working the whole problem out again in each particular case. The saving of time thus effected is of more ethical importance than would seem at first sight, for, as we are always acting in some way or other, we could not decide altogether afresh about each particular case of action without taking up our whole time in deciding and leaving none for doing. Everybody acts mainly on general rules (or, as they are often called, habits), framed in the course of his life, thus he does not need to decide afresh every minute whether he should continue to carry on his professional work or to obey each particular command of his employer ; but this does not eliminate the necessity of being ready to perceive exceptions and act accordingly. There is nothing inconsistent in a man following the general rule of obeying his employers and yet recognising in some exceptional circumstances that a certain command of theirs ought not to be obeyed.

Secondly, general rules are useful because it is often far more difficult to know whether the consequences of a particular act are good or bad than it is to know whether the consequences of similar acts are good or bad on the average ; in these cases we may be less likely to go wrong if we trust to the rule which expresses the average, especially where we are biased by desire in favour of making an exception or where an adequate judgment of the consequences is not possible without more " expert " knowledge than we possess. Finally, much as I dislike an excessive insistence on authority in moral matters, I am bound to admit that it is sometimes a duty to accept a general law on authority even though one is not able to see its justification, *e.g.*, a man who saw no wrong in polygamy himself would not, therefore, be justified in committing it. We must take into account the moral judgment and the moral experience of the race embodied in the general rules of ethics as well as the importance, where current practice is wrong, of intelligent reform. When we are to obey authority, and when not, cannot be decided in advance, but must be left like all particular ethical problems to the judgment of the individual at the time, helped but not entirely determined by general considerations.

We may, however, see an act to be wrong " immediately " both without detailed consideration of consequences and without appealing to a general rule. This applies to most of the acts belonging to the class commonly known as " dishonourable," especially acts involving deceit or treachery. Any man with a tolerably developed capacity for moral knowledge can see these acts to be wrong without calculating the consequences at all. In such cases our knowledge as to what is right or wrong seems *prima facie* quite independent of the good or evil produced, and therefore they form the stronghold of a Kantian or of an intuitionist theory of ethics. We must remember, however, that they constitute only a small minority of moral decisions. Further, though it is possible to maintain that in these cases the wrongness of the act does not depend on any evil produced, it is equally possible to give a different explanation. Certainly it does not depend entirely on any evil consequences, but if we include under the evil produced the evil in the act itself we may say that we see the act to be so intrinsically evil as to outweigh any good that we have the least reason to suppose could be done by the consequences ; but then, though we have not examined the consequences, we know or assume that they are not likely to involve an extraordinarily great amount of evil, *e.g.*, I pronounce it wrong to cheat a man of 10s., knowing or assuming that my abstention from cheating will not produce a great catastrophe like another war. If I did not assume this, the case would at once be totally altered. It is also true that it would be positively undesirable in these simple cases to reason about the particular consequences at length, because they are not the chief factor in deciding here and therefore it would give them an undue importance and obscure the issue, especially as they are difficult to determine and prediction is uncertain at the best.  Besides it may tempt a man to examine them not with a view honestly to deciding what is right but with a view to finding excuses for what is wrong.  Added to this is the fact that the evil of, *e.g.*, a lie is certain, while any good in its consequences that may out-balance the evil is uncertain, a consideration which must be applied, *mutatis mutandis*, to other questions.

In some cases preliminary reasoning may be required before we perceive the wrongness of the act, *e.g.*, it may take some " argument " before a man sees that a certain act would involve disloyalty to somebody who trusted him, yet once he has seen this he may realise at once that the act is wrong without any consideration of its consequences.  This is not merely applying a general law, because there are cases where " disloyalty " may be right as the lesser evil, (*e.g.*, not keeping a promise to help a friend where it cannot be done without grave injury to somebody else), but is a non-inferential cognition that *this particular* " disloyalty " is wrong.

These considerations have a special importance for the problem of punishment.  We know that unfair[1] punishments in general are likely to produce bad results, we know that deliberately to inflict such a punishment is intrinsically evil and that we are justified in accepting a general rule which prohibits such punishment without considering the exact consequences in each particular case.  Yet we cannot say that it is *never* justifiable to inflict unfair punishments, *e.g.*, make a whole class stop in because some of them have misbehaved, or punish one offence more than another equally serious for reasons of deterrence, so we must—alas !—admit some exceptions.  Where the question is whether to make an exception to the rule or not we have to balance other consequences against the intrinsic evil of unfairness and the further bad effects that the mere fact of unfairness is likely to bring in its train (*e.g.*, the embitterment of the men who are punished too severely).  If we do so honestly, remembering the uncertainty that unfairness will really produce the result which we wish and looking for other means of securing a desired result, it will very rarely happen that we have to make use of punishments which offend against fairness ; but we have no right to convert " rarely " into " never," for fairness, important as it is, is not the only thing to be considered.  But to decide whether a punishment is fair we have to consider not primarily its effects but the action for which it

.[1] " Fair " is to be taken in the sense defined on pp. 90-91, *v*. also pp. 104-7.

is inflicted, *i.e.*, we have to go by a method different from that of consequences. Similarly in deciding whether I ought to pay A some money, I may have to consider prior obligations rather than consequences. Sometimes the decision is simple, as when there is a definite debt ; sometimes it may be the subject of a more complicated argument, as when a man is in doubt which of two relatives has a stronger " claim " on him.

But let us pass on to other methods of determining what is right (including under this term both what is one's " duty " and what goes merely under the name of " prudent," provided the latter is not actually wrong).[1] In some cases no doubt the rational way to decide is by estimating degrees of pleasure, *e.g.*, in choosing an amusement or in finding how " to make things most comfortable " for somebody else. This method is justified because *sometimes* pleasure seems to be either the only value considerably affected by a choice, or a rough criterion of the degree in which other values are realised. For instance, the value of study (or even sport) is not merely hedonistic, but a man may be justified in choosing to study the subject which gives him most pleasure, not only because his pleasure is an important good but because the other values attained in the pursuit of it are likely to be greater than if he chooses a subject, otherwise somewhat more valuable, which gives him considerably less pleasure.

Or it may be simpler to act on our desires,[2] provided we are clear that there is no important factor leading in the other direction. It is a commonplace that in choosing a friend or a profession at least one of the chief things to consider is one's own desires, not because nothing else matters, but because other values are likely to be best furthered in these particular cases if we act in accordance with our desires. Often we must act not on our actual desires but on the desire we predict we

---

[1] All the methods given below, with the possible exception of the second, may be used to answer questions of duty ; some may be also used to answer questions of " prudence." It is, however, difficult to separate the two kinds of questions, at least as far as methods of decision go ; both turn on the realisation of values. " Prudence " consists in realising pleasure or other values for oneself ; but it is impossible to do this without indirectly affecting others, which suggests that all questions of prudence are also moral questions, although there may still be a vast difference between prudent acts and moral acts.

[2] It may be held that where we are justified in simply acting on our desires there is no *moral* question at stake, but at any rate it is a question of deciding which of various actions is preferable, *i.e.*, a question of right and wrong, though, it may be said, not of moral or immoral.

should feel at the time, *e.g.*, though I may at the present moment desire to have a week's holiday next month more than I desire to have a fortnight's holiday next year, I realise that I shall desire the second holiday more when the time comes. But the reason for following our desires is only that it will produce more good for ourselves and others, or rather that it seems likely to do so.

Or again we may decide on the action which we think will best satisfy our desires (or even most people's desires) in the end.

Or we may act on the desire that we think we should feel strongest if we were better men. This presupposes prior ethical conceptions, but granting these (as we must do in any case) it may be a more useful method in certain contingencies than the method of analysing the consequences would be.

Sometimes we regard one end as paramount, assuming or having previously decided that it is good, and just discover the best means to the attainment of it, a procedure which is perfectly justifiable *as long as* the means are not likely seriously to affect other ends, *e.g.*, in deciding what is the best medicine to give a patient a doctor can generally assume that whether he gives one medicine or another will not seriously affect other ends than the health of the patient and through that those values dependent thereon.

Sometimes again an action would produce or render likely some consequence which seems so obviously evil in a high degree that we at once realise that it outweighs any good likely to be produced by the action, *e.g.*, where life is endangered.

Sometimes the main consideration that influences us may be analogy with certain actions about which we have already made a decision, *e.g.*, a man may not realise the dishonourable character of an act which he desires to do till it is pointed out to him that it is nearly as bad as stealing, or that it is just like the act which he condemned so strongly when done by Mr. X.

In other cases a man simply takes it for granted that an action is bad because it excites in him an emotion (or, as it is loosely called, " feeling ") of a peculiar kind ;[1] and even this may be sometimes justified on the ground that, although the

---

[1] *i.e.*, disgust, contempt, shame, etc. We must not confuse this with the method of deciding by reference to our desires. What matters here is the specific character (qualitative) of the emotion, not the intensity with which it is felt.

emotion does not necessarily correspond to real wrongness, many men are far less likely to be wrong in many kinds of decision if they trust to their " feelings " than if they try to reason, because the former faculty is much better developed in them than the latter. Thus the " moral sense " and " feeling " theories have a certain partial justification. They have more justification still if by " feeling " (or " moral sense ") is meant " non-inferential cognition," as is often the case, but then they are guilty of a confusion between this and emotion.[1]

Or we may decide according to the motive we take to be highest (Martineau's theory) ; or we may choose to do the act which would, if done by somebody else, be taken as giving an indication of the most praiseworthy spirit. This again presupposes prior ethical conceptions, but involves genuine inference from those conceptions.

Again there is the method commonly inculcated of deciding " by looking at it from the other man's point of view." The advantages of this are (a) that it counteracts our individual bias and helps us to be impartial, (b) that the good and evil in the consequences for the man who is affected most closely by our action is one of the chief data in determining what we ought to do.

In other cases and for other people it may be best just to ask which of the acts proposed would be more compatible with the character of an ideal man, of which we already have some conception, or even with what we could imagine a perfect God to will.

Or we may ask, like T. H. Green, which alternative will make more in the direction of an ideal society. The drawback of this method is that it is not always the case that conduct which is more *like* the ideal will, therefore, be better, because the actions which suit an ideal environment will not necessarily suit an unideal one like the present, and if it is meant only that we should do the things which tend most to produce (cause) an ideal society, we can only decide which acts these are by asking which acts have the best proximate effects ; but within limits the method is exceedingly useful.

Sometimes we ought to have recourse to Kant's method and consider what would happen if everybody acted in the way proposed. This will work in some cases where a calculation of the consequences of the act would lead us definitely astray. For instance, the payment of taxes by any particular

[1] *v.* below, p. 215.

individual is likely to cause him more annoyance and loss than it causes the community pleasure and gain, because the money he contributes makes an appreciable difference to himself, while it does not to the community as a whole, therefore the State in enforcing payment commits an act which, taken by itself, does more harm than good. Yet the State is justified because, if it exempted the man on these grounds, the only consistent course would be to exempt everybody except perhaps a few millionaires, and the results would be evil in the extreme.[1] Here Kant's law—Act as if the maxim of thy act were to become by thy will law universal —supplies a truth which is in danger of being overlooked by a morality based on consequences.

This point is of some special importance in relation to punishment (and reward). There may be cases where the pardon of a particular man would in itself do more good than harm, and yet he ought not to be pardoned, simply because, if punishment were remitted in all similar cases or all cases where there was an equal justification, the effects would be very bad indeed. Someone might say, " Why punish this man ? He seems to have repented, and it is very doubtful whether punishment will do more good than harm in the way of reforming him. There is its deterrent effect to consider, too, I admit ; but then whether one crime more or less is punished will make little difference to the general deterrent effect of punishment or its other moral effects on the community. Why make the man incur the evil of suffering where it is likely to do him harm, if anything, rather than good and will do no appreciable good to anybody else ? " The answer is that if we let him off in this case we shall have equal justification for letting off the delinquent in all cases where this could be said, and if that were done the harmful effects might be very obvious indeed. If it is right to act like this with A, it must be right to act like this wherever there is equal justification, and if we act like this wherever there is equal justification we shall do much more harm than good, therefore it cannot be right to act like this with A. That is the form of the argument. It does not apply, however, where there is a *special* justification for pardoning A which would not equally justify the pardon of many others. Similar considerations apply, *e.g.*, to the reward for the sake of expediency of those who do not deserve it.

We also may have recourse to the method of the coherence

[1] This principle is admitted even by Bentham.

theory. We may frame the question whether a proposed act is capable of forming part of a truly coherent plan of life. But we should distinguish between three senses of " coherence " as applied in Ethics. In the first place it may stand for bare logical consistency, or non-contradiction, in which case the theory can put forward no claim to be applicable in all instances though useful in some. Or, secondly, the word may signify a deeper kind of harmony, just as in metaphysics the theory that reality is a coherent system means a great deal more than that it includes nothing which is at the same time both X and not—X. But again by this harmony may be meant either a specifically ethical harmony or a logical system. In the latter case the criterion will be merely the possibility of ordering our moral judgments in such a way that they depend on each other reciprocally and are seen to be expressions of the same general principles running through our whole life. This is very valuable if we have already decided that the principles are right, and, even in cases of doubt, we may derive additional assurance if different moral judgments confirm each other in this way ; but such a test could only be completely conclusive if it were possible to *prove* all moral judgments, which it is not. We may further note that so far no specifically ethical element has been introduced into the method at all. But coherence may be understood in a deeper sense as signifying not only a logical system but a truly ethical harmony, as meaning that a right action is an action which furthers that harmony between different tendencies in the soul which we call peace of mind and that harmony between different human beings which we call love. It is to be regretted that both advocates and opponents of the theory generally fail to distinguish these different senses of " coherence." But it remains true that the doctrine both describes at least a very important aspect of rightness and supplies two of the most important tests to help us in determining whether an act is right. We are helped (1) by considering whether a proposed act is logically consistent either with other ethical principles or with what we have already adopted as the settled policy of our life ;[1] (2) by asking whether it is such as to make for a genuine harmony both within the soul and without. Any objection that may be made to the view in either sense as a universal principle does not prevent it from being applicable in *some* cases, though

[1] Naturally this policy itself may be wrong, but we obviously are not required to reconsider it every time we decide a fresh case.

it must be remembered that we require non-inferential cognition to see when this harmony is achieved. We can always have recourse to another method where it is very doubtful which of two states is more of a harmony or whether we ought to sacrifice a present imperfect harmony for one that is problematical but nearer perfection. *To prove* what particular acts are right the coherence theory wisely does not even claim to attempt, *unless* we (as Bosanquet apparently does) understand proof so widely as to include the same non-inferential cognition of which I have spoken at length above. This cognition itself may, however, be interpreted as the perception of a kind of (more than logical) coherence between the act and the general situation as a whole, and this view of it is, as we shall see below,[1] essential to an adequate moral philosophy.

However in ethical decisions we are not usually presented with a few " cut-and-dried " alternatives, so here Aristotle's doctrine of the Mean comes in. Whether ultimately true or not, the doctrine does not furnish a method that can help us much in cases where the choice is between doing and not doing some definite act, *e.g.*, lying to save a friend ; and its chief application will naturally be where excess and defect are susceptible of quantitative expression. Here we may decide by reasoning like this : " 8 hours is too long, 4 hours is too short, 7 hours is still too long, 5 hours too short. What about 6 hours then ? Yes, 6 hours seems right."[2] But definite numerical treatment is not necessary for the application of the method ; we in fact very often decide our behaviour mainly by trying to avoid both excess and defect, keeping both dangers at once clearly in view. Whether interpreted in the narrower or the wider sense, the method of " the Mean " is very important.

All the above methods are actually employed and capable of providing valid arguments. I have naturally only discussed what we *decide* to be right, not what we will to do in fact, or do simply out of habit, tradition or desire ; and I have also excluded the cases in which ethical decisions are influenced by religious or metaphysical beliefs. But it is clear that even in genuinely ethical decisions alone the modes of arriving at a conclusion are very manifold. The most important method remains, I think, analysis of the value of

[1] *v.* p. 217.
[2] *Cf.* Ross, *Commentary on Aristotle*, p. 196.

consequences,[1] but we have seen that it is far from being the only one. All of the methods given are used and are of help ; they ought, therefore, to be studied by Ethics as having at least limited validity.

We need not deny that men's ethical beliefs are in the main rather derived from their social environment than produced by their own reflection ; but to state this fact cannot possibly be an answer to the question how they are justified. It is this problem that we are facing now, and the Hegelian philosophers' talk about the dependence of our beliefs on society cannot possibly tell us which beliefs inculcated by society are right and which wrong. Further even the most unreflective person has to perform genuine moral thinking, at least in particular cases, for, as the same philosophers themselves insist, we cannot settle particular cases beforehand by any general rules or standards, however much these may *help* in deciding. Nor must we neglect the duty of at least trying to see for ourselves the truth of the moral beliefs handed down to us and, if we can, improving on them. That most moral judgments are the result merely of habit and tradition may possibly be a fact but cannot possibly be an ideal. Our morality is the fruit of education, but this education has failed unless it enables us to see for ourselves why the acts which it teaches to be wrong are wrong, and if we see this we shall be able to apply the knowledge in fresh cases. I do not mean that everybody is expected to develop a fresh system of ethics for himself, but that any man must be capable of real moral thinking in particular cases if his life is to be satisfactory, though he need not necessarily be able to formulate this thinking even to himself. For two reasons tradition is not enough. In the first place it is not adequate to meet new cases, and no two cases are exactly alike ; and secondly a man who merely does right acts without realising their rightness himself is not really moral, and to realise their rightness he must do some moral thinking on his own account and not merely accept what tradition tells him.

Which of the methods given should be applied varies according to the circumstances, I doubt whether a single one of them is suitable under all circumstances, but it varies also according to the individual judging. For, although I should firmly maintain that an act is not made right merely

---

[1] In emphasising the importance of consequences I do not mean that the morality of an act is determined by its *actual* consequences.

by being thought so, it remains true that there are alternative methods of coming to learn that the same act is right, and one may suit one man better than it suits another.[1]  A man with a " Kantian " frame of mind will be most helped by an appeal to universal laws, a more imaginative and less purely rational type by a picture of an ideal man, a " practical " type by a consideration of consequences and so on, though the morality of all these will no doubt suffer if they confine themselves entirely to the one mode of thinking most natural to themselves.  But they are all legitimate methods *in their proper place*, though some are no doubt capable of more extended application than others.  Some would give a completely wrong result if applied to any except a very limited class of actions, *e.g.*, the method of deciding by one's own desires ; others might claim almost universal applicability but are liable to become very obscure and require to be supplemented by simpler methods.

This sketch shows at any rate that there is plenty of scope left for moral reasoning.  It also has the advantage of bringing Ethics a good deal more into touch with the ways in which we *actually do reason*.  The types of argument I have given are clearly all valid in some degree—everybody is influenced by them—and further they surely are capable of scientific treatment, in the best and widest sense of that much abused adjective.  It is a sadly neglected task of Ethics to fix the scope of all these methods and determine more closely their logical nature, an enterprise of which moralists have commonly lost sight in their eagerness to arrive at ultimate questions about the nature of the good and the right.  A " logic " of Ethics is badly needed ; such a work might both have some influence on those of our practical decisions which allow considerable time for deliberation and help towards the construction of a system of Moral Philosophy.  For I did not say that there was no " logic " of Ethics ; I said that it could not decide everything.  Ethics as a science must remember two things if it is to avoid the errors of the past : (1) it must not claim to effect the decision itself, but only to submit considerations which will *help* us in deciding ; (2) it must remember that the methods of ethical thought are manifold.  In the past theories of Ethics have generally either dismissed as unanswerable the question what we

---

[1] This does not mean that their acts of non-inferential cognition differ, only that the men vary in the modes of approach they find the easiest to them.

ought to do in particular cases, or professed that all particular acts could be proved right or wrong by applying *one* of these criteria. But there is a mean between claiming omnipotence and denying any power at all ; and if Ethics as a science recognises this and is content to advise rather than dictate to our practical judgment, its prestige and influence may be revived and again reach their rightful dimensions. All the methods suggested by moral philosophers in the past find their place in a view like this—they are helps in deciding, they have a certain part to play, but none of them must claim either to decide what is right completely by inference or to supersede all other helps and become the only one.

We need not suggest that Ethics as a science should revolutionise established moral codes ; to it belongs the humbler but still valuable task of putting us into a better position gradually to amend them where faulty and helping us to decide rightly on the open questions which still perplex. The task requires great patience and long investigation, we have no right to suppose that ethical, any more than scientific, discoveries can be made in a day. Nor must we underrate the extent to which some of the more difficult ethical decisions are matters of guesswork, though this is due, mainly at least, to the difficulty of predicting consequences. We are often driven to grope in the dark ; but this does not exempt us from the duty of at any rate groping as rationally as we can. For this we need all the helps that ethical reasoning can give, and the fact that we are unable to reach certainty by means of it is no ground for rejecting contemptuously the assistance which it can still give us. After all it remains true that in general we find less difficulty in deciding what is right than in doing it when we have decided ; in this way we prove *ambulando* that the problem of ethical knowledge is at least partially soluble by us.

Which of the methods we select to help us is in practice left to our judgment, almost unaided by general principles, but there is no reason why Ethics should not be able to advise us as to which is in a given case most useful. It is a most important (though not the only) function of Ethics to fix the scope and analyse the logic of each method ; and it is a function that has been grossly neglected in the past. I do not suppose that Ethics as a science can always decide by inference what method should be applied and when the results that method suggests are valid ; but surely it can give us some suggestions. (That it can *prove* what is right in all cases

I have denied *ad nauseam*, but I should be prepared to assert equally *ad nauseam* that it can help in the matter).

What I have said does not necessarily exclude in advance the logical possibility of ultimately synthesizing all these methods into one ; but if that is to come at all it must come after and not before their examination as separate, though related, and of this hardly anything has been done.   For most philosophers have just examined one or two of them as though they were the only ones.   Nor again does my statement that we cannot prove the rightness of particular acts exclude the possibility that it is ultimately provable in a way which would give a larger part to inference than I have been able to admit, but it is impossible to discuss what future philosophers or what minds of a superhuman type might do in the matter.   I take my stand on the fact that at present we do know something about what acts are right without being able to give this proof.   By all means do as much as you can by inference, but you must not pretend that you are doing more than you really are.   If the scope of inference in ethics can be extended, the best way to do it is by developing a science of the inference we now practise.

I have not overlooked the fact that, since practical ethics is a matter not only of ends but of means, the task cannot be fulfilled without the close co-operation of other sciences which tell us by ordinary causal reasoning the consequences that our acts are likely to have.   It is the business of Ethics as a specific branch of knowledge not to predict these consequences and supply these data as to facts, but to say what use is to be made of the information when supplied by other sciences, how it bears on the rightness or wrongness of an act.   In the business of ordinary life prediction sufficient for the purpose in question generally does not require the special knowledge of a science as to facts ; but where it does Ethics must certainly call in the help of that science before pronouncing on particular cases.   That is why it is not possible for me to be more directly " practical " in my theory of punishment and reward ;  this book could not be " directly practical " in such a subject without including several other sciences besides Ethics in itself, but part of the conditions necessary for any rational decision in the matter are still provided by Ethics. In this capacity it deserves study as much as any science which helps us practically by supplying facts.   Both knowledge of facts without knowledge of values and knowledge of values without knowledge of facts are blind and will produce evil ; but in complicated social questions there must be specialisation. One man may investigate the question from the point of view of Ethics as a science, another from the point of view of some other branch of knowledge, either not indeed ignoring but refraining from deciding on the questions of the other. Their joint contribution is necessary for reform ; but the work may be divided.

To return, most of the methods I have mentioned carry their incompleteness on their face : thus the appeal to pleasure only introduces *one* particular kind of value ; the appeal to consequences ignores the value of the act *per se* ; other methods ignore the importance of consequences ; some patently presuppose prior ethical knowledge and are only means of clarifying it in our mind. Yet, despite that, they are all of use on occasion. Pleasure is not the only good, but it may be the only point to consider in *some* cases, because it happens in these cases that none of the other goods are known to be seriously affected, or because we may assume that the pleasure is roughly in proportion to the degree in which these other goods are promoted. The method of appealing to desire may be used in similar cases and for similar reasons, although as a universal criterion it would be quite inadmissible. Again there are cases where it is right to think of nothing but the consequences. This is true of those acts which fall under the heading of " prudence," and of most of those which would be described primarily as " benevolent." In other cases, as with lies or " unjust acts " in general, we do and perhaps ought to reject a course as wrong rather on account of its intrinsic evil than on account of its consequences to humanity.

Most of the other methods are debarred from any claim to sole authority by the fact that they obviously presuppose prior ethical knowledge if they are to be applied at all. We cannot make it an ultimate criterion of rightness that an act conforms to a law which may satisfactorily be universalised, because we can only decide whether it may be universalised by seeing whether the consequent state of the world would be good or bad ; nor can we decide entirely by the test of non-contradiction, since wrong actions may be consistent among themselves. Appeals to analogy with other actions known to be right, or to the ideal man or society, or to " the right spirit in which to act " still more obviously presuppose prior ethical knowledge. Nor can it be a sufficient answer to say, " Find the Mean," both because some actions are not susceptible of this quantitative treatment, and because, as Aristotle would no doubt admit at once, the mean must be fixed by reference to the likely consequences as well as to the intrinsic character of the act. But this does not in any way impair the validity and value of any of the methods when applied in a limited sphere. The criticisms I have just given are quite obviously suited to show that none of them can claim to be the only method, not that any of them are invalid.

If I am now asked the old question whether ethical judgments are the work of reason or feeling, I can only reply that these terms are ambiguous and my answer must vary according to the sense in which they are used. If by reason is meant explicit reasoning and by feeling a kind of non-inferential, though more or less confused, cognition, all ethical conclusions certainly neither are nor ought to be the work of " reason." As I have said, in Ethics we cannot *prove* much. On the other hand, if reason and feeling are used in the more correct sense in which they stand for the whole cognitive and the whole sensitive side of our nature[1] respectively, all ethical judgments must be the work of reason, otherwise they would not be judgments at all. A mere feeling (*i.e.*, emotion), for example, of admiration, is not a judgment. On the other hand I should be perfectly willing to concede to the advocate of " feeling " that we could not discern values or make ethical judgments at all if we did not have certain emotions. Although we may very well make a particular ethical judgment without emotion, it still seems to be true that, if we were purely rational beings and had no emotional element in our nature at all, we could not know either what is good or what is right. But all acts of thinking, forming opinions or knowing, whether inferential or not, still fall on the cognitive side of the self, and are therefore essentially different from mere feelings or emotions. We must not be deluded by the popular use of the term " feel " for " believe " into ignoring this important distinction.

Is ethical knowledge then empirical or *a priori*? If we conceive *a priori* as Kant did, namely as a set of universal laws deducible from the mere form of law as such and valid quite independently of all empirical circumstances, it certainly seems not to be *a priori*. Nor is it *a priori* in the sense that it can be proved by any kind of discursive reasoning ;

---

[1] If the traditional threefold division of the self is maintained we shall have to class under " feeling " both (a) emotion, (b) sensation. It is (a) rather than (b) that has been confused with ethical cognition.

nor again in the sense that we are ever exempted from taking account of the concrete situations with which actions are concerned.   On the other hand to say without qualification that Ethics is empirical is open to objection, because it suggests that ethical knowledge is derived entirely from some feelings (*i.e.*, emotions, or pleasure and pain, or those together with the so-called " moral sense," conceived as analogous to the outer senses), and ignores the distinction between judgments of fact and judgments of value, proceeding on the supposition that we can arrive at Ethics by studying what is an empirical fact.   It is essential to recognise that " good " and " right " are specific attributes which we can apprehend and which must not be reduced to anything else that is not itself ethical.   If this is recognised, I do not much mind whether we call our apprehension of the qualities empirical or *a priori*.   In any case it must be conceded that we do not apprehend them by our five senses and that they are qualities of a unique kind.   If the theory expounded above be true, it is quite clear that our arrival at this apprehension presupposes both empirical knowledge and (generally at least) inference, but that our final judgment as to the rightness or wrongness of an act is not *completely deducible* by mediate inference without the help of " intuition," or non-inferential cognition.   Often what is meant by calling ethical knowledge *a priori* is that it is partly non-inferential, and with that we must agree ; but at the same time it is important to remember that any non-inferential cognition of the good presupposes previous experience either of what is apprehended as good in this instance or at any rate of something else of the same kind.

Duty, or the right in action, has three different aspects which need not be ultimately irreconcilable.   In the first place it must be viewed as unconditionally obligatory just because it is the right act ; we cannot regard it as our duty at all without taking this aspect into account.   But this is not incompatible with its obligatoriness being due partly to the value of its consequences ; it is right partly (though not wholly) because of them, but once granted that it is right its rightness is an absolutely sufficient reason for doing it.[1] We may ask questions as to what is our duty ; but the question why we should do our duty is fundamentally immoral. No " sanctions " need or can be used to account for the obligation to do it, any more than any further evidence is needed to justify us in believing what has already been proved

[1] *Cf.* p. 167.

to be true. Moreover, the performance of right actions because they are right and not *merely* because one likes them is itself of all values realised in human life the highest, besides being a means to the best results. So far I should agree with Kant.

Secondly, the right act appears as an act which fits, harmonises, coheres with the whole situation. This is grasped especially vividly by the coherence theory, and also by those who tend to assimilate moral perception to æsthetic taste. It was the aspect which appealed most to Aristotle and perhaps to the Greek mind generally. If we were totally blind to this side of the question, we should be quite unable to judge the intrinsic value either of particular acts or of any kind of life which ethics holds up as an ideal. We should be always ignoring the importance of our concrete social setting for the application of ethical principles and developing the part at the expense of the whole. The dangers of the view are that it will lapse into undue conservatism by stressing " facts " too much and " ideals " too little, and that it will destroy the specific character of ethical ideas by either trying to treat them in terms of purely logical categories (as often seems to be the case with the " Absolute Idealists ") or reducing them to mere æsthetic good taste. But this is not a necessary consequence of the standpoint ; and it is clearly true that the right action must be the one that best fits into the situation, whatever other properties it may have besides.

Thirdly, the right act is viewed as the act which produces " the greatest good." To decide whether this is tenable would require a long and difficult investigation for which the present is hardly a suitable place ; but at any rate it is certain that right action is always a creation of values. To act rightly is to produce good both as a consequence and as an intrinsic property of the act itself. The world is richer for right acts both because they produce other good and because they are good themselves. Further we can never decide the question of rightness without some reference to the good[1] (or evil), either immediately or ultimately, either in the consequences or in the act. If we look at right action from this standpoint as well as from the other two, we can avoid the formalistic, negative and unjoyful character of the Kantian view or any other which speaks too much of obligation and too little of

---

[1] Whether the right act is always necessarily the act which produces the greatest good is a question that I must leave open here, but in any case a right act must produce some good.

good, and can regard ethical principles not as primarily a set of cramping restrictions but as a method of producing all the good that is in our power, of achieving and appreciating the best that is in us to achieve and appreciate. Many people think of " ethics " and " morality " as a matter merely of prohibitions and laws; and this has naturally led to a reaction, for mere restrictions, unjustified by the good they do, can hardly lay claim to be rational or worthy of a free man. But, as soon as the reaction becomes an attack on ethics or morality as a whole, it commits suicide, for it is denying the validity of ethics on the ground that something else, *e.g.*, " self-realisation " is better; and this is a contradiction in terms, as much as it would be to say that error is preferable to truth because it is truer than truth. The business of Ethics as applied to practice is the discussion of what life is good (in the widest sense of the term); and to assert that some other life is preferable to that usually inculcated by moral teachers is not to repudiate ethics but to propose a new ethics. If it were realised that right action means the achievement and production of the good, of values of every kind, for ourselves and for others, of all that is most worth doing and enjoying, then no one could reject morality as such on principle, whatever he might be tempted to do in practice. We may differ as to what is worth most or as to the way of attaining it; but since the question is one of values and right action we can only differ within ethics itself. Real self-sacrifice is a duty sometimes; but it is always sacrifice for a good though it may not be our own good.

# CHAPTER VII

## Conclusion

PUNISHMENT as externally inflicted is a help towards making either the offender himself or others realise the wrongness of certain acts. It is, however, a quite subordinate and an extremely imperfect means. It does sometimes partially attain this end, but it perhaps even more often totally fails, and it is certainly not the only and very far from being the most satisfactory means. This disparaging view as to its importance may be regarded as typical of modern times ; but in earlier theories it tended to occupy a far more exalted position as the sanction of all morality and even together with reward the main object of the whole universe as created by God. With the modern repudiation of this gross exaggeration of its significance I entirely agree. To base ethics on punishment is to say that the only reason for not doing wrong is because you will suffer pain for it, *i.e.*, to adopt a view of egoistic hedonism in almost its purest form ; nor is it reasonable to make just punishment a primary end of the universe unless you are prepared to maintain not only that punishment is an end-in-itself but that it is a more important end than the improvement of the offender. To justify the ways of God to man it would not be enough for the sinner to be punished ; he must be saved by his punishment.

Has the principle of punishment then no wider ethical or metaphysical significance at all ? Perhaps it would be wiser to call a halt here and say that it has not. Punishment means properly pain inflicted by an external agent as a mark of disapproval for wrong done ; and this can at best only be a subordinate means of bringing crude minds to a state in which it will not be necessary. But it may by a very pardonable analogy be regarded as symbolical of a process which constitutes a fundamental and very often neglected side of moral life. For emphasising its importance in this wider sense we have the authority of Hegel. In the interests of correct terminology it is, however, desirable to state quite clearly that the wider sense of punishment is not the same as the narrower sense. Apart from any externally inflicted penalty there is a psychological process by which men sometimes come to realise the wrong which they have done and are, as is said, reformed. Punishment in its strict sense is an attempt to bring about this end by external means, but it can only succeed by initiating an internal psychological process of " repentance," and this process may occur without external punishment. Further, as thus occurring it has a certain analogy with punishment in the stricter sense, which has seemed to many to entitle it to be regarded as " self-punishment," or even as the only true form, the best example of punishment as such. What is the nature of this process, and what is its relation to external punishment ? In what sense may sin be regarded as its own punishment, and what is the moral significance of this fact ? We are dealing here with no less a subject than the overcoming or checking of evil in general, a process which plays at least as large a part in the universe as its opposite, the deterioration beloved of pessimists.

Now it is a recognised fact that a wrong action makes a man worse, *i.e.*, more likely to commit wrong acts of a similar kind in the future, and this is sometimes what is meant by saying that sin is its own punishment. But, if this is a punishment, it is one that, by universal admission, nobody could rightly try to inflict ; on the contrary it is this evil which all reformatory measures and moral education seek to avert. Also it is not necessarily dreaded by its victim. So its resemblance to external punishment is limited to the fact that it is an evil consequence of sin which falls on the sinner. It is not evil in general but pain that characterises punishment in any proper sense of the term.

By the statement that wrongdoing carries with it its own punishment is more generally meant that it brings consequences which are not only bad but painful for the wrongdoer Whether the degree of unhappiness can be said in any way to correspond to the degree of moral badness we need not discuss here, but to bring pain to the wrongdoer is certainly an important characteristic of wrongdoing. In this sense it resembles external punishment much more closely and may produce or help to produce the change of mind which we call repentance. We hear a great deal about " vicious circles," or evil producing evil ; but there must also be a way of breaking the circle, otherwise everything would always go from bad to worse without cease. To do wrong once makes one more likely to do it again ; but if we were to stop here there would be no such thing as ever overcoming one's faults. Each bad act intensifies a bad habit, the bad habit leads to further bad acts, and so on *ad infinitum.* Yes, but this is not what invariably happens at any rate, sometimes bad habits are cured, sometimes their development is checked. How does this take place ?

Well, I should suggest that besides the tendency for evil to produce evil there is also a tendency for evil to be followed by a reaction towards good. Which tendency prevails will depend on the character of the individual (or the State, for the same factors are at work in political life). To elaborate this statement, which may appear paradoxical, it is sufficient to bring together two facts, first, that evil actions will produce evil effects and that as the habit which leads to these actions is strengthened they will produce worse effects ; secondly, that the evil effects will, or at least may, arouse disgust and revulsion on the part of the wrongdoer, which again may be strong enough to stop him from doing wrong again in future. The first will be generally admitted ; but the second may be met by the rejoinder that he did not feel sufficient repulsion to pre-vent him committing the first acts which initiated the habit, and, if so, he is *a fortiori* still less likely to feel it when the habit has been established and is developing. But, in the first place, he may not have known that the act would produce bad conse-quences. It is generally considered unjust to punish people for purely intellectual errors, but in the course of nature they do suffer from these errors and may be made more cautious in the future thereby. Further, if foolish acts did not have evil consequences, it would be difficult to see how either the race or the individual could have evolved what intellectual qualities they possess, and in fact in its elementary stages it is a well enough recognised principle of biology. Even an animal tends to avoid kinds of action which lead to painful results. This learning by evil consequences is obviously a factor in life of the greatest importance, and it may be regarded even in its most elementary forms as a natural analogue of punishment.[1]

[1] It will be said that this has nothing to do with Ethics, meaning that it is not a question of moral or immoral action. But, if pleasure is a good at all and pain the opposite, it is certainly a question of good or evil in the wider sense, and as such must be a subject of interest for Ethics. We are concerned with all good and evil, and must not limit ourselves to considering one type only, *i.e.*, moral good and evil, even though it be the most important. Besides, I am not saying that the process here has all the features of punishment but only that it bears a certain analogy to punishment as the nearest approach to it on a lower plane, or the embryo out of which it developed.

We have not, however, yet taken a case of deliberate wrong-doing. Here the man who performed the act knew or believed it to be wrong at the time he did it, but he may still learn from its evil consequences. For (1) he may have known or believed it to be wrong and yet not have expected it would have these evil consequences, *e.g.*, a man who embarks on a course of deceit may know it to be wrong at the time and yet imagine that he can avoid any very bad consequences either for himself or for others. Then later he may discover that his action has brought great suffering on his family, and if the knowledge of this brings suffering to himself it like human punishment is the direct result of his wrongdoing ; further, in this case it is wrongdoing for which he certainly is morally responsible as much as for anything, though he did not anticipate all the consequences. The lie was not wrong merely because of these consequences, yet the experience of them is likely to be a more effective way of bringing home to him the evil of lying than the mere cognition that it is bad in itself or any sermon on its wickedness. The man ought to have abstained from the lie even without the knowledge that these consequences were likely, for even apart from them the lie would still be wrong, and therefore he is morally to blame, though he did not foresee them. In fact nobody when he does a wrong act is ever likely to anticipate the full consequences of his wrongdoing.[1] Moreover, secondly, even if the man anticipates these consequences intellectually this is a very different thing from experiencing and feeling them, and though the former was not sufficient to stop him the latter may be.[2] This, unfortunately, does not happen always, but it clearly does sometimes.

But are we not merely considering selfish expediency ?

[1] If the more utilitarian view be accepted and it be held that the only reason why these acts are wrong is because of their bad consequences, this would still leave the man responsible, though he did not anticipate the consequences, for (a) even if that is the *ratio essendi* it is certainly not always the *ratio cognoscendi* ; people do, in fact, believe that an act is bad without having considered its consequences ; (b) they may know that its consequences in general are likely to be bad without knowing the degree or the particular nature of this badness.

[2] The reader must remember that I have not yet dealt with the opposing tendency of habit which counteracts this tendency in most cases. I am here only speaking of those cases where a man does over-come or check the evil and explaining how he can do that. These are psychological facts and require explanation like any other. Even if we ascribe them to an undetermined " free-will," we must do our best to understand the conditions under which this free-will occurs. *We* cannot hope to explain everything by causal laws, whether it is really

The fact that the consequences of a wrong act are painful to the doer is not what makes the act wrong, and if the man merely repents of the bad act on account of these painful consequences to himself, is he in any way made the *better* man thereby, though he may be made more *prudent* in future ? Is it not true that he is still acting from entirely the same motives as those which prompted the bad act ? But we have already found ourselves able to answer the same objection in regard to external punishment, and I must refer the readers to the passage in question[1] for a full reply. A course of action begun with these low motives may end with higher, and experience of suffering *may* intensify the man's consciousness not only that the act was unfortunate but that it was wrong. Our answer given earlier would indeed apply with greater strength in the present case, because the numerous objections and drawbacks to the interference by external force involved in ordinary punishment obviously do not apply here. If a man's misdoing leads by a natural process to painful consequences for himself, it cannot well be resented as an interference with freedom, it does not lead to a confusion of the moral law with external force and it is far more likely to make the offender dislike immorality than to make him dislike morality, as external constraint may. Most of the drawbacks of punishment of which I drew up a list[2] do not apply to this inner analogue of punishment with anything like the same strength. A man may and often does become bitter and blames " Fate " or others rather than himself, but at any rate he is much less likely to do so than in the case of punishment inflicted from outside. If punishment inflicted from without may bring home to a man his badness, why should not these natural consequences ? In one respect external punishment is superior as a reformatory measure, in that it has the moral authority of society behind it ; but if the offender knows when he suffers the natural consequences that the authority of society is also against the act the two may work together. Also apart from deliberate punishment one of the natural consequences of recognised badness is that others think less well of the man and treat him accordingly. Here the two factors are combined, for this effect is both a natural conse--quence of the act and an expression of society's moral author-

so explicable or not, but in either case we must try to explain as much as possible. There will be a great deal left unexplained by us at any rate, however far we succeed in that attempt.

[1] *v.* pp. 80-84.  [2] *v.* pp. 121-2.

ity. (Like external punishment, however, this " sanction " only applies effectively to actions which fall below the average practice of a man's social group.) [1]

But, when I spoke of the consequences of the wrong acts, I did not include and would have had no right to include only pain to the agent himself. Almost all bad acts also bring pain to others, and if a man is moved to improve himself by a realisation of their sufferings this cannot be said to be mere selfish expediency. The man who is induced to overcome a fault because he sees the pain it gives others is not acting selfishly. His motive, if not the highest of all, is at any rate very much higher than the motive which prompted the fault. Further in many cases at least he is now being influenced by the factor that really makes the act wrong, because very often the only or main reason which makes an act wrong is that it brings suffering to others.

But, thirdly, it is quite possible that such a repentance may be in the fullest sense moral. After all the act cannot be altogether separated from its consequences, and therefore a realisation of the badness of the consequences may easily be a realisation of the badness of the act. It is not always merely that a man is pained by the consequences but that he sees them to be bad. In seeing vice at work he may first learn what vice really is, and if he learns that before the habit has him sufficiently in its grip he will overcome it. He knew " intellectually " beforehand that it was bad, but he did not, as we say, " realise " its badness. After all, we can only make clear the nature of virtue or vice by depicting them in their working, as Plato showed in the Republic. The consequences of bad acts include the state of moral degradation to which they lead, and when a man sees himself drifting into this state, may well realise the badness of his offence for the first time.

So we must distinguish between three senses in which this natural consequence of wrongdoing has been described as punishment :—

1. As making the offender more sinful.
2. As making him less happy.
3. As making him realise his sin.

[1] Not necessarily below the average in society as a whole. A thief who lives among thieves may not feel the natural condemnation of honest people till he is sent to prison, and in fact we all feel the approval and disapproval of our own " set " far more than that of society in general. Whether this is good or bad depends on whether our " set " is above or below the average moral level. How many good families have a much higher standard than surrounding society !

CONCLUSION 225

The first sense is not at all analogous to external punishment, but the second is. This second kind of natural consequence is, however, only of considerable importance if it is followed by the third, in fact it bears but little resemblance to punishment unless the man is at least conscious that it is a necessary and natural, not only an accidental, effect of his wrongdoing. We may add further that the object of external punishment as a reformatory measure is to bring on (2) artificially in the hope of producing (3).

The process we have sketched shows how evil *may* in a sense give rise to good ; but we must add that it is only a " Pickwickian " sense, because it is not the evil but the good in the man's character reacting against the evil that produces the good results. It remains true that from sheer unmitigated evil one could obtain no good. The reaction arises not because the man has become bad but because he is too good to stand the increasing evil once he really sees what it is. It arises because he dislikes moral evil or because he feels sympathy with the sufferings of others and shame for having caused them, *i.e.*, because of good traits. But these may be insufficient in strength till they are intensified sufficiently to cause action by a strong taste and vivid experience of the bad. Evil as such cannot produce good, but the reaction against it may do so.

On the other hand it is no doubt an indisputable fact that a repetition of bad acts leads to bad habits, and in so far makes it progressively more difficult to act rightly in the future, so that the two tendencies run against each other, and experience seems to show that in the majority of cases of evil habits the tendency which proves the stronger is the less desirable of the two. But it is not by any means certain that it will win the day, and the presence of the other tendency must not be forgotten. It is in fact necessary to account for the moral improvement that does sometimes take place. It is true, unfortunately, that habit *qua* habit tends to blunt a man's sensibility to the evil, but it also strengthens the data for appreciating its badness ; he feels an *equal* evil less but he has experienced a *greater* evil through the repetition of the act, which is liable to make his state progressively worse with considerable rapidity. Few very bad acts would be done if the doer had any genuine realisation of their consequences at all, but he may be forced to realise them when the consequences are upon him.

This must not be regarded as a mechanical tendency operating on the man from outside, but as a statement of the fact that increased knowledge of the badness of a given course may rouse the whole man against this course.   I do not assert this to be an inevitable consequence, but only one tendency which may be counteracted by others.   That there is a tendency of this kind has been deduced as a logical consequence of the nature of bad acts, and it is needed also to explain the admitted fact that bad habits frequently are cured.

The same tendency operates on a larger scale in society, and here it often has more chance of success because a man's bad habits are not transmitted in the same strength to his children.   The following example of this tendency will be plain to all.   War is an evil, and " the Great War " is by far the worst example of this evil that humanity has experienced.[1] But, just because it was so evil, it has been followed by a reaction against war which, though far from universal, must at any rate be admitted to be stronger than any that the world has known before.[2]   It may be that this reaction will yet not lead to the abolition of war, but at any rate it is true that, human nature being what it is, there was no chance at all of its being abolished till its evils had reached such a pitch of magnitude as they did in the years 1914–1918, whatever chance there is now.   For very many even this amount of evil

[1] At one point the analogy breaks down.   The last war was not the worst because men have become more bellicose than they used to be (they have in general become less so), but because of the accidental circumstance that scientific discoveries have increased their power of destruction.   It is not that the vice itself is increasing, but that its physical effects are becoming more serious for humanity.

[2] It may be said that this merely means that we are afraid of the consequences of war, but I cannot agree.   However pessimistic we may be about the outlook, it is hardly disputable that far more people think of war as a crime against humanity, as morally wrong, than ever did before, and those who already thought of it as wrong realise its wrongness incomparably more fully now.   Besides, apart from its actual and *intended* consequences war would not be an evil : the evil of *war* is not indeed merely the destruction and death which it *actually* produces, but war would not be morally evil at all if it did not involve at least the *intention* to compel others by producing destruction, harm and death.   The primary moral evil of war is constituted by the hatred and disregard to others' interests involved, but they are only involved because war is both in intention and action an attempt for the sake of the imagined good of one's own country to coerce others and bring terrible consequences upon them.   Nor, however comparatively weak and undeveloped the League of Nations may still be held to be, can it be denied that the War has been followed by more practical achievements in the way of institutions and agreements for rendering another war less likely than have ever been known before.

seems insufficient to make them change their minds, but at any rate nothing less could have been sufficient, and if civilisation is saved from the menace of war it is this that will be the reason of its deliverance. Till we saw the effects of war "writ large" we most of us accepted its periodic occurrence as something necessary and glorious. It would obviously have been very much better if humanity could have learnt the lesson without trying war so often and so long, but we being what we are this was the only way of learning even the poor fragment of the lesson that we have learnt by now.

To appreciate the situation adequately we must note that the effects of war carried to its extreme are such as no man could desire; the danger is not that anybody will deliberately choose to destroy European civilisation rather than give up war, but that men may choose war thinking its effects will be indeed evil but "not so evil as all that" and then be unable to stop themselves in time to avert the catastrophe. Similarly no one would desire to be in the degraded state which is the result of vice carried to an extreme, though he might find a lesser degree of the vice very pleasing. Evil is of such a nature that when carried to its extreme it must disgust and cannot be desired, therefore when it is practised consistently it will eventually become so bad that the man wishes to overcome it and will overcome it *if* it has not first broken his power to do so. It is a race between habit and the acquisition of understanding through experience. If habit wins, the man's efforts will be paralysed so that he cannot cure the evil though he would wish to do so; if the other competitor he will as a result of his experience of evil see whither he is going before it is too late to avert disaster.

The situation is complicated in a way favourable to the evil tendency by the fact that habit not only makes it more difficult to avoid committing bad acts but blunts a man's sensibility to their badness. Thus, though the evil becomes progressively worse, the man often does not feel its badness so keenly. Thus habit often prevents the first tendency from taking effect, but it cannot always do so, and where evil is cured or checked this is the explanation.

There are in fact two kinds of progress which bear an analogy to reward and punishment respectively. There is the progress from good to better, virtuous acts confirming and strengthening virtue, good institutions in a State improving character and the improvement in character leading to a further improvement in institutions. Here habit works on the right side, and in addition to the effects of habit there are the further facts that good causes in general produce good results and that as a man knows the good better through practising it he will come to like it more.    This simple kind of progress may be compared to reward, *i.e.*, the principle that good shall bear as its fruit further good.

But there is a second kind of progress, the progress by reaction, and this is the kind I have just been describing.    It is a progress not direct to good from good but to good only by reaction from evil, and this is analogous to punishment. If, as I hold, the formation of the League of Nations is a step in advance, and if this event was a result of the war and would not have taken place without it, the war may be said to have contributed in this respect to progress ;  but this does not make the war a good thing, any more than it is a good thing to beat one's wife because a man may repent so bitterly of having done this that in consequence he never even loses his temper with her again.    If evil subserves good, it does so in a way radically and completely different from the way in which good subserves itself.    Evil can only help good through its own defeat, yet, given a certain disposition in a man or a race, it may be a necessary precondition of its opposing good, the man or the race may only learn by evil that good is best. We must, however, again insist that this good is produced by good reacting against evil, not by evil alone, otherwise it would be the most incomprehensible of miracles.    Nor does it make the evil good, but only a means to the good.    If we take the evil effects of evil acts as analogous to punishment we must not therefore think of them as good-in-themselves.

Should we then seek evil so that good may come ?    It is possible that sophistries of this kind may be used to excuse and perhaps half-convince oneself, but the state of mind implied in the suggestion is a self-contradictory one.    For a man who did this would be willing to do wrong in order that he should be stopped by suffering from doing the wrong.    If he wished to do the wrong he could not be doing it for the sake of the good which is simply its own suppression, and if he did not wish to do the wrong he could attain the good without having any need first to give way to the evil.    The evil is not a necessary means to the good unless it is sought otherwise than for that reason.    Besides, as I have said, it is neither the only means nor a certain means of attaining the good in view.    A man is more likely to escape the harm of a confirmed bad habit if he never falls into it at all than if he falls into it, though even in the latter case he may subsequently be cured. Further, even if the same goal were attained in either case, that would not do away with the evil incurred on the road thither. *Granted that* a man wills bad acts, experience of the evil which these bring about may be necessary to cure him ; but this leaves him responsible for the bad acts in question. When I said that it was a necessary means, I only meant that it was necessary granting a certain evil will ; and the man is responsible for this will if he is responsible for anything.[1]

Evil thus produces what may fitly be called its own punishment ; and this not because external events are so arranged that happiness must be in proportion to virtue and suffering to vice, but because the nature of evil is such as either to disgust or destroy. This punishment may reform the offender ; but unless we postulate a future life we cannot say that it always does so.[2] The theory of punishment must be content with insisting that the processes described are of great significance for our life on earth while leaving it to metaphysics to say whether they are also of importance for the Universe.

A study of external punishment as of reward in the ordinary sense of the terms does not usually carry one into the most exalted regions of moral thought ; but even in their most sordid forms they are expressions, if perverted expressions, of the principle which underlies all morality. Evil is worth

[1] I agree that man has " freedom," though I do not think myself that this freedom involves acts which are undetermined, but for my views on the subject *v.* Chapter VIII of my book on *Kant's Treatment of Causality* (Kegan Paul, 1924).

[2] *i.e.*, the " punishment" seems to be universal, but not the reformation. Similarly with reward in the widest sense of the term. But though wrongdoing always brings with it *some* punishment (pain or loss of happiness) and virtue *some* happiness, this is not necessarily in proportion to desert, and may be outweighed hedonistically by other circumstances. For no one can maintain that these are the only factors in happiness or misery, unless they suppose that external circumstances, which also affect our happiness, are adjusted so as to be in proportion to our deserts ; and for this supposition I can see no grounds. Even if we take the view that Nature is created by God for the best, we have no right to infer from this that Nature is exactly fitted to serve the ends of retributive justice, for this is at best a very subordinate good and might have to be sacrificed to other more important ends. If a future life is to be established by moral arguments at all, these must be based not on the need that the bad should be punished and the good rewarded, but on the need that all men should be cured of their faults and continue to develop what is good in them more and more fully. The principal object of justice must be not to punish but to reform, to improve.

fighting, therefore we have punishment; good is worth encouraging, therefore we have reward. Are they only temporary human makeshifts or are they the expression and imperfect analogues of a fundamental law of the cosmos? Many have thought that, in order to justify the dealings of God with man, the universe must be so ordered that happiness and suffering are always exactly in proportion to desert. But, if we think reformation much more important than retribution, the same premises ought to suggest the conclusion that happiness and suffering are always so ordered as ultimately to be the means of moral regeneration. The supposition that to justify Providence it is enough that the wicked should be punished in proportion to their deserts and not necessary that they should be cured of their wickedness, whether made by an orthodox theologian or a follower of Kant, is one of the evil effects of a retributive theory which virtually made retribution more important than moral improvement. Hegel seems more on the right track when he lays down as a metaphysical principle the nullity (" Nichtigkeit ") of evil by which it must through its own nature cease to satisfy and so give place to good. The metaphysical significance of this tendency we cannot discuss here, but at any rate the theory of punishment has thrown some little light on " the problem of evil " by suggesting that it may sometimes be curable and only curable through its own development, so that it would be no real conquest for a God artificially and miraculously to stop it by external intervention. The evil in a man may sometimes only be cured by letting the man develop it till it becomes so serious that it disgusts him, just as we may sometimes teach a child not to be naughty by letting it experience on a small scale the natural effects of its naughtiness.

But, however that may be, and whether the world-process can be viewed as essentially a showing-up of the " Nichtigkeit " (nullity) of evil or not, it remains true that punishment is our way of expressing and realising in action the conviction of the moral " Nichtigkeit " of the evil act for which it is inflicted. Similarly reward may be regarded both as a metaphysical principle by which virtue through its own inherent nature brings with it satisfaction and peace, and as our mode of expressing our belief in values and our estimate of their relative importance.

# INDEX